MY FRIENDS,
THE NEW GUINEA HEADHUNTERS

MY FRIENDS, THE NEW GUINEA HEADHUNTERS

by

BENJAMIN T. BUTCHER

With a Foreword by

H. LEONARD MURRAY, C.B.E.

Former Administrator of Papua

Doubleday & Company, Inc.

Garden City, New York

1964

FOREWORD

by H. Leonard Murray, C.B.E.
former Administrator of Papua

I AM happy to write this foreword because I am convinced that this is a valuable book, and because I knew Mr. Butcher well and visited him frequently on his lonely station when he "lived with headhunters". I also knew the natives, and was familiar with their villages in this huge district.

It was over half a century ago when I first came into contact with Mr. Butcher and his work. His station was then at Aird Hill in the midst of the mangrove and nipa palm swamps of the delta country at the head of the Gulf of Papua. The natives around him for over fifty miles were headhunters and cannibals and completely wild. The rainfall was over 300 inches a year. Malaria and other tropical diseases were widespread. Added to the risk of health, and even life, was the real danger of attack by headhunters resentful of the intrusion of this puzzling white man. Mr. Butcher's tiny settlement would have had small chance of survival in the event of such an attack.

After that first contact I visited Mr. Butcher at intervals until he eventually left Papua, and I had the opportunity to observe the progress he was making as teacher, friend and adviser to the thousands of surrounding natives. His work was of valuable help to the government in the difficult task of trying to ease the passage of a very primitive people from the stone age to the twentieth century. He was constantly watching for any exploitation, ill-treatment or injustice to natives, and in that way also he was of real help to the government.

It is no part of this foreword to attempt any comment on his Christian teachings. Indeed it would be an impertinence to do so. But perhaps I may mention an occasion when I introduced an important representative of a foreign government to one of Mr. Butcher's brother missionaries in another part of the territory.

During the visit the foreign investigator asked: "You and your wife have now lived and worked for many years among these natives. During that time, Sir, how many converts have you made?"

The missionary replied: "Converts? None. Not one. It is too early to make any true converts. But, if the example of our way of life among these people improves their own way of life at all; if we can persuade them to give up some of their cruel and revolting ways; if we can heal some of the sick, reduce the appalling infant mortality, and induce them to adopt some of the rudimentary rules of sanitation; and generally make them happier and healthier natives, our work will not be in vain.

"Of course, as is our duty, we are also trying to lay the foundations of understanding and acceptance of the Christian faith. But we are only paving the way. It is for those who come after us to make true converts."

The foreign investigator was deeply impressed, and so was I. I have no qualifications to comment on what that missionary said about converts, but as regards all the rest, it seemed to me as fine a thing as a man could do.

A similar high endeavour inspired much of Mr. Butcher's work, and he is entitled to feel proud of the measure of success he attained. In his case, this work was done in surroundings of most primitive savagery, loneliness, most austere conditions of living, and often real danger.

Mr. Butcher has an easy style of writing and a happy gift of literary expression. The book gives an accurate description of much of the territory, and what he writes about the natives is always interesting, often entertaining, and sometimes quite exciting.

The whole book is a fascinating record of the life of a dedicated man.

PREFACE

THOUGH commenced as an autobiography, this has now shortened to a story of Papua as I knew it during the earlier years of this century.

James Chalmers, Oliver Tomkins and eleven Papuans who were with them had been killed by the headhunters and cannibals of the Kikori delta in 1901 and I was privileged to open up work among these wild people and am one of the last links with the earliest pioneers, for Ruatoka and Dr. W. G. Lawes were still in the country when I reached Port Moresby.

I lived among these people for thirty-four years and was the first white man many had ever seen. Learning their language and seeking to understand their outlook on life, I was often touched with wonder and admiration at the achievements of a stone age race though troubled by its darker side.

Much that is described in these pages no one will ever see again. Even when I started work early in 1905, the effects of contact with the West were already evident in places such as Daru. They became still more widespread after the first World War while what has followed the second has revolutionized the life of tens of thousands of Papuans who in increasing numbers are being brought into the main streams of Western life. The Papuan scene is changing rapidly and the old tribal life with its wonderful buildings and amazing ceremonies is swiftly disappearing.

We of the Western world have destroyed much that was picturesque and good as well as much that was evil, and this story of Papua deals with the changes and has something to say of what is being done to help the Papuans discover a new and richer way of life.

CONTENTS

MY FRIENDS,
THE NEW GUINEA HEADHUNTERS

1

THE CALL

THE rugged grandeur of the Blue Mountains, transformed into soft loveliness by the azure haze that fills the distance, draws many visitors from Sydney, though most prefer to make their homes in warmer areas near the sea.

Here, only sixty miles from the coast, the winter brings us frost and snow, but as I tread the silent mountain paths and look across tree covered valleys unbroken by sign of human habitation, I feel closer to the wild places of old Papua where I spent so many years, only then I was often alone or surrounded by folk living in a stone age environment, while nowadays I am never alone but surrounded by invisible waves bringing sound and sight of places and peoples far away. The busy world is always close to us and I switch on my T.V. set and watch what is happening or live again through days long past.

Recently under the title A Time to Remember, events since 1896 came alive once more but my mind travelled back still further and as I watched and listened memories crowded in of the England I knew as a boy and of a world vastly different from that we know today.

My grandchildren and their parents have many things we old folk never dreamed of at their age but I doubt if their life brings them greater happiness than we enjoyed.

Ours were the dreams of Jules Verne, with a world so big that to circumnavigate it in eighty days was dreamed fantastic, and we eagerly followed the adventures of the *Clipper of the Clouds* and the *Nautilus* travelling 20,000 leagues under the sea when planes and submarines seemed much more visionary than space ships do today. Ours too were the days of great explorers, with the North and South Poles still unconquered and Central Africa and many other parts of the world largely unknown. Tales of great explorers such as Livingstone and Stanley of Africa and James Chalmers of New Guinea, and stories of Buffalo Bill and the Wild West stirred our blood and filled us with longing to follow in their steps. It was a wonderful time for boys with the spirit of adventure, yet life in mid-Victorian England was at times rather primitive.

I was born in London in 1877. Ours was a large house near the Old Kent Road, built for a family in comfortable circumstances, yet there was no bathroom. Bath night was once a week when a big tub was filled with hot water from black cast-iron kettles heated on an open fire in our large but dingy kitchen. We knew nothing of electric light. The better rooms had naked gas jets while most bedrooms relied on candles, and these we lit in the hall and lighted ourselves up dark stairways to bed. Cooking was a hot and lengthy job, the joint being hung from a clockwork spit and roasted before the blazing coals. Wages were low and hours long, housemaids averaging about £1 a month and labourers about £1 a week, and instead of a half-day holiday on Saturday, the streets and shops were crowded until ten or eleven at night.

We were on one of the main roads, little more than three miles from London Bridge, but London was still so small that there were fields quite near to which my father would take us to fly our kites. Trams drawn by mules or horses passed our home and horse-drawn buses provided cheap transport through the city. I envied the favoured few who, seated beside the driver, could look down upon the horses, while small boys and others who were on top sat on a long wooden seat back to back all facing outwards. There was no protection from rain apart from the umbrellas some folk carried, from which water dripped down the necks of those behind or soaked the knees of those in front.

Tarred or sealed roads were unknown, and in dry weather the dust was thick and in wet weather the mud was deep. Hence the need for the Crossing Sweeper who earned a scanty living by sweeping paths from kerb to kerb. We always looked for these crossings for boot cleaning was a messy business. The lasting wax polish of today was unknown and we used a semi-liquid mixture called blacking which required a lot of elbow grease and never gave a lasting shine. The streets were dimly lit by naked gas jets and every evening the lamplighter would light each separately and every morning reverse the process.

The fastest vehicle on the roads, which were often full of ruts, was the bicycle. I saw its development from the rather dangerous, high wheeled, solid tyred contraption, to the safety bicycle, heavily built and of various shapes until the present diamond frame ousted all the rest. About that time Dunlop invented the pneumatic tyre. There was much scepticism concerning its merits but in a year the solid tyre had gone and pneumatic-tyred bicycles were breaking all records. This led to the imposition of a speed limit and to my getting into the hands of the police and subsequent appearances in Court, where I was charged, convicted and fined for exceeding ten miles an hour on a public road.

I had ceased to be a small boy by then but was still living in the hey-day of the Victorian era, when Britain ruled the waves and boasted of an Empire on which the sun never set. The coloured peoples were regarded as subject races, incapable of governing themselves, while the white races parcelled out their lands as if they were theirs for the taking. No one considered America a great power and few thought there could ever come a challenge to Western supremacy from such lands as China and Japan. It was the white man's world and the British thought themselves in charge of it; and for lads like myself it was a world full of boundless possibilities with vast areas unknown and waiting to be explored.

Among the middle classes in those days church attendance was the rule, non-church-goers being viewed with considerable suspicion and coming in for much unfavourable comment. My family observed the rule, although Marlborough Chapel in the Old Kent Road meant a walk of over a mile each way. It was quite a business to marshal the family and get us started and we frequently arrived breathless and barely on time. There we lined up and marched in and as there were usually about eight children, the procession up the aisle created considerable interest. We relished this and could not understand our parents' concern at being late since it assured us of a goodly congregation to watch our progress.

We always enjoyed Sunday even if the sermon was beyond our understanding, and it was probably the interest of the minister in work overseas that first turned my thoughts in that direction. In addition, I have vivid memories of a collection box with a picture of a nicely dressed missionary standing under a coconut palm surrounded by a crowd of very respectable brown people, and we all delighted in the pictures found in book prizes won when collecting for the missionary ship *John Williams*. Like many another lad, I wanted adventure and my search for it often landed me into trouble and caused my parents much concern. I had a love for tools and handicrafts and thoughts of one day being an engineer, yet as I dreamed of the days ahead, other thoughts would come not usually associated with childish dreams and I felt I had to do something to help others. Though at the time quite unaware of it, even as a child I was being led towards a life of service and before I left school I was definitely pledged to be a missionary.

I was educated at Aske's, the school of the Haberdashers' Company, but left there soon after I was sixteen to help my father. We are a very old London family and by patrimony I am a Freeman of the City of London, my father having been a liveryman of the Clockmakers' Company or Guild, of which our family name is the oldest on the role. My father, however, was linked with another branch of the family that had been in Billingsgate Fish Market for generations and I found myself in the wholesale fish trade though I had no intention of staying in it.

For four years I worked in that none too salubrious market and also took part in the life and work of Hanover Chapel, a Congregational church in which the Duke of Kent, father of Queen Victoria, had been interested. At the same time I was studying Latin and Greek, knowledge of both being required from one seeking entry into a theological college, and attending a technical school where I added a course in blacksmithing to my knowledge of wood-working.

In 1896 I entered Cheshunt College. I have often envied the men of the new Cheshunt with their splendid buildings and wonderful opportunities at Cambridge. We lacked so much the present men enjoy and missed the wider interests of a university, but probably worked as hard as most and turned with the same zest from our studies to great days on the cricket or football grounds where I played for my college during five seasons as centre half. To widen our experience some of us were placed in charge of village churches of which we were known as Deans. I became the Dean of Whittlesford, near Cambridge, and while there, the people decided to build a new and larger church, of which I was asked to lay one of the foundation stones. I conducted its fifty-third anniversary services when visiting England in 1956 and found few of my old friends left to welcome me. Among those who had gone on was one I missed very greatly— Mrs. Robert Maynard, a cultured lady, whose leadership had meant so much in Whittlesford and whose friendship and help enriched my early years abroad.

It was in 1901 that news reached England of tragic happenings in New Guinea which were to affect the whole of my future. At that time most people knew little about the country, though one of the earliest mentions of it is by a Portuguese explorer who in 1511 reached it from the Moluccas Islands, and after seeing its people, called the land Papua, a Moluccan word for frizzy hair. Later a Spaniard in 1541 renamed the island Novo Guinea as the inhabitants reminded him of those on the Guinea coast of Africa. Still later during the nineteenth century process of seeking colonies or spheres of influence, while the Dutch were already in possession of the western half, the British took over the south-eastern quarter and the Germans the north-eastern. In 1906 Australia undertook the administration of the British section and changed the name from British New Guinea to Papua; while after the first World War, the German territory became known as the Mandated Territory of New Guinea usually shortened to New Guinea. Thus the names once given to the whole country are now but those of separate quarters.

The London Missionary Society entered Papua in 1874, some ten years before the British Administration, by which time its missionaries were settled at various points along the coast. The interior was unexplored and even when I went out little was known of the region between the Fly and Purari rivers save that some of the wildest tribes in the country had their homes there. The whole of this area of thousands of square miles is a vast expanse of forest-covered swampy country where big rivers linked by cross streams transform the whole into a lacework of land and water with channels between innumerable islands and broad stretches of open water. Thousands of wild folk practising cannibalism had their villages in these parts and here one April day in 1901 something happened that was to affect the rest of my life.

It began one afternoon when the people watched with mounting excitement a strange craft approaching slowly as it felt its way between the shoals and mud banks.

The watchers were used to travelling in canoes, some quite small and others sixty or seventy feet in length, but this was something other with white sails instead of paddles, and as it came nearer it swung up into the wind as the anchor dropped. At once crowds of men fully armed with bows and clubs set off in their great canoes and, surrounding the little ship, closed in and clambered aboard.

Two white men faced them, and others with dark skins like themselves. The younger of the two was Oliver Tomkins to whom I had said good-bye a year before. The other, white haired with deeply lined face, was James Chalmers, known to multitudes as Tamate. He had ranged from east to west of British New Guinea and the story of his adventures had made his name a household word all round the world. He had faced many dangers and endured much privation and looked much older than he was, but he was still a pioneer. Here was a bit of unexplored country where he had never been and he had come among these cannibals hoping to make friends and settle for a time among them.

The wild men urged him to come ashore at once, but it was toward evening and Chalmers shook his head and by signs led them to understand that he would visit their villages in the morning. For him it was no new experience to be surrounded by fearsome looking crowds, and he and his fellow adventurers had their evening meal with canoes circling round the ship, then after evening prayers, turned in to rest. In the village, however, there was mounting excitement as canoes made for Dopima where there was much debate through the night.

Soon after dawn Tamate went on deck. Here and there he could see a village but most were hidden by the mangrove forest that fringed the shores. As Tomkins stood beside him, the whale-boat they had been towing had drawn alongside and they got into it with eleven of their helpers from the Fly River district. They made for Goaribari Island and pulled up a small creek leading to Dopima. Here a great house known as the *dubu-daimo* or men's house had just been completed, and this must have made Chalmers aware of danger, for such places were often dedicated with the blood of human victims, and he had seen the floors of similar buildings in the Purari delta glazed with the blood of the slain who had been dragged along their length. But he had faced danger too often to be deterred, and had he wanted to turn back, the way was closed by hundreds of armed men. So they went on and into the great house and almost immediately were attacked. A man standing behind Tamate raised his club and beat the old man to the ground, and as pandemonium broke out Tomkins and the rest of the party were clubbed, speared or stabbed to death.

At once the clothes were stripped from the bodies and the heads cut off, for these were prized tokens of the prowess of the killers, and in these great houses the skulls of victims hung in scores before the sacred images known as Agibe. News of the killing was shouted through the village and as the braves dragged out the headless bodies and began to cut them up, women and girls who had rushed from their houses carried the pieces off to roast on the fires for a cannibal feast. One body, the people have always declared, was left untouched. It was the body of Tamate that lay in the sunlight stripped of all clothes, with one who told me the story standing beside it. Dauwa at that time was a young man, a headhunter like the rest, but as he stood there some strange feeling gripped him and looking on the headless body it seemed all wrong to have killed so old a man. Thus they had died, Chalmers looking back on a life crammed with adventure, and Tomkins dreaming of all he was hoping to do, and eleven men of the Fly River who had accompanied them.

There were still the crew on board the *Niue* and strange to say these were not molested. Men came out to tell them what had happened, proud of their share in the killing, for this was part of their tribal life and bound up with age-long rites. They looted the ship but left the crew unhurt and these, in spite of danger, waited on, hoping some of their friends might yet return. Then, when at last hope died, they weighed anchor and brought the news to Daru from whence it was carried to Australia and flashed all round the world. Tamate was dead.

Since then two great wars have made us familiar with far greater tragedies, but in 1901 the loss of those men stirred the English-speaking world, since Tamate was so widely known. His adventurous life, his experiences among cannibal tribes, his vivid personality had caught the imagination of many thousands and to some of these his death seemed a horrid waste and an end to all he stood for. But for us who mourned the passing of our friends this was not the end. Their passing brought a challenge and we knew that we who live must take the place of those who fall.

2

OFF TO NEW GUINEA

WHEN Chalmers was killed I was still at Cheshunt College and serving the church at Whittlesford. The news which had shocked and saddened us had also brought a challenge and I volunteered for service with the London Missionary Society. Some of those dealing with my application were hesitant about accepting it owing to what they deemed my unorthodox views on sundry doctrinal matters but after a wait of twelve months they took the risk and I was appointed to the New Guinea Mission. No other appointment could have given me such satisfaction though quite a number of people had most exaggerated ideas of the dangers ahead.

"You will be eaten by cannibals," was the remark of more than one who seemed shocked when I suggested that to be eaten by worms was still more horrid. I could never see why people should be so concerned about the body when the occupant has moved out.

Insurance companies though unconcerned about these things were very concerned about my chance of surviving which they reckoned so slight that they would not take me on. I had a special introduction to the general manager of one of the largest Australian offices but when I asked for a life policy he held up his hands in horror; the deaths of a number of gold miners through malaria and hard liquor, followed by the deaths of Chalmers and Tomkins, had led the insurance people to view a man in New Guinea as a bad risk. Youth, however, does not worry over much when strange peoples and unexplored lands are beckoning and the dangers seemed small compared with the opportunities.

Thus it was that in 1904 I set out on a journey that was to take me where Chalmers had been working and at last to the people who had slain him.

Even today a long voyage is a wonderful experience but it was much more so before cinema and television had made us familiar

with the peoples of the world and aeroplanes and radio had made
that world so small. I have made over a dozen such voyages since
but no other was as crammed with interest as this first, with real
excitement added as we went through the Suez Canal. The Russo-
Japanese War was raging and just ahead of us was the Russian
fleet which had shot up our fishing fleet in the North Sea and was
on its way to disaster in the Sea of Japan. All day long we
followed it and as we entered the Red Sea the Russian search-
lights were sweeping over the water on the alert against the surprise attack they feared.

We were on the route familiar to many but Aden, Colombo,
Perth, Adelaide and Melbourne were all new and wonderful to
me, and after these the rocky cliffs of Sydney Heads and the end
of a long voyage and the beginning of new adventures.

In those days there was no harbour bridge but at a wharf near
where one of its great arms now rises we saw a little steamer
looking very small among the big vessels all around. It bore a
name crammed with romance and island story, *John William IV*.
Her earliest forerunner was a barque, the *Duff*, which in 1796
left England in the days of the Napoleonic wars to carry a company of missionaries and their wives to Tahiti and other islands
of the South Pacific. Following her, other ships went their way
in the same service until the pioneer missionary John Williams,
ranging among the islands, landed at Erromanga and was killed
by the clubs of wild men.

His death brought a challenge to the Church and a ship named
after him was built to keep his memory green. She was a sailing
ship and travelled far before piling up on a coral reef. By then
the children of our Sunday schools had claimed her and on hearing of her loss raised funds for her successor. Her career was very
short for *John Williams II* was wrecked off Niue Island on her
maiden voyage. *John Williams III* was more fortunate and,
known as the Children's ship, sailed among the islands of the
South Pacific and along the shores of New Guinea for many years
until her place was taken by the steamer *John Williams IV* we
saw looking trim and neat but very small among the big ships. I
watched them loading her. The crew of Rarotongans were stow-
ing a strange assortment of goods for the New Guinea Mission.
Flour, rice, hard biscuits, a whale-boat, a horse, some sheep and
one or two cows, cases of hardware, knives, axes, cotton prints,

tools, buckets, fishing-lines and hooks, roofing iron, sewing cotton and sail-cloth, something of everything for a land where there were no shops, and men and women were cut off from the outside world.

Then came sailing day and a crowd gathered to wish us good-bye. Wharf labourers and sailors from other craft seemed rather intrigued by a ship that commenced its voyage with an act of worship but the port authorities always showed special consideration for the little steamer whose story held for Sydney people so much of romance and adventure. Flying a navy-blue flag on which were emblazoned the white doves of peace we steamed down the harbour past ships that dipped their colours, the passengers on ferry steamers waving their farewells, until at last we passed through Sydney Heads and out to sea. We had left Australia and I had no regrets, no longing to go back. I was launched at last on a great adventure and eager to learn what lay ahead.

For a week or more we sailed on and at night I would listen to the crew singing as I had never heard men sing before. The tunes had once belonged to us but the islanders had altered them to harmonise with their own sense of music until one could scarcely recognize their source, but felt deeply moved by the deep, rolling voices and the wild beauty of their singing.

Soon we were in tropical seas passing great coral reefs where the waters that cover them are shot by vivid shades of yellow, green and blue reefs that rise sheer from the deeps like some great precipice against which an unwary ship can come to quick disaster. Above the water, flying fish glittering in the sunlight would travel far before slipping back again into the ocean, while dolphins would come hurrying towards us and play around the ship.

Up in the cross-trees a Rarotongan was stationed on the look out for isolated patches of reef but suddenly we heard him cry "Land oh", and soon after saw a smudge on the horizon growing ever larger until mountain ranges, hills and islands took shape, and there was New Guinea where I was to live and work and meet the sorrows and the joys of life and find new avenues of service.

Ahead was Samarai, an island gem with a small settlement of Europeans, and as the *John Williams* dropped anchor a whale-boat manned by Papuans in blue serge jumpers and loincloths

trimmed with red put off from the tiny jetty. They were bringing
the doctor and customs officers, for this was the port of entry
for Eastern New Guinea and as soon as formalities were completed we were free to go ashore.

Across the water was the island of Kwato where one of our
men, Charles Abel, was doing a remarkable work. We saw him
coming over to welcome us in a whale-boat built by the lads he
was training, and as he came on board with a fine-looking band
of young men, I had no doubts concerning the worthwhileness
of the work to which I had been called. Soon they were taking us
to Kwato where crowds of excited boys and girls swarmed round
vying with each other to carry our luggage and taking even the
smallest parcels from us just to have a hand in the welcome.

We walked across a cricket field that had been reclaimed from
a swamp and here Abel, a keen cricketer, had so coached his
Papuans that they were ready to meet any team the white
residents of the country could get together. Beyond the field was
a saw-mill and in the workshops, carpenters had been trained,
capable of putting up homes or building and repairing boats.

It was hard to believe that these were the children of 'savages',
yet one day I stood among the palm trees with two men: on the
body of one were ugly scars of wounds inflicted by the other
when they fought as chiefs of rival tribes, but they were standing
together with smiles on their dark faces; and the people they
had led to fight and kill now met to work and play and feast and
dance together.

The memory of those two men and of my first Sunday in their
country did much to cheer me when, in the years that followed,
the going was hard and the odds almost impossible. I had
wandered over the island among the palms and shady mango
trees and looked across the sunlit sea, where beyond the little
islands with their coral beaches, the mountains of the mainland
rose range on range as far as eye could reach. From where I
stood I looked down on a little channel between Kwato and the
island of Logea with numerous thatched dwellings lining its
shores. Hardly a soul was in sight and the island seemed drenched
in sleep until a bell rang out and the shores of Logea burst into
activity. The whole population seemed to be hurrying to their
canoes, dragging them over the sand and paddling across the
channel. Then, landing, they came up the hill in long procession,

the women clothed in rather long grass skirts seemed to be wearing about a dozen apiece and looked rather like animated haystacks. The men were less burdened and had reduced their clothing to a fine art and I wondered how men could wear so little and still feel dressed. As for the children, many wore nothing but smiles, yet all fitted well into the Papuan scene, with one exception. It was a man taller than most, but as he strode past me I was amazed to see his only garment was a white man's waistcoat tightly buttoned. How he came by it I have no idea but his bare arms and legs protruding from that waistcoat looked so peculiar that I had to pull myself together lest my mirth should hurt his feelings.

I was soon to discover that the Papuan had his own ideas on how white men's clothes are shown to best advantage, and have seen a pair of white men's trousers draped round the wearer's neck with the legs hanging gracefully behind, while a friend of mine noticing that a member of his congregation was strangely clad learnt that the wearer had a brother with no clothes so they had shared a pair of trousers between them and came to church each wearing one leg. It reminded me of a chief who on entering church had, at Tamate's command, very reluctantly removed a sadly battered tall hat, but later expostulated, "You made me feel very ashamed, Tamate; didn't you see it was all I had on?"

Recovering from the appearance of the waistcoat I followed the procession to the church, a grass-thatched building with openings in the walls in place of windows. There were no chairs or pews but mats of plaited palm leaves on which the people sat, men and boys on one side, women and girls on the other, and peering through the openings in the walls were the heads of those who could not find a place within. At first I felt a stranger among people of different colour, language and culture, but as they began to sing, the strangeness changed to wonder. Their voices had been trained and the tune, though wedded to Papuan words, was one I knew, and if for a moment my mind was with my own folk, I was soon back among these people with the glad feeling of belonging to a family that in many languages worshipped the one God and Father of us all.

The singing ceased and a young Papuan woman rose, and as she stood the heads of men, who once owned their women as they did their pigs, were bowed in silence whilst a woman prayed for them and us. She spoke to God as simply as a child speaks to her father and one sentence of that prayer has remained with me ever since: "O God," she said, "our hearts are so small and Thy love so big; enlarge our hearts that we may hold more of the love that is Thine." She was not far removed from days filled with lust and strife: her father had lived in them but she had made a great discovery which had brought to her and her tribe a happier life, and drawn her people with ours into a world-wide family. Strange how she had so quickly learnt what the historic creeds missed and failed to teach, that "God is Love".

Our fathers thought that men without our Gospel were far from God, but I have always felt when "the heathen in his blindness bows down to wood or stone" he is coming very near to Him as he seeks after the meaning that lies behind the mystery of life, and I have always been impressed by the persistence of that search and the discoveries made by the seeker. There are many lovely folk tales that reveal this and Charles Abel tells of one belonging to the Eastern Papuans. He came across it after a man had committed suicide. He had hanged himself after a quarrel with his wife and from then onwards his name was not mentioned but he became *Naniwa* or Someone. The body had been brought to the village and lay in state on a platform while the mourners sat around. Naniwa's body shone with the coconut oil rubbed over it, his face was painted red and a shell stick thrust through the septum of his nose. His hair was combed and decorated with red and yellow hibiscus flowers and he lay propped up for all to see while around him a circle of women howled the death wail and cut themselves with flints that blood might run down their faces. A great feast was being prepared and as Abel watched he asked if Naniwa was really dead.

"No," came the reply, "we say he is not dead; only his body dies."

"Where then is his spirit?"

"It is still here, but when the feast is eaten it will go."

"But where will it go?"

There was some hesitation before the answer came and then it was Dilomi the Christian Chief I had met at Kwato who took up the story.

"They say", he replied, "that all spirits of the dead go to Biula. It lies across the seas and the only way is beneath the water. The feast will help the spirit on the journey and give Naniwa strength for the way he must go. Yonder is the rocky cape from whence they say all spirits depart when they leave this world. A great snake lies there. Its slimy body stretches far beneath the sea, and while its tail is here, its head rests on Biula. The way is long and full of peril and so they make the feast, for if the mourners' grief is great and the food plentiful, Naniwa will be strong and walk along the slimy snake with ease, but if his friends neglect him, he will be weak and his feet will sleep and he will fall into the sea and be changed into a fish. But the feast today is big and the mourners wail loudly and Naniwa will arrive at Biula and one named Sanga will receive him and light a fire under a frame of split cane and lay him on it and Naniwa will come to life again and find his friends who have already reached Biula, and they will know him and welcome him with a great feast."

Dilomi loved the story and could tell it well and maybe believed some of it, but had discovered something more, and as he finished he turned away saying, "Farewell, master, I must go. The feast is ready, but there is only one way to Biula. I will tell them that He is the way."

3

ON TO PORT MORESBY

My work lay in Western Papua and the journey from Kwato provided an introduction to the country and its people as we called at our stations along the coast. In those days we looked to the steamer to bring all our supplies for the next twelve months and among these, tobacco bulked largely. This surprised me until I found that money was practically unknown among the people who conducted most transactions by barter. Tobacco formed a useful medium of exchange and served as a currency throughout the then known country. It arrived in cases usually holding about thirty pounds, the tobacco being twisted and compressed into thin sticks weighing roughly twenty to the pound. This enabled us to work out approximate costs on the basis of so many sticks for a day's work, or bundle of sago or basket of crabs or fish. Kerosene or paraffin was another important line, bottles of it being a popular form of barter once the Papuan became acquainted with hurricane lamps. A year's supply of the above, plus foodstuffs, drugs and bandages, etc., for the medical work at each station, together with building materials, household goods, school requisites, etc., meant landing a large amount of cargo by canoes or the ship's whale-boats. At times they loaded their canoes so heavily that one feared they must sink, but they usually got safely back to the beach where men, women, boys and girls would carry the cases up to the station.

Thus it was I became acquainted with peoples along the coast whose customs and costumes differed widely. These have changed greatly since those days as I realized when reading a letter written about this time. "Some", I wrote, "have tight bands of fibre or human hair fastened round their legs and arms, others have black stripes painted across their faces which as the day passes and perspiration does its work tend to make the painted savage look more like a dirty boy. Most slit their ears and many have fine wooden combs fastened in their bushy heads of hair. Women and girls wear grass skirts of varying design and length and the men of the east have strips of palm leaf drawn between the legs and tucked into belts of bark or woven raffia or cane. The men at Kerepunu, however, were the most lightly clad of all, as a piece of string was literally their only garment and if while working the string came undone they seemed most embarrassed."

The village houses were, and I believe still are, built on piles, but I doubt if those of today have as much time and trouble spent on their decoration as some I saw with coloured patterns worked all over the front. Yet those same houses had no windows or chimneys and the smoke from the fire on the clay hearth would fill the place and blacken the underside of the thatched roof. Maybe that was one reason why each home had a platform in front on which the folk would sit and chatter or doze.

Nearer Port Moresby we passed some of the marine villages built well out in the sea where one can paddle a canoe down the main street or fish from one's home. At first it looked as if such a village would be wiped out should a storm arise, but it had faced many a storm, for it was protected by a great coral reef under the shelter of which the houses stood secure.

We took the ship's whale-boat through Kapakapa, where on the hills inland Dr. Lawes had established the first Training Institution for Papuans. It was here that I acquired a new name. The Papuan has no sound in his language akin to our "ch" and as the students and their wives came to greet me I discovered I was known to them as Buta, and to my friends and many others that is still my name. A church was to be opened and a brown-skinned man was to open it. He was not very big and seemed old and worn to my young eyes but his life had been crammed with adventure. Ruatoka had lived on the lovely island of Rarotonga and was one of the first to come to New Guinea, and was at work in Port Moresby when William Lawes arrived. He, the South Sea Islander, was the pioneer and I think built the first church in that place. It was a quaint building far better suited to the climate than many more pretentious places for it consisted of a thatched roof supported on wooden pillars and in the tropics no cooler house could be designed.

Ruatoka had been trained by James Chalmers during the ten years that fearless man had spent in Rarotonga and volunteered for mission work in New Guinea when those who did so knew they took their lives in their hands. When I met him he was nearing the end of his long years of service among tribes then constantly at war and when life was cheap and there was no white government to give protection. He had pioneered in the Manu-manu district where his companions died of fever and then moved on to start work in Port Moresby. Though he had seen many of his countrymen die and known some killed, he had held on through the years winning respect and affection from white and brown alike.

Here I met him, an old man standing by the door of another church he was to open. This was no thatched shed but a lovely little timbered building and we white folk stood back waiting for his lead as well we might, for he was in this land before us all, and through danger and sickness had borne his witness down the years. Thinking many things as we watched, we saw him insert a key into the lock and swing the door wide open. But he did not enter. He drew back as if standing aside for someone else, and we heard him saying very quietly, "Go in first, Lord Jesus," and so the Christ came into His own, and in awed silence we followed Ruatoka into the House of God. A fresh breeze was blowing as we left Kapakapa for Port Moresby and the barrier reef that fringed the coast was plainly marked by the waves that broke upon it in a line of foam, though on calm days there is no such warning. A rough beacon marked the passage through the coral and we steamed between the reef and the shore, and rounding a point entered the harbour.

Everybody knows of Port Moresby now. Australian and American troops fought to keep it from the Japanese, and from its aerodromes rose the planes that drove enemy fighters and bombers from the skies. From this place also the forces set out on that hard fight that finally flung the Japanese back in terrible defeat.

There were no aeroplanes in the world when I first saw the little township and the Japanese had only started on their amazing march to power. It was a very small and undeveloped place with a few government offices and the homes of the governor and sundry officials and traders. There was a wharf where small ships could come alongside, a couple of stores and a little church of which our man at Hanuabada was the minister but which welcomed representatives of every denomination. All the buildings were of timber with corrugated iron roofs, which as the sun beat down upon them became unbearably hot, and the largest was an unpretentious place calling itself an hotel. Gold miners, traders and venturesome travellers made it their home when passing through, and drinking was heavy and life pretty wild at times. A novelist once described it as the sink of the Pacific, but I doubt if it was worse than or even as bad as many places nearer civilization and my memories of it are lit up with happy friendships and kindnesses received from those who, separated from their kith and kin, lived in a trying climate and did their work under difficult conditions. Port Moresby changes with the seasons. The wet season was well advanced when I first saw it and the foothills and forest-covered mountains were beautifully green, but sometimes for six months or more there is no rain and all the hills are parched and brown. Yet even drought could not take away the beauty of the sea or the greatness of the harbour with its picturesque villages built above the water.

In those early days the men and boys were wearing little, but the women and girls wore what are often called grass skirts but which are made from the very young leaves of the sago palm teased out and dyed to lovely shades of brown and yellow. No European garment suits the Motuan girl so well and we have tried to instil in them such pride in their native costume as not to wish to copy ours. Unfortunately the trading stores tempt them with brightly coloured cotton prints and slowly the lovely Papuan skirt gives place to less attractive dress. We may deplore the change but cannot stop it, though I believe there is now a strong movement among the Papuans themselves to encourage the use of these native garments on all special occasions.

The men were born seamen and their fishing craft with their crab-claw sails both picturesque and speedy. The hull consisted of a single canoe to which were lashed two or more poles extending some feet beyond one side. Some decking was laid on these on which the mast was stepped with an outrigger fashioned from a log of light wood beyond the deck, towards which the crew would run should the wind threaten to capsize their craft. They had a much larger sea-going ship called a 'lakatoi' and this was made of two or more big canoes, lashed side by side and decked all over. Many of these two-masted vessels with large crab-claw sails traded along the coast. They served as freighters for the pottery made by the Motuans, who bartered it for sago made by the western tribes living in low-lying country where the sago palm flourishes. In the villages around Port Moresby the long, dry spells often ruined the gardens and left them short of food: hence the long voyages taken by the men to get extra supplies.

Among the Motuans, the making of pottery was a major industry. The potter, always a woman, having first prepared the clay, worked it up with her hands while smoothing the surface with a wooden spatula until the completed pot looked almost as symmetrical as one turned on a wheel. Each pot was put in the sun to dry and when a number were ready the woman piled wood round them and started a fire, carefully tending them until they were burnt a brick red. Some were used in cooking, being placed on big stones with fire beneath, others to carry water from the waterholes; but most were used as barter, and before they were sent away, the pottery was displayed outside the houses, each woman proud to show others the work of her own hands.

All this fragile cargo was stacked in deck houses fore and aft on the *lakatoi* and then to the accompaniment of ceremonial dances the men would set off on their long trip to the west. They took this journey only once a year, for these two-masted craft could not sail close hauled but had to run before the wind, so they waited until the south-east monsoon was drawing to a close and as the winds grew light, travelled before them. Their arrival was not unexpected for this was the season at which they always came, and since the goods they brought were much in demand, a truce was called to fighting and the tribes of the west met the men of the east to feast and dance and barter. During their stay the Motuans felled great trees and shaped them into rough canoes and eventually the *lakatoi* that on the journey out consisted of three or four big canoes lashed together, was rebuilt with perhaps a dozen. During the rebuilding the sago was coming in, for when the pottery was bartered, two sticks had been put in every pot, one for the buyer, the other for the seller, the buyer having to bring in a bundle of sago weighing about thirty pounds for each stick he possessed, his womenfolk working day after day in the swamps to prepare it. When at last the tally and rebuilding of the *lakatoi* were complete and the north-west winds had become less boisterous, the vessel, laden with tons of sago, would set off on her homeward journey, a longer and more dangerous voyage in heavily laden and much more unwieldy craft. They tried to keep close to the coast but would sometimes be blown far out to sea or the south-east monsoon would start earlier than usual and storms arise and their ungainly boat be broken into pieces. But the trading went on and these primitive voyagers continued to face great risks with cheerful courage. I saw them first at Port Moresby preparing their ships and then in the west where they bartered their pottery, and I have seen the *lakatoi* at sea, each with crab-claw sails hoisted and a drummer for'ard beating out some rhythm to secure a fine passage and a safe return.

The Motuans are far from black. Many in fact are a light copper colour and the patterns tattooed on their bodies showed up well—too well I often felt when I saw a pleasant-looking face sadly disfigured by the markings. Yet no woman regarded the patterns as a disfigurement, rather the reverse, for in her eyes the designs she bore through life added to her charm and proclaimed her status. They were not merely decorations but writings all could read. A pattern found on most women was begun when as a girl she was betrothed, but it remained unfinished until just before the wedding when the markings then became her marriage lines. A girl with markings on her legs and thighs wore her skirt slightly open down the side that they might be better seen, for these and perhaps others proudly displayed upon her abdomen proclaimed her a daughter of the master of a *lakatoi,* a notable man of the tribe, a Papuan Drake or Frobisher. Other markings tattooed under the eyes, or a line beginning from her chin and running down the middle of her chest, proclaimed her father's prowess in a fight. He had killed a man, and she shared the honour of his deed and wore these tokens of it. A sharp sago thorn was used to make the necessary punctures into which charcoal powdered in oil or water was rubbed and although the process must have been painful, no girl would miss it, for only thus would she be regarded as properly adorned.

In those days most Papuans had their ears punctured or split and the holes made were so enlarged that the lobes sometimes hung down close to the shoulder. In other cases the slit was just large enough for shells or other ornaments to be fastened to it or to serve as a useful clip for a piece of tobacco. Being without trouser pockets the slit in the ears became very useful and no self-respecting man would leave his ears as nature made them.

Another almost universal custom was the piercing of the septum of the nose. Among some tribes this was done when the child was still a baby but among the Motuans the piercing did not take place until the boy or girl was ten or twelve. The ceremony was of religious significance and the child prepared to face it by observing certain taboos, for much hung upon it being properly carried out. If it was not done there was no hope of heaven, for no one could hope to enter the Good Place of departed spirits with nose unpierced. Consequently if a child died before the operation, the hole was made after death to ensure a safe entry.

Often I would hear the death wail in the village, for the mortality among the people was fairly high, and would sometimes see a widow smeared with mud and hung about with grass garments which were literally widow's weeds. Many of their burial customs seem strange to us but I was always aware that in them they expressed their belief that death was not an end but a new beginning and an entrance into another world with larger freedom.

The Motuans bury their dead, and before the body was placed in the grave a relative would whisper in the ear of the deceased, "Do not be angry with us but watch over us and bless and prosper us," for to these people the dead became gods. They were *Dirava* and this word is now used for God in translations of the Bible. The pots, spears, lime gourd and a small bag containing betel nut would be buried with the man (or in the case of a woman, her grass skirt), and some food, a large bag, a short stick for digging and a tomahawk were placed on the grave. Later, this might be covered by a hut which would be kept sweet and clean for a time in the hope that the spirit would return, though if he did so he would be minus his nose, and if scolded for not coming sooner would go away ashamed and never come again.

In common with other tribes these people believed in a heaven and a hell, obedience to a tribal custom being the passport to heaven which could only be entered by those whose noses had been pierced. Those who had missed this operation went to Mamaro, the bad place—bad, not in the sense of evil but because it is the place of hunger and want. The elect or nose-pierced went to Tauro, away to the west, and the story concerning this bears. some resemblance to that told by Dilomi.

"Far out to where the sun goes down the spirit travels along a length of thick cane reaching on and on under the sea, and as he goes, he balances himself with the support of a short bit of cane he carried with him. His ancestors will be waiting for him in Tauro for when in the village the drums begin to beat to tell all who live that one has died, out there the spirits of the departed hear the throbbing, and opening the gates, come out to meet the one who comes to them. They bring him in and place him on a stage beneath which fires burn, and turn him over and over until all the moisture of the earthly body is dispelled and he becomes light and airy, able to fly like a bird wherever he will. He has reached his heaven and met his friends of other days, with whom to fish and plant, hunt and talk and never know what hunger means. He has become a God to those who remain on earth. The spirits of the dead are strong. They touch our lives in many ways and hear our prayers and can reward or punish."

We may think their customs strange, but as I learned these thing I sensed how God has never left man without some gleam of light and hope beyond the darkness of the grave. Sometimes I wondered if the Papuan savage was not nearer the truth than many of the white men who came to live in his land.

The folk-tales often reveal more than glimmerings of great truths as does the story of Dausia and Mauvai.

"The two girls lived in an eastern village and Dausia was plain, while Mauvai was most beautiful. Though plain, Dausia was full of energy and ever ready to lend a helping hand. She would be off in the early morning to the garden or to catch the tide when the people went to fish. She would be away in the afternoon and return with a heavy load of firewood or garden produce in the great string bag she carried on her back, supported by a band across her forehead. Always she was among the workers. Mauvai though beautiful was lazy and vain and spent much time oiling her body that it might shine in the sunlight and combing her frizzy hair into which she would stick the red hibiscus flowers before walking through the village to revel in the admiration of the men.

"One day Dausia was sitting on a tree trunk that bent over the sea sewing up a mat with the aid of a needle made from the wing-bone of a flying fox. She sang as she worked, until the needle slipped from her fingers and fell into the waves beneath. Without hesitating she dived after it, following its slim whiteness through the water. Soon she found herself in a cave where the white, red and yellow coral made the place a fairyland of beauty and little fish of many colours darted among the sea-weeds or played among the coral branches. Suddenly the girl met an old woman. 'Where are you going, Dausia?' asked the woman, and Dausia replied, 'To find my needle which I've lost.' 'Very good,' said the old woman, 'but don't eat anything you see.'

"So Dausia swam on, and came to where a bunch of ripe bananas hung from the cavern's roof. She was hungry, but as she stretched out her hand to take and eat, she remembered the warning and left them behind. Then she found a basket full of ripe pawpaws and again hesitated, but with the words of the old woman in her ears left them untouched. Next she found an earthenware cooking pot in which yam and taro were floating in rich coconut milk so appetizing that they tempted her, but still remembering the warning she went on. She had gone far but now at last right ahead she saw the needle, and retrieving it, started to return the way she had come. So long was the way that though it was evening when she had dived into the sea it was now morning as she stepped from the water. The birds were calling to one another, the sun was near to rising and men from the village were coming towards her with their nets and fish spears. Dausia took little notice of them, nor did she expect they would notice her. She knew she was plain and unattractive, and looked round in surprise when one cried out, 'Whence comes this maiden all so beautiful, with eyes like stars and lips like the red hibiscus and hair that ripples like the sea?' She looked around in vain to see this lovely girl and then caught sight of her reflection in a rocky pool and started back in sheer amazement for she was utterly changed. She was no longer plain. All that the men said was true; she had become most beautiful and the villages gathered round her full of wondering admiration while she shyly hung her head as the best boy followed her, wanting her to be his bride.

"Mauvai was watching and jealously filled her heart with bitterness, for the people had ceased to notice her and all their talk was of Dausia, the loveliest of all the girls. She made enquiries and, thinking she had found the secret, took a needle, and sitting where Dausia had sat, dropped it into the water. Down it went with Mauvai swimming after it right into the coral cavern where she was met by the strange old woman. 'Where are you going, Mauvai?' she asked, and Mauvai replied, 'I'm seeking my needle which fell into the water.' 'Very well,' said the woman, 'but don't eat anything you see.' Mauvai swam on. Soon she saw the ripe bananas hanging from the cavern's roof and Mauvai, heedless of the warning, for she had always pleased herself, picked and ate them. Next she found the pawpaws and again stayed to take her fill, and so on to the cooking pot with its coconut milk and yam and taro where once more she feasted, and well satisfied, continued her search and swam on. At last she found the needle and with a sense of triumph started back along the watery way.

"It was morning when she had dived beneath the sea but night had already fallen as she came out and made for the village. A number of men were sitting around a fire and she walked proudly towards them, for now, she thought, I am more beautiful than Dausia and they will love to see me. But as the firelight shone upon her she saw the men jump up in horror and as they ran away, one cried to the others, 'Whence comes this horrid creature, with no hair on its head and a skin like the soot on a cooking pot?' Mauvai stood trembling, wondering what had happened, then felt her head and found her hair was gone, she felt her body and found her skin was rough and hard, and as the moon rose over the palms she saw herself reflected in the rocky pool and shrieked in misery, for all her beauty had departed.

"With a cry of despair she fled into the forest and no one has ever seen her since, but at times you hear a cry among the trees; some think it is the cry of a night bird or flying fox, but it is the cry of Mauvai and she is weeping for her lost beauty that will never return."

Such a story makes one feel that even the primitive man senses that it is better to be kind than beautiful and that there is a loveliness of life worth more than all the good looks in the world.

4

WESTWARD HO!

THE pioneers with whom I worked, before the world was shattered by two great wars, have long since gone from us. I think it was on my second visit to Port Moresby that we said good-bye to Dr. Lawes, the first white missionary to live among these people. Papuans from all the villages around had gathered for a last sight of their friend. Long years before, they had met him with more suspicion than friendship, but he had ministered to their sick and stood between them and their enemies; he had reduced their language to writing, translated the Scriptures into it and compiled a grammar to help those who followed him. Over the years he had won the confidence and affection of the Motuans and they came in long procession, each carrying some gift or token to express what they found so hard to say. They were strange gifts: bows and arrows once used in the fight; carved drums that had so often sounded in the dance; plumes of the bird of paradise that once beautified their head-dresses; spoons and bowls carved from coconut shell, or larger bowls carved from wood; mats plaited by the women, and clubs with stone heads brought by the warriors. I watched them piling their presents in a great heap before the white-haired man who stood there with his wife, his faithful comrade through the years, and when at last they left for Australia, the crowds stood weeping by the shore knowing they would see their friends no more.

At Port Moresby I met the men from all our districts, gathering as they did each year to plan for the tasks that lay ahead. Their homes were spread along seven hundred miles of coast, a tiny company attempting an enormous job. All have gone from us and I alone am left with my memories of old comrades. Charles Abel of Kwato, Rich, then commencing his work at Isuleilei, and Saville starting his at Millport Harbour; Pierce growing old in the work at Kerepunu and Schlencker working among hill tribes of the Owen Stanley range. Lister Turner preparing to take over the work from Dr. Lawes, and beyond Port Moresby Dauncey at

Delena, Pryce Jones at Moru and Holmes at Orokolo but preparing to move on to the Purari delta. Still further west Baxter
Riley was making his home at Daru. And these ten men held a
coastline that would reach farther than from Land's End to John
o'Groats. I had come to join the company to work with Baxter
Riley among the islands of Torres Strait and the tribes east and
west of the Great Fly River, where Chalmers and Tomkins had
been working before they met their deaths.

Travelling west we landed with Dauncey at Delena. Across the
waters of Hall Sound could be seen the church and houses of the
Roman Catholic Mission that from there worked up the St.
Joseph River to the mountain ranges. At that time about seventy
priests, brothers and nuns worked from this centre. Often I have
felt humbled by the sacrifice they make, leaving kith and kin and
staying at their posts until death carried them away, yet I have
been saddened that so much devotion should be linked with so
much intolerance.

We humans are so unlike and God made us thus. He has small
place for uniformity, and fills the world with birds and beasts,
with flowers and trees full of glorious variety, and made us in
many moulds. What meets the need of one fails to satisfy
another. Some worship best in silence and others with a song;
some find help in simple forms and others in ornate cermonial.
There is no one answer to man's search for God, yet this diversity
brings much perplexity. A group of Papuans came to a government officer with a question they had long debated: "Which was
the true religion?" Some were Methodist, some Church of
England, others were Romans and others attached to the London
Missionary Society, usually known as L.M.S. "Which was the
true faith?" they asked. The officer was a wise and tolerant man
and told them a story to make things clear. It was published in
the Papuan Villager, a periodical issued by the government to
encourage the use of English as the lingua franca. Speaking of the
confusion in the minds of those who spoke to him, he likened
them to four companies of men and women setting out to climb
Mount Yule, a mountain known to them all.

They started from north, south, east and west by different
routes, climbing the steep ascent hid from each other by dense
forest but ever moving up until at last they reached the summit
and there they met. The ways were different but at the top they

were together, lost in wonder at the glory of God's world. I felt that here was the answer of a man who understood and I was grateful, but when I visited the editor I found him much perturbed. A letter had come from the Roman bishop, a letter of stern protest against the story, and a warning that should another be published, all his people would be forbidden to read the paper. So among those once divided by tribal enmities a new and horrible division is being enforced. Yet we are all God's children, seeking Him along many ways with the assurance that those who seek will surely find. Something just as tragic happened at Isuleilei. There had been a great gathering of young people, Anglicans, Methodist and L.M.S. rival teams had competed in cricket and football and they had shared together in evening sing-songs and then at the end of a week of happy fellowship it was suggested that they should all gather together for the service of the Holy Communion. The suggestion came to nothing, for the leaders of the Anglicans forbade their followers to share in this, and the fellowship was rudely shattered where it should have been most real. I wondered what those beginners in the Christian way thought of such denial of fellowship between those who loved the same Lord and I have always felt that those who seek to force uniformity of creed and dogma upon the minds and hearts of men are creating the very schisms they deplore.

Walking through the villages in this part of the country we noticed many of the houses had two separate ladders by which to reach the entrance platform, sometimes six feet above the ground. One was of normal but rough construction and used by the family, but the other was backed by slats made from the midrib of the sago palm and used by the dogs. There is a delightful folk tale concerning this which I learnt from Dauncey.

"In the days of very long ago," the story runs, "the people of the land possessed no fire. They could cook no food nor could they warm themselves at night when the winds from the mountains made them shiver. Yet there was fire in the land. Far up on the mountain top it blazed, guarded by Haiavaha, a creature great and terrible, with long hairy arms, ever on the watch lest men should come and steal it. Often they had tried to get it, but they had always failed.

"Almost in despair, they sent messengers to the people of the forest calling them to conference; and from the long grass and the shade of many trees they came—the pig, the wallaby, the cassowary and the dog. As they gathered, the old man of the village spoke:

"'We are tired,' he said, 'tired of eating uncooked food. We shiver when the rains come and the winds at night blow cold from the mountains. Oh, people of the forest and the long grass, we want you to help us. Who will go and get the fire that Haiavaha guards? Oh, pig, will you do this for us?'

"'No,' said the pig, 'I could never get through, for whenever I find a thing I want I always grunt; I just can't help it, and if I grunt up there, it will be the end of me. I cannot get the fire for you.'

"They turned to the wallaby. 'Oh, wallaby, will you go for us? You could do it, for you could jump right over Haiavaha's arms.'

"'No, no, it is no good,' said the wallaby. 'He would hear me coming, for whenever I jump I come down with a bump. I cannot get the fire for you.'

"The old man looked at the tall, strong cassowary and cried to him, 'Oh, cassowary, will you go? You travel quickly and you can run fast and Haiavaha will never catch you.'

"'No,' said the cassowary, 'I am too tall. My head sticks out above the long grass, and Haiavaha will see me coming. It is no good, I cannot go.'

"Only the dog was left. He sat there, short-haired, reddish-brown and with a pointed nose.

"'Dog,' said the old man, and the dog looked up. 'Oh, dog, you are our last hope. These others are all afraid but you are brave and clever; will you go and get the fire for us?'

"'I will try,' said the dog, 'and I might manage it if only I can keep my mouth shut, but I so often want to howl and I must be quiet. Farewell, and watch for my return, perhaps I will bring the fire.'

"Into the forest he went and up the mountain-side, beyond the trees and through the tall grass until close to the edge of a clearing he stopped and thrust his pointed nose out from the grass. There was the fire and there was Haiavaha nodding; he was asleep. The dog stifled a howl of delight and crept silently in, grabbed the firestick in his jaws and ran. Then Haiavaha awoke and reached after him with his long arms, but they were now too short. The dog was away and as he ran he shouted back, 'I have your fire, Haiavaha, I have your fire. Why did you sleep, oh foolish one?'

"Then down the hill he came, running in triumph, and the village people shouted with joy as they saw him break from the forest with the firestick blazing in his jaws.

"'The fire, the fire, at last we have the fire,' they cried. 'Now we can cook our food and warm our bodies in the heat and never more be cold at night. We have the fire but what shall we do for the dog who brought it?'

"'This we will do, my people,' said the wise old man. 'We will make him one of us. He will live in our homes and travel and hunt with us and at night he will sleep by the fire he brought.'

"So they built the second ladder that the dog might come into the house and share its comfort with his friends."

Old and young listen eagerly to such tales as this and every tribe has its stories, stories of the way the lands were made, and of how the fish came in the rivers, of great spirits who brought the coconut or showed them how to build their homes; stories of heroes who fought great fights and did many mighty works. They knew nothing of writing and had no books; but at night by their fires as the bamboo pipe was passed round, tales such as that of the dog who brought the fire would be told or an old man would start a song or chant, which all the rest would join in, singing stanza by stanza some story of old.

5
OROKOLO

NOT many miles beyond Delena lies Cape Possession, separating the two main races of Papua. East are the Melanesian peoples with the copper-coloured skins and west the Papuasians or Negroid peoples, a darker and on the whole taller race. The Melanesians came from far, and made their homes in different lands. Some think they first belonged to India and others to Africa, and they seem to be linked with tribes in Madagascar as well as in the South Pacific. The western peoples dwell in villages which in my time were quite unlike those east of Cape Possession and they speak different languages. After leaving Delena I found myself amongst them.

It is never easy to land on their coasts when the south-east monsoon is blowing, for the Gulf of Papua has few sheltered spots, and when the *John Williams* anchored off Orokolo the current swung her broadside to a heavy swell and we began to roll in a manner that made the hazards of getting ashore through the surf appear preferable to the discomforts of staying on board. It was a long pull but once ashore and standing on the hard, black sand I felt as if I had entered a dream world. Here were villages unspoilt by the touch of the West and the people living much as their ancestors had lived centuries ago.

Towering over all the other houses were the *eravo* with their sloping, overarching roofs rising sixty to seventy feet above the ground. The *eravo* were sacred places where the men of the clan foregathered, but into which no woman dared to enter. Here the gods might dwell, and here were kept the bull-roarers and dancing masks, and here the young men were instructed and initiated into the secrets of the tribe. As soon as possible I visited one of the largest. The great roof, thatched with palm leaves, arched over the entrance platform and come to a point far above it, and from this pointed roof dangled a totem shield. A screen hid the interior from the gaze of passers-by and shut off much of the light so that the end of the hall was lost in the shadows; but the sight that greeted me on entering was an amazing one.

Hanging from the rafters on either side, were long rows of fantastic dancing masks. Some must have been ten or twelve feet in length and the men using such would get inside to be hidden from all spectators. The masks consisted of cane frames covered with tapa cloth on which were worked curious patterns outlined by thin strips of cane and painted in with red, yellow, black or white. One had a snake running down its length, others had long projecting beaks like prehistoric birds. Some had representations of human faces and others various tribal marks, but no two were alike. A man seated on the floor was working the strips of cane into a pattern on the mask he was making while another was filling in the colours on the one he had almost completed. The paints, made from clays or the juice of roots or berries, were in small plates of coconut shell placed beside him and his brush was a piece of cane with the end well stubbed, but with these crude tools he worked with real artistic sense. Later on these masks would be used in a wonderful festival, the preparations for which took months and were then going forward; I was privileged to see something of its greatness in later years. Near the dancing masks totem shields hung from the walls or stood against partitions that divided both sides of the hall into a series of cubicles, where the owners kept their weapons and personal possessions. It was an awe-inspiring place, and as I stood in this home of primitive Papuans, their achievements filled me with wonder.

Outside, the children were swarming. I never saw such numbers in all Papua as on the black sands of Orokolo beach. They had crowded round as we landed, shouting aloud in wild excitement and escorting us to the mission house, and then, like children all round the world, gone off to play.

They made sand villages, the overhanging roof of the *eravo* being constructed by piling wet sand against the bent back of a small boy who, when the shaping was complete, would slide gently from under, leaving the sand house a remarkable model of the real thing. Having made two villages at some distance from each other, the owners of each would stand close to it and with balls of wet sand try to batter the other to pieces. They had whip tops made from seeds, balls made by plaiting leaves of coconut fronds and very interesting spinning tops with long spindles.

These they held between the palms of their hands and gave them a twisting motion, spinning them on plates of shell and competing as to whose would spin the longest. They played with toy bows and arrows and became clever marksmen; they had a game of touch and another of hide-and-seek and, most exciting of all, a form of hockey. It seemed to have no rules nor any limitation to the length of the hockey stick, and women, boys and girls all took part. The ball was a very young coconut or hard, round seed and the aim was to drive the ball through the territory of the other side. They might start with teams fairly equal but as all liked to be on the winning side there was an increasing number of deserters from the weaker party until, with tremendous shouting, all seemed to be driving the same way.

To the casual observer the children seemed to be growing up with no training or education but, actually, they were always at school. Their school was the forest, the seashore and the village where they lived, and day by day they learned to fish and hunt and garden. The girls learned string-making and basket-weaving from the women, the care of the gardens, the preparation of food, the taboos and rights and duties that were theirs. The boys learned from the men how to make their bows and arrows and fashion the masks, build houses, fell trees, shape canoes. They were always at school until, well prepared for the stern duties of life, they married and soon were teaching their children.

At the end of the *eravo* I noticed a rough structure of plaited palm fronds extending from the house. The entrance was closed by a screen and within were a number of lads, their bodies shining with coconut oil and looking sleek, well fed and happy. They were going through their final initiation during which they were taught the secrets of the tribe and the duties of its members. They were shut away from the village for many weeks and no woman or girl was allowed to see them. So terrible was the taboo that they believed sickness or death might come to any female who looked upon the face of an initiate. Hence the enclosure to guard the youths from prying eyes. Still, the lads needs must take their walks abroad, and so they constructed a cage of plaited leaves that looked something like the shell of a giant cocoon and within this they could shuffle to the seashore still hidden from the gaze of women.

During these weeks of seclusion young braves who had already been initiated went dancing along the sands each wearing a peculiar high-pointed mask with a long-toothed beak projecting from it and sometimes fashioned as a bird. From the mask supported on the shoulders of the dancer a grass skirt was suspended, which covered his body so that only his legs could be seen, plus a longish stick that he carried. As the dancers came along, stopping here and there to prance around, people on the sands moved quickly for the dancers had the right to thrash any loiterers with their sticks, and a crowd of screaming girls and women would often be seen fleeing from the masked men. Yet these dancers could be great workers and the building of the *eravo* was a tremendous task that made heavy demands upon the strength of the whole clan.

The house, built on piles well off the ground, might be two or three hundred feet long and all the timber and materials had to be cut and brought in from places often far away. The overhanging front was supported on two great posts sixty or seventy feet in length and the lifting of these was no mean feat. Scaffolding was erected on either side of a post as it lay prone on the ground with one end close to a hole dug to receive it. Long lengths of cane for use as rope were brought in from the forest and poles were lashed together to form crutches to help with the lifting. Then gangs would climb the scaffolding and catch the cane ropes already fastened to the post and as they pulled, a gang on the ground lifted, and as soon as the top was high enough, one of the crutches would be slipped beneath it, and as it went higher, yet another, with everyone calling to the rest in a tumult of shouting.

I have held my breath as a post rose slowly and swayed dangerously, with the crowd growing more and more excited. Men, sweating and yelling, were, I feared, finding the task too great for them; but they kept at it, and the post went on rising until, with a tremendous shout from the workers, it slipped into the hole and was made secure. This was the most ticklish job, and once accomplished, the framework was erected with all the timbers lashed by strips of cane or home-made cord and not a nail or iron fastening in the whole structure. The floor of palm bark was laid on joists of mangrove and the roof and walls thatched with sago or nipa palm leaves, and when completed, such a building stood firm and secure, able to defy the heavy winds of the south-east monsoon and remain dry within through a tropical deluge.

6

DARU

AFTER leaving Orokolo for Daru where I was to make my home, we steamed on through the night and next morning picked up Bramble Cay, an outlying fragment of the great Barrier Reef of Australia. There was not much to see save a low sandy inlet on which stood a beacon to warn shipping, for the Cay lies in the path of ships from the East bound to Australia or Suva. Later we saw land, just a long, low line of mangrove, which as we neared it separated into the islands of Bobo and Daru with a small channel between them. There were no hills to be seen and the blue sea changed to the muddy waters swept out of the Great Fly River. After the beauty of the east it looked a most depressing spot. Later, the ship slowed down as the leadsman called the depths. There were no buoys to mark the passage, but we had a fine leadsman, an old Rarotongan of great experience. He would stand at the top of the gangway swinging the heavy lead to and fro, well ahead of the ship's bows and down into the water, while he called out the marks on the line. "By the deep nine, sir"; "By the mark eight, sir"; so it went on as we felt our way in. Ahead were some small craft in the roadstead and as we rounded a bend, a few houses on the shore. It was from here that Chalmers and Tomkins had set out on their last voyage, and Riley and I were to carry on the work they had been doing.

Daru is the port of entry from Thursday Island, over a hundred miles away on the other side of Torres Strait, and between the two are numerous islands whose peoples are closely linked with the Papuans but are under Queensland jurisdiction. The Papuan Mission began on these islands and with Murray Island as a base, started work on the Papuan mainland. Known then as British New Guinea, Chalmers explored its coast and later established work among the Toaripi tribes in the Gulf of Papua. From there he moved west to Saguane on Kiwai Island at the mouth of the Fly River. It proved a most unsatisfactory base and it was while moving on to Daru that Mrs. Chalmers died. The house he built there and lived in after her death became my first home. It was a rather primitive place and I had hardly settled in before I contracted my first dose of malaria. The old hands said that if you got malaria early you suffered less from it later on, and that certainly was my experience. I had a bad dose to start with, but when, after some months of recurrence, I shook it off, I had far fewer attacks than most of my colleagues. It is a miserable experience and the first time it hit me I hardly knew what was happening. I had found life full of excitement and each day well worth living, and then suddenly the zest of it all went from me and the days seemed heavy, and walking a burden. My head ached terribly and I shivered under blankets, while my skin was burning hot. I shivered so much that the bed shook and then the shivering gave place to heat and I would perspire so profusely that pyjamas and sheets needed changing two or three times in a few hours. Then the attack would pass, leaving me exhausted and seeing life through jaundiced eyes.

Daru is low and swampy, but its few white inhabitants slowly transformed it. They planted crotons whose many-coloured leaves shone in the sunlight, and hibiscus shrubs with glorious blossoms, and the frangipani with its sweet-scented clusters. Poinciana trees in flaming red fringed the shore and made a wonderful splash of colour against the dark green of the mangoes that lined the main street. Most of this came later and it seemed a most desolate place when I first lived there. Perhaps the after effects of fever had something to do with that for they say the fever convalescent sees life at its blackest and everything as vile.

There was, however, much of interest in the island. The administration of the law was taken with tremendous seriousness by the administrators who would add to the gaiety of the other whites by their disputes on methods of administration, while at one time the wives of the two government officers were seriously at loggerheads owing to a dispute which assumed dangerous proportions and centred round an argument as to which of them was the leader of society. As the population consisted of themselves, a number of Papuans, a sprinkling of half-castes and a few white folk including one trader with a white wife and another with a coloured one, and a sailor with several, there did not seem to be a lot of society to worry about. All the same, the dispute convulsed the island and provided much entertainment in the days before radio.

The native population was unlike any I had seen along the coast. Here changes were taking place that were transforming the life of the village communities. The Papuan was copying the ways and dress of white men and the result was far from pleasing. Many were wearing European clothes which were old, torn and very dirty and contrasted ill with the crowds I had seen further east who still retained their native dress. Their villages, too, were changing, and native architecture was giving place to imitations of traders' shacks far less beautiful. The Papuan was trying to be like the white man and apt to think the ways of the latter were always worth imitating, and one of our tasks was to help him discern between the good and the bad; to make his own that which would enrich his life and to refuse that which would destroy the good he had.

Many had picked up pidgin English but Riley had set his face against this horrible jargon and was training a number of young people on Daru to speak and read correctly in addition to training them in the vernacular Kiwai language. I was in full agreement with him and failed to see why the people could not be taught to use simple English instead of the vile gibberish they had acquired. I therefore set myself to cultivate the habit of using the simplest words possible to express my meaning and found if I did this, the man who spoke pidgin not only understood me but began to copy me. As Colonel Ainsworth said when reporting on the Mandated Territory of New Guinea, "There is no reason why it should be easier for a native to say 'one feller boy' than it would be to say 'one boy', yet the Authorities there have made this horrible jargon the official *lingua franca*. They were until recently doing all they could to encourage it and what is still worse have, with the aid of certain missionaries who should know better, committed a crime against all decent language by fixing it in writing."

Fortunately, under the more enlightened leadership of those who have followed that great administrator, the late Sir Hubert Murray, the aim in Papua, as distinct from New Guinea, is to develop the use of correct and simple English and thus open the door to the wide range of literature already available and being used in Africa and other parts of the world. It will, I fear, take a long time to undo the mischief already done by those who have followed the bad example of the Germans before them and encouraged what J. W. Burton calls "this awful jargon—utterly useless in conveying any accurate ideas".

7

AMONG THE ISLANDERS

AFTER a short stay on Daru I set out in the *Niue* to visit the Torres Strait Islands. This was the boat in which Chalmers and Tomkins had sailed to Goaribari. She was an old craft and had carried sago, much of which had got into the bilges, and when she rolled and churned up the bilge water, the stench in the cabin became almost unbearable. She was also full of cockroaches of a large and ferocious variety. On hot, still nights they often got excited and chased each other through the cabin and over my face, and I always knew when they were getting busy by the queer rustling they made. I discovered that they were literally man-eaters, so before turning in at night I would pull on a heavy pair of socks and tuck my pyjama legs into them to prevent the creatures eating the skin of my toes while I slept.

This most lively and evil smelling ship was my home for weeks until in order to get into closer touch with the islanders, I settled for a time on Mabuiag, an island midway between Papua and Cape York. Here I lived with a Samoan mission teacher and his wife in their very simple home among the palms.

The situation sounds attractive, but a coconut grove can be a dangerous place for the unwary, and not a few have been badly hurt by nuts falling on their unprotected heads. Moreover we were close to the beach, and through the south-east monsoon, the winds would roar around the house or whistle through its many crevices, while day and night we would hear the noise of the sea pounding on the coral reef.

The island was very hilly and I frequently took long tramps over the hills and through the bush where the bamboo grew luxuriantly, or down some ravine beautiful with masses of maidenhair fern. Sometimes I climbed the hills behind our house, from which I could look across the sea to the islands of Nagi, Moa and Badu and others so far off that only on very clear days could they be seen. No two days were alike and at times the scene was unforgettably beautiful: a wild, stormy sky; and in the west, the heavy rainclouds a pure deep violet; the sea changing all the time, reflecting back the violet of the clouds, and then, when the sun broke through and shone upon the reefs, becoming alive with every shade of green and many a tint of blue and gold. Where the dark hills of Moa rose, a white cloud often crowned the summit of the highest and sometimes along the horizon a bar of light would stretch from east to west, edging the multi-coloured, foam-flecked sea with a line of lightest green. Such scenes brought me very close to God and sent me back to the village refreshed and thankful that life could be so good.

These islanders were not heathen folk. Thirty years before I met them the pioneers had planted the Church in island after island. Most of the early missionaries were Samoans, Lifuans, Rarotongans, who had left the loveliness of their own islands to bring these Torres Strait folk the Gospel that had changed so utterly the life of their own people. I was there to give a lead to the young church, but as I look back, I have my doubts as to the wisdom of entrusting such a task to young, untried men, and often think how much more I could have done for the people had I but known what the years since have taught me.

My work demanded much that is never included in the curriculum of a theological college, and during the years spent in Torres Strait, I was doctor, dentist, builder, carpenter, sailor and teacher by turns.

Soon after settling on Mabuiag, a girl whose body was covered by queer spots was brought to me. "Measles," cried the teacher who had children of his own, and on this island measles meant something far more serious than in a white community, for populations in the South Seas have been devastated by it. These islanders knew nothing of infection or of the danger of a chill and when the fever was upon them they would run into the sea and then sit in the wind to cool off, and as a result frequently died of pneumonia. Knowing an epidemic was probable, the headmen were warned of the dangers and the beaches patrolled to keep sufferers from the water, while I kept a look-out for fresh cases. They came quickly and my time was fully occupied going from house to house to see my patients.

I was not well myself and still suffering from malaria, and, after visiting the patients, would come back to my humpy and go between blankets as another shivering attack shook me from head to foot and left me limp and weary.

We had sent a warning to the government resident at Thursday Island and were put in quarantine while I was supplied with the necessary drugs, and so alternately treating the people for measles and its complications and myself for malaria we won through and lost only one man. We would not have lost him if he had not sat at the door of his hut so that the heavy wind then blowing might cool his fevered body. All the sick and suffering looked to me for help and I had to be oculist, optician and dentist as well as physician and surgeon. If practice makes perfect I certainly had plenty of practice. I won some reputation in treating or removing aching teeth. This latter operation became a popular diversion for all except the one undergoing the experience.

Life on the whole was pretty uneventful, and a tooth extraction provided both excitement and entertainment. It interested me to note how more people had troublesome teeth after the Sunday morning service than at any other time. Whether twinges of conscience had started twinges elsewhere I never discovered but as I came from church I frequently found some sufferer waiting to be relieved of a troublesome molar, and it was on one of these occasions that I was greatly humbled. My patient was a fine, buxom woman, black of skin, comely and strong, but looking very sorry for herself, for her tooth gave her no rest and ached horribly. Would I relieve her of her enemy? She had no need to ask twice; but I soon realized that this thing was not going to be done in a corner. The verandah of our house was about three feet above the ground and provided a splendid stage. I fetched a chair and seated Balo upon it while I prepared instruments, antiseptics, etc. By the time all was ready, a big and what promised to be a most appreciative crowd had gathered full of eager anticipation. Having located the cause of the trouble and selected the appropriate forceps I prepared to get a grip. All would have gone well had not the patient, to the amusement of the watchers, suddenly shut her mouth. It took all the encouragement the audience could shout to get her to open it again and much persuasion on my part for her to keep it open. Each time the forceps came near, the mouth would shut fast to keep them out, but at last I got them in and hastily gripped the tooth.

Balo was both stout and strong and the tooth a back molar and I prepared for a tussle while the crowd which had been steadily increasing seemed full of excited expectation. As I began to pull, the woman began to grunt and the crowd to yell encouragement. Then Balo flung her arms around my neck and held me fast and the more she grunted and the more I pulled the more the audience enjoyed it, showing their appreciation with shouts of delight. In the face of such applause I could not admit defeat and held on doggedly until out came the tooth. The spectators gave a round of applause and I was feeling really pleased with myself until I looked carefully and realized with a shock of horror and remorse that I had got the wrong tooth. My humiliation was complete and my sorrow profound but nothing I could do could put it back, and to my amazement no one seemed to regard it half as tragically as I did; they probably felt they had had a glorious time and a little thing like a tooth was not worth worrying about. Even Balo bore me no grudge and became a real friend, greeting me with a wide smile of welcome whenever I came her way, which proved that she had a very forgiving nature.

My parish was widespread, calling for sea journeys of hundreds of miles through what were often very stormy waters, and I felt I should never get around it effectively until I had a boat of my own. My financial position was such that under normal conditions I saw no hope of securing even a dinghy, but at that time conditions were very abnormal.

Thursday Island was one of the chief centres of the pearling industry with various fleets of pearling vessels based on it. All were in trouble, for the Russo-Japanese War had so upset the market that there was no demand for the shell that kept the fleets in being, and the boats were laid up, and numbers of them for sale.

A pearler named Cowling, with whom I had become friendly, but who had lost everything, told me that one of his cutters which had only been built three years was now in the hands of the receivers. He had seen it lying half sunk in shallow water looking as if it might become a total wreck, and thought the receivers would be glad to get it off their hands. I accordingly took a trip to Thursday Island and when I offered the receiver fifteen pounds for the boat as she lay in the water, he gave me such a look that I hurriedly raised the offer by a pound and gave him a day to think about it. The cutter did not look up to much as she lay half sunken in the water, and I suspect that he thought sixteen pounds better than nothing as next morning I found myself its owner. We had to put her on the slip and get her caulked and re-coppered but even then she was a gift, a splendid little craft some thirty-five feet long in which, as captain and owner, I sailed thousands of miles and had some great adventures.

As a splendid site was available on Darnley Island, I decided to move from Mabuiag and make my headquarters there, and started to build my first house. Carpentry and joinery had always been my hobby, a fact that served me in good stead, as I became architect and builder of churches, schools, workshops, houses and boats. I was young and strong and in a short time had a band of young men around me eager to share in the work I was doing. They travelled with me on *Pearl* as our cutter was named, and worked with me ashore. They were born sailors and also quick to learn the use of tools, though they sometimes astonished me by their unconventional methods. While building my house, some of the bolts used in fixing the top plates to the verandah posts had rusted and I went off to fetch a spanner to free the nuts from the end of them. Returning, I saw a fine young fellow named Aragu already on the job, and shuddered at the sight. He had the nut firmly held between his teeth while with both hands he gripped the bolt and so unscrewed it. All my teeth were on edge as he, quite indifferent to my vicarious suffering, went calmly on to complete his task.

While at work, men came rushing to me with the news that one of their number had fallen from the top of a tall coconut palm. I hurried down and found the poor fellow in agony. His nose was smashed and face and body cut, and worst of all, both femurs were broken and the bones sticking through the flesh. Making him as comfortable as possible, I ran up the hill, studied my books and went to my bench to make a couple of Liston splints, while the patient lay where he had fallen, his friends around him discussing the doubtful possibility of his recovery. As soon as the carpenter's job was completed, I pulled the legs into position, fitted the splints, dressed the wounds, and bandaged all up neatly. Everything looked quite workmanlike and some time later the man was again walking freely among his friends though one of his legs was not as straight as the other.

There were a number of young men eager to be trained for missionary and teacher service and the islanders, glad to have a training centre in their midst, set to work to help us build a school hall and row of houses where the students might live with their wives and families. The training varied, for they shared in the work of the station and travelled with me when I visited other islands or went across to Papua, but I think the variety of their training made better men of them and enabled them to give sound leadership to their people.

The Queensland government had taken over the day schools and with the spread of English, Sankey's revival hymns with their bright choruses had become very popular, though to me they did not seem very appropriate for weddings. The people on Yam Island had no such misgivings and no hymn that I knew tackled the question so directly as the one they used, for the first verse pointedly attacked the groom with, "Why do you wait, dear brother? Why do you tarry so long?" The chorus drew attention to the bride, as the people roared, "Why not? Why not? Why not come to him now?" and sung twice over it was irresistible. In the second verse the groom was again challenged with, "What do you hope, dear brother, to gain by a further delay?" and the bride could join in that and sing with all the rest until the rafters rang. The thought of that hymn in such a setting has always been a sheer delight but to my amazement no one else seemed to sense the humour of it.

From my home at Darnley we could see the hills of Murray, the most fertile and beautiful of all the islands, and with the largest population.

They had erected a splendid church with thick limestone walls but an earthquake had so damaged it that the roof was unsafe and the walls in bad condition. With plenty of willing helpers I was able to devise means by which the structure and roof were effectively repaired and at the same time I learnt a lot about limestone walls from the workers. The first South Sea missionaries had taught the people how to use their coral for building purposes and I watched them preparing it. A wide, deep hole was dug in the sand and in this were placed alternate layers of wood and coral until the pile rose high above the ground. This when fired reduced the coral to lime which when mixed with sand made splendid mortar. Lumps of limestone and coral were bedded in it and the result was a fine white durable building with thick walls that made for coolness. When at long last our task was completed the roof was stronger and safer than it had ever been and the whole building with its limestone buttresses much more impressive. Everyone was delighted and there was a wonderful re-opening ceremony with crowds from other islands sharing in the great thanksgiving service and mighty feast followed by songs and dancing that went on through the night. The work on the Murray church was so successful that other islands wanted similar buildings and the coral limestone churches we built will probably be in service long after I am forgotten.

Though these islanders were adopting a way of life far other than that of their fathers, they still retained many of their old customs and beliefs, with the result that old and new were strangely mingled. Their burial places, for instance, revealed that many still cherished the belief that the dead had need of all they used in life, but its expression took strange forms owing to the people possessing articles in common use among white folk. It never struck me as strange or incongruous that beside the dead warrior in Papua was laid his bow and arrows and dancing head-dress, but it did seem strange to find upon the grave of some woman the sewing machine she used in life, or above another a four post iron bedstead with, still more surprising, a chamber beneath it. Evidently in the minds of the mourners the dead had many needs.

8

THE GREAT FLY RIVER

BEFORE south-east New Guinea was made a British protectorate, there was direct communication between the Torres Strait Islands and the mainland, but once the latter had an administration of its own, regulations restricting this came into being. These were not rigidly enforced when I went to Darnley and I had permission to run to Daru and the Fly River without first clearing from Thursday Island, but I knew this arrangement could not continue. Both Queensland and British New Guinea were insisting on stricter compliance with normal procedure and it became evident that our work in the Strait would have to be separated from that on the mainland. As a matter of fact, a few years after I left, the supervision of the island churches was handed over to the Anglicans who were already well established on Thursday Island. This seemed a wise move when so much was waiting to be done up the great rivers and along the coast of Papua. I would set sail from Darnley and after visiting various islands, go on to Daru and the Great Fly River with its many villages.

The *Pearl* was a fine sea-boat but it had few conveniences and my cabin was seven feet long, eight feet wide and four feet high and like an oven when the sun beat down on us. We faced all weathers and when beating up against a gale would have the seas coming over the bows and sweeping the deck from stem to stern with never a chance to cook a meal or even boil some water for a drink of tea. Our ship would be loaded with everything we needed for ourselves and the villages we hoped to visit. Drugs, bandages, surgical instruments and dressings, dental forceps, and things summed up in the word trade; all had to be taken. Money was unnecessary, for we would be among people who did not use it. What we needed was less portable: twist tobacco, fish lines and hooks, looking-glasses and beads, knives and hatchets, and brightly coloured cotton print. With these we could pay carriers, buy food and make friends with new folk. In addition, we took what no one in those parts had ever seen, a magic lantern and boxes of coloured slides.

From Daru to the Fly River the coast is just a long line of mangrove forest with nothing to relieve its dull monotony. Toward the east, a narrow channel runs between Parama Island and the mainland which saves small sailing boats from two or three days' journey round a great reef through what are often very heavy seas. The Pass was a haunt for crocodiles and on one occasion I shot no less than nine as we went through. We entered the river which at that point is over forty miles wide and landed in the rain on Parama Island and for three miles tramped through mud and water to the village. It was a nightmare journey as the tide came in, for the deepening water drove us among the mangroves, where their roots mingle with those of the pandanus to form an obstacle almost as difficult to negotiate as barbed wire entanglements. The people crowded round as we entered the village wet and tired, and Manga, a Christian teacher from Mabuiag, took me to his home. Thirty years before, his people were savages, but Manga had found a better way of life and was, in that most inhospitable spot, trying to help others find it also.

We took the lantern ashore and rigged the sheet in one of the largest houses but had a job to steady the projector, for the floor seemed to have the jitters. These homes were built on piles six feet above the ground and the floor consisted of slabs of palm tree bark laid on mangrove saplings, and moved up and down as the people walked along it. No one who could walk or crawl stayed away; the village turned out *en masse*, and the finest film ever shown never had a more enthusiastic audience than that which watched with breathless wonder our series of pictures which were often very crude. I had been ashamed of them but now I was glad I could take them with me, as we travelled up the great waterway visiting many villages and enduring vast discomfort.

We sailed for miles across the river to the island of Kiwai and anchored off Iasa. It looked an interesting village when the tide was up, but as it fell, what seemed a mile of black slime lay between us and the shore. Donning my sea boots, I stepped from the dinghy into the soft horror wondering when I was going to stop sinking and speculating what would happen if my boots stuck fast and I had to leave them behind. It was dark when we reached the shore but men with flaming torches of dry palm leaves came down and led us to the village. Here there was an immense *auwo-moto* four or five hundred feet long and to this we took the lantern gear. It made a magnificent hall, partly illuminated by the torches, but stretching far beyond into the gloom with its fine, thatched roof lost in the shadows overhead.

It was easy to fix the sheet from the rafters, but as at Parama, not so easy to steady the lantern, and while we worked, the audience assembled. With pictures of places and animals I had some ingenious moving slides, including a London coster using a skipping rope, and Punch, whose nose grew longer and longer until an imp appeared sitting on the end of it, and a Red Indian who opened his mouth and rolled his eyes in a horrible manner. When the man with the skipping rope appeared there was a dead silence, then a startled grunt of amazement as he skipped and a grunt with each skip as they followed in quick succession, until peals of laughter rang through the building. The Red Indian with the rolling eyes had a different reception. At first he startled them, and they shouted at him and clung to one another as if afraid, but finding him harmless, made fun of those who had shown most fear. Punch was the greatest success. I discovered it was better to proceed in stages. Punch with a short nose appeared in silence. When it suddenly grew an inch there would be a gasp of surprise, another inch and a loud grunt, another, and a shout, and so on with the excitement growing until the imp appeared sitting at the end, when grown men and women would rock to and fro and roll on the ground convulsed with laughter. Never had they seen anything to equal this and no picture theatre ever had a more appreciative crowd.

Later, the laughter would be hushed as another story unfolded before their wondering eyes, and no sense of incongruity oppressed their minds. They enjoyed to the full all the fun and laughter, and then turned to follow with eager interest a story that fascinated more than all that had gone before. I had a set of slides telling the story of the Prodigal Son and another of the life of Christ. Both were highly coloured and crudely drawn and offended my sense of the artistic, but when later I secured a world famous series in which each slide was a work of art, I was bitterly disappointed to find that these beautiful pictures never made the appeal of the cruder drawings. They were too beautiful, too full of wonderful detail, and the untrained eye of primitive people could not appreciate them. The bold outlines and few simple figures of the earlier pictures stood out clearly and were easy to see and understand, and though I put them on the screen feeling I must apologize for them, I found the audience filled with wonder and touched with awe. In these simple pictures they saw the things Manga had taught them, and seemed to feel that the prodigal son was travelling the hard road quite close to them and that Christ was teaching, healing and dying on a cross while they watched. After such a night many of them never went to sleep. They sat around the fires going over all they had seen, talking and asking questions. This coming of Christ to men had never seemed so real before, and over and over again they recalled the ways he went, and the things he had done, and the story of the cross, and the wonder of the resurrection. These were the pictures they were most anxious to see. The moving figures filled the place with laughter, but this other story was one that held their wonder and touched their hearts with awe and was still talked about when the memory of all the rest grew dim.

After repacking our gear I went by a path among the palms to another great building, a communal dwelling where all the members of the clan lived under the same roof. On either side were cubicles, most of which were open to the gaze of passers-by, like a great cow-shed with human beings in the place of cattle. Before the cubicles, fires were burning on hearths of clay or mud, and here they broiled their fish, roasted their crabs and baked the sago that was their staple food. Men and women, boys and girls were sitting around or lying on their mats, while some were already fast asleep. Their possessions were hanging from the roof or stacked in corners, canoe paddles, wooden spades, water bottles made from coconut shells or gourds or short lengths of the giant bamboo, long and beautifully woven raffia bags through which the sago is strained, fishing nets and bows and arrows, all could be seen in the flickering light of the fires, arranged around and above the compartments of their owners. Slowly I wandered through this amazing place where the smoke from many fires curled upward to the high, arched roof and finding no outlet, hung in a blue fog above our heads. The flames lit up the wild home and the faces of its occupants, and the years seemed

to drop away, and I was looking at the homes of my own
people who in the distant past lived in the swamps of England
much as these were living here. I listened to the murmur of
voices, the cry of a babe, the laughter of young folk talking
of what they had seen, and caught a smile of friendship from
one who looked up at me. Everything changed, the savages had
gone, and these were people like ourselves with their hopes and
fears, theirs loves and hates, their joys and sorrows, and not just
strange, wild things.

Rounding the southern end of Kiwai Island a day or so later,
we passed Saguane where James Chalmers had once made his
home. His wife had been used to all the comforts of a lovely
English home and it hurt to think of her at Saguane, for it was a
dreadful place. The mouth of the river is fifty miles across and
the south-east monsoon drives the muddy water before it, and at
high tide swept it under the mission houses and into the
swamps at the back, while day and night the wind howled
through the palm trees and the mangroves. Tamate made his
home here to be near the peoples of the river, and here his wife
faced loneliness and fever and watched the destruction of all the
things she treasured as reminders of her English home. Like many
another brave soul she held on through the years, until stricken
with fever, they carried her to the mission boat and as the
anchor dropped off Daru, she breathed her last; one more life
given over in the service of a wild, cruel land. As we sailed past,
we knew no other would make a home where she had lived, for
the encroaching sea was washing all the land away, and where
the mission house once stood the water was fathoms deep.

During this journey I was inspecting the very elementary village schools and encouraging the pastor-teachers, and we made
for Ipisia where two Samoans, Tovia and his wife, were working.
They had had a lovely home on one of the two most beautiful
islands of the Southern Seas, where food was plentiful, and life
easy and happy, with all the friends around them; yet they had
left it all, to work among a people who gave them little, without
expecting much in return, and where food was often poor and
the climate cruel. Asked why, they said with no heroics that
they had to come, for this was God's call to them and there was
no other way.

There was a time when the men of Ipisia had driven a missionary from their village, but Tovia had won their friendship. He had built his home from timber cut from the forest and thatched it with palm leaves and covered the floor with the lovely mats given to them by their friends in Samoa. There was little furniture save a table and a stool and a bed with webbing made from cords of coir fibre and covered by a half-a-dozen soft mats. Hibiscus and frangipani blossoms were used to beautify the room, and on the table was a young coconut with the husk stripped and the top cut off, so that it formed a cup full of its own sweet, cool milk into which had been squeezed the juice of a lime. Here was a bit of Samoa with its lovely welcome amid the uncouthness of wild New Guinea, and as I rested, Tovia's wife prepared a delightful Samoan meal, something quite different from a European feast.

These people had never seen pictures, and I found at times they could not understand them. When I threw upon the screen the picture of a cow there was no response, nothing but a dead silence. I realized it was because they saw nothing but a blur of meaningless colour. Here was the primitive man I had read of who could not understand a picture, and I set out to teach them what it meant. "Look," I cried, pointing to the different parts, "here are its eyes, its ears, its nose. This is the body, these the legs, and this the tail." There was a moment's silence as they took it in and then a roar of delight with one explaining to another and all shouting as they saw it. Some, however, were terrified, for to them these pictures of men were spirits brought to the screen by the magic of the white man, and they lay upon the floor and hid their faces from the sight.

All the time the show was on the dogs were everywhere, mangy creatures for ever snarling and fighting. They seldom bark, and their finest musical effort is a long, plaintive howl that fills the air with resounding horror, for when one starts, all the rest follow, until a hundred sharp noses are lifted skywards as all join in the chorus. As the noise grew in intensity I found it impossible to compete, so would give up the struggle and wait for the storm to pass. Nature, however, is full of surprises, and as I left the howling dogs and fever-stricken village, there by the river was a dream of loveliness. Around us the dark night was alive with fireflies and we seemed to be surrounded by a world of fairies, lighting their way with their tiny lights. These lovely insects, actually tiny beetles, seem to delight in gathering

together, and I have noticed that they return to the same tree
night after night. The light they give is never still but pulsates
like the beating of a heart, and the tree seems ablaze with shining
jewels, flashing and flickering, while all around are thousands of
other lights, like the lamps of fairies patrolling round the place
where the queen holds court. The loveliness made us hold our
breath in wonder and forget the swamps behind those trees and
give thanks to Him who has made even the dark places of the
earth so full of beauty.

My crew were getting rather bored with the lantern and glad
when at last we set sail for Darnley. We left the Fly River with
a good following wind, expecting to pick up Bramble Cay before
dark and anchor under its shelter. We were well out of sight
of land when the wind eased and then died right away and we
drifted helplessly until nightfall, unable to anchor in the very
deep water and knowing the strong currents would be setting us
off our course. Then we saw the stars swiftly disappearing behind a black mass of cloud and knew a *guba*, or very heavy
squall, was on the way. The rain came in torrents as the wind
roared down on us, and with close-reefed jib and mainsail we
ran before it. Somewhere ahead was the Cay where more than
one big ship had struck, and if we hit it, our small craft would
be smashed to pieces with small chance of any escaping with
their lives. We drove on, with one of my best boys well for'ard,
clinging to the jib-stay and looking ahead through the rain and
darkness of the night. The crew were on the alert and very
fearful, and I kept by the steersman with a long, light pole
handy, for in shallow water a pole gets soundings more quickly
than the lead. Suddenly there was a cry from the look-out:
"Keep away! Keep away", and a white line of breakers appeared
right ahead. We jammed the helm hard over and the boat heeled
steeply as she swung round. I thrust the pole into the water and
the helmsman gave a shuddering grunt, for it struck the rocks
beneath and we held our breath waiting for the crash as we piled
up. It never came; instead the *Pearl* held on her way with the sea
deepening rapidly, for we had met the Cay at the point where
the reef turned north, and we drove round it and on to leeward.
Only a few yards lay between us and disaster that night and all
on board felt that God had been with us, guiding our little boat
through the storm to safety.

9

REGIONS BEYOND

Our early contacts with villages on the Fly were always bringing news of other peoples and adding to our travels as we tried to
reach them. The Bamu River at that time was little known and
still awaiting exploration, and beyond it, the Gama and Turama,
the Omate and Kikori and vast delta country connected with
these rivers. The Bamu has five mouths, one of which connects
with the Fly, and all the country is low and swampy, yet in this
uninviting land were many villages, while higher up where the
land was better, the villages were few. Food supplies were one of
the reasons for this, as the lower reaches abounded in fish and
crabs with big sago swamps near at hand. The enemies of the
coastal tribes who lived higher up provided a further reason, as
a kind of no man's land lay between which all avoided.

One of the lower villages was Buniki whose men had the
reputation for being great fighters, and we set out to get in touch
with them. Entering from the Fly River we worked our way
along streams fringed by nipa palm and mangrove. The *Pearl*
boasted no engine, as in those days marine motors were little
known, and we often had to wait for the tide to help us, but
eventually we dropped anchor off the narrow creek that led to
the village. Ashore everything seemed strangely quiet and when
no answer came to all our shouting, we set off in the dinghy to
investigate. The crew were not happy, for they knew the place
had a bad reputation, and as we pulled up-stream they were
anxiously scanning the nipa palms that walled us, fearful of the
arrows they thought might be let loose by hidden braves. Rounding a bend, we saw the village in a clearing and jumped ashore
near the communal house. For all our shouting there was no
answering call; the place seemed deserted and we clambered on
to the entrance platform to investigate. It was dark within, after
coming from the sunlight, and we stood for a while to let our
eyes get used to the gloom. The great place was empty and the
silence eerie, for the possessions of the people, mats and baskets

fishing nets and spears and much else told us this was no ordinary deserted village. Seeing on a clay hearth in front of a cubicle the white ashes of a burnt out fire, I stooped to touch them and found them hot. Men were not far away and my boys, thinking things looked suspicious, wanted to return to the boat. Back on the entrance platform we began once more to call to the villagers, and suddenly caught sight of a man among the forest trees. He was a fearsome figure, a warrior with painted face and feather head-dress and bow and arrows in his hand. We knew others like him were not far off and wondered what they were contemplating. I signed to him that we were friends, and held out a piece of trade tobacco. He hesitated, then turned and gave a call, and out from the forest came groups of men, armed and ready for trouble. They were very suspicious but slowly gathered round, and after I had given each a smoke one raised his voice and shouted something and out from the bush trooped crowds of women and children and we knew all was well. They stopped some distance from us talking excitedly, but gathered round when reassured by their menfolk, eager to get the bits of tobacco I handed out. Later we learnt the reason for their fears. The men had been fighting and had killed members of another tribe and all knew that as surely as night follows day, the friends of the slain would exact payment by raiding them and murdering as many as they could.

Further up the river we caught another glimpse of their wild life. We were tacking from bank to bank and saw a large village ahead of us and soon realized that our appearance was creating tremendous excitement for crowds of armed men came rushing together and lined up near the water. The closer we came, the greater became the excitement, and we were sharing in it for none of us had ever seen a sight like it before. The men were wearing strange feather head-dresses and their faces and bodies were painted in fantastic patterns while all carried their bows and man-killer arrows. As we stood in towards them on our next tack we could hear their yells as they raised their bows and threatened us. Then a man jumped into a canoe and started paddling towards us and told us we must on no account attempt to land, for the people were celebrating the *Moguru*, a ceremony no strange eyes must ever look upon, and the men were there to drive us off should we try. Though there was much we would have given a lot to see, to have gone there against their wishes would have been to antagonize those we were out to win, so with a wave to the crowd lining the bank with their half-drawn bows, we kept on our way, steering as close as possible to see what we could of a truly wonderful sight.

During these journeys we often heard of many villages in the country between the Fly and Bamu, and I made plans to visit them and try to discover an overland route between the two great rivers. Leaving Darnley in the *Pearl* we made for the Fly and at Ipisia met an interesting young scientist named Landtman, a Finlander who was investigating the customs and folk lore of the peoples of western Papua. As soon as he heard of my plans he was so anxious to see something of the inland tribes that I agreed to take him with me and found him a most interesting companion.

About eighty miles up the river, the mud flats gave place to high banks of reddish clay and we landed on solid ground at a village named Gaima. The people were very different from those lower down the river and related to the inland tribes we wanted to visit. They were a very undressed crowd, the women wearing almost nothing save a belt and a band of fibres while many of the men wore hats and nothing else.

These were the first hats of tribal origin I had ever seen and were cone-shaped like the dunce caps worn by dull boys in the dark ages of our educational system. They were made of cane and fibre wound round and round and spiralling to a point from which projected a plume of feathers of a bird of paradise. The hat was then finished off with native paints, red and black on a white ground. At first I wondered how the thing kept in position but discovered that the man, having made his hat, would collect the gum from certain trees or the sticky wax of the wild bee and, working it into his hair, glue the hat firmly in position. Once there it stayed put, secure no matter how the wild winds blew. He wore it by day and slept with it by night, his head resting on a strange wooden pillow lest in his sleep his hat should suffer. He wore it until things underneath made him feel a change might improve matters. I bought one off a man's head and shook it very carefully before taking it on board. The transaction was interesting. I explained what I wanted and offered a stick of tobacco and some hooks but the owner seemed unimpressed. I added a fish line and small mirror and he looked interested, and when a bit more tobacco and some extra hooks went with the rest, a smile and a nod told me we had at last arrived. The price was right but the hat remained securely fixed to his head. To complete the transaction he called a friend and the latter took a shell with a sharp edge from his raffia woven bag, and as my man stooped down, started to use it to cut the hat away, and by the time he had finished, the late owner had had a hat off and a hair cut in one operation.

The community lived in one great communal house very different from those on the lower reaches of the river, save that, like all Papuan homes, it was raised well off the ground on piles. The steps leading to the entrance platform were made from a log into which notches had been cut but on reaching the platform I was surprised at the small size of the front entrance, and though I was then much slimmer than I am now, I had to squeeze myself through what was little more than a hole in the wall. It was a simple method of protecting the inmates from a rush of hostile invaders. Within was a fine lofty hall with the walls on either side built from the midrib of giant sago fronds, neatly lashed by thin strips of cane and reaching from floor to ceiling. It was a most imposing place with its high arching roof and great floor space unencumbered by stalls or cubicles. The living apartments behind the walls were on three floors approached by ladders of notched logs like the one at the entrance. The lower rooms were used as kitchens and approached from outside; the second floor provided apartments for women and children, while the topmost was occupied by the men and older boys who had free run of the great hall into which women did not seem to enter save for special ceremonies. Outside the house, neatly arranged down either side, were gardens lined with croton and flowering shrubs and in all my wanderings among primitive people I never found such careful planning of the surroundings as among these people who seemed to take a delight in bright flowers and shrubs and in the arrangement of the gardens.

There was, however, a dark streak in their social habits, for children were not numerous owing to homosexual practices. I knew there was little hope for their future unless a new way of life and the power to live it were revealed to them, and it was to open a way for the Christian Gospel that I planned this journey.

At first it looked as if we might have to turn back, for very heavy rains had fallen and the people said the swamps would be impassable. It certainly was wet but fear as well as rain made them try to dissuade us, for ahead were unfriendly tribes among whom life was very insecure. Consequently, we had difficulty in getting the carriers required for the food, barter goods and other things we had to take with us. It took much persuasion to get even a few to help us, and even these would only come as far as a village one day's march from Gaima.

As we set off, the rain started and the track was deep in mud through which we squelched hour after hour until the low lands began to give place to undulating country and we broke out from the forest into a stretch of grassland. It was not the kindly grass of an English countryside, but hard, coarse stuff that cut the hand and reached above our waists until we were weary with forcing our way through. Later on, descending into another stretch of low-lying country, we reached the swamps of which we had heard so much. The rains had transformed them into a vast lake and we waded in with the water ever deepening until in places it reached our armpits and even called for a bit of swimming. I began to feel uneasy as I thought of the things I had shot in the rivers, so turned to one of the carriers to ask if there were any crocodiles about. "Plenty," was the cheerful reply, and I felt still more uncomfortable, but waded on, hoping for the best and glad when after hours in the dark swamp, the muddy forest welcomed us again.

It was a very wet and weary crowd that reached Nida where we piled our gear at one end of the great hall and after a meal turned in for the night. The floor on which we lay was made of black palm laid in strips side by side, something like corrugated iron, and no matter how or where we turned there was always something sticking into us. I slept at last through sheer exhaustion but my crew were snoring almost as soon as they hit the floor, for the Papuan can sleep almost anywhere, and in my time his favourite pillow was a bit of wood.

We had little difficulty in securing fresh carriers and eventually we reached Baia with its communal building between fifty and sixty feet wide and the great hall some four hundred feet long. Little was to be seen on first entering, as what light there was filtered in through various holes and chinks, there being no windows anywhere. The thatched roof was almost lost in the shadows but presented a fine appearance when torches were lit and the fires blazed up.

No women were to be seen, but they could be heard as, hidden in their apartments, they were watching us through crevices in the walls, and there was audible evidence of much excitement. Later, I met some outside the building who promptly fled, and then, overcome by curiosity, suddenly stopped and turned to have a better look at me. Some tobacco offered to the nearest soon brought scores around, and when I rolled up my sleeve and they saw the white skin untanned by the sun, the noise was deafening as they marvelled at it. Some had nets over their heads which sometimes reached to the waists, the nets being a sign of mourning, the widows wearing the larger ones. Someone had died quite recently so, with the aid of an interpreter, I spoke of the Christian faith while all the crowd listened in hushed silence. When I stopped, they began to talk earnestly among themselves. They had always known, they said, that the dead lived on, but had wondered how and where, and the word they had heard that night came to them like light breaking in upon their darkness.

After leaving Baia we found the going very hard for a time and nowhere worse than when we worked our way through a sago swamp, for the midrib of the sago palm has sharp spikes all down its length and these cause many a nasty wound.

The country grew more attractive further inland, the track winding among low hills, and the scenery reminded me of that in Sussex through which the Arun runs.

We had travelled a long way without seeing any people, but suddenly came upon a crowd of women off to their fishing grounds. They were as surprised as we were, and fled back, screaming at the tops of their voices. We soon reached their village which was situated in one of the prettiest places I had seen in Papua. A wide road ran past the great communal house, from which the ground sloped steeply to the stream which entered an extensive lake dotted with lovely little islets. On a low hill far on the other side we saw Barimu, of which we had already heard, as it was one of the largest villages of the Girara tribe through whose country we had been passing. The chief of Warigi, the village we had reached, came out to welcome us and the women who had fled from us gathered round still carrying their fishing nets. These were fastened to hoops of cane four or five feet in diameter and made from fibres the women had first worked up into a splendid cord. Like all primitive people they made everything they needed and, wild and untutored as these folk appeared, they were far from ignorant and much less dependent on others than those living in civilized lands.

The chief offered to take us over the lake and led us to a splendid canoe, at the same time calling to some of his men. They came with their paddles, each a work of art, carefully shaped, carved and painted and about six feet long. The canoe matched the paddles and was one of the finest I had seen. Hewn from a great tree and sixty-nine feet long, it was carved from end to end and also painted with elaborate figuring. The bows for the first six feet were fashioned with scroll work and conventional designs carved with great care and finished off with a projecting figurehead, somewhat resembling a boar with curving tusks but wearing the conical hat favoured by the men. There was ample room for all, and my crowd, who were at the end of their tether, were glad to let others paddle. The men of Warigi, led by their chief, stood upright in the canoe, swinging their paddles in unison as they drove us across the lake. It was evening and the sun, low in the sky, was shining across waters studded with tiny islets, each an emerald gem. At times they seemed to merge together, and then a passage opened and we slid through it and on among other islets beyond which on the far shore lay Barimu. The great house built on a hill stood out on the sky-line like some huge church without a spire. Some time elapsed before the canoe reached the shore and while the men of Warigi went on to announce our coming, we had a bath in the clear water and then discovered our helpers had taken our clothes up the hill where we eventually made an undignified appearance. Nania, the chief, gave us a grave but friendly welcome and assigned us a place within the hall. He was a fine man and his house the greatest I had seen among these tribes, at least 450 feet long with the roof rising some forty feet above the ground. It was too late to see much that evening so we prepared our evening meal, fixed our blankets and mosquito nets, and got ready for the night.

Groups of men were also having an evening meal while the women were chattering excitedly in their apartments.

Later we joined Nania and his men and Boidam, a mission

teacher who had come with us as interpreter, started to tell them why we had come and where we hoped to go, and after he had explained our custom, all the men gathered round us and listened as we sang a hymn and joined in our evening prayer. That was the first act of Christian worship they had ever seen, yet even the chattering of the women ceased and there was a strange quietness all around us. They could understand little or nothing of its meaning save one thing and that of tremendous import, that men like themselves could speak to the Great Spirit and He could hear them. I always found the act of prayer was one of the first things the Papuan could enter into, and though they might understand little of the Christian faith, they knew enough to speak to a Spirit greater than themselves of their daily needs and call to Him when fear or sorrow touched their lives.

We had that day tramped through swamps and forest for twenty miles or more in the heat of the tropics and were more than ready to turn in for the night. For a time I lay awake thinking of the way we had come and of these people whose guests we were. High above me was the arching roof black with the smoke of many fires, outside my net sounded the ping of mosquitoes thirsting for blood, and from the far end of the hall came the murmur of men's voices as I fell asleep. Soon I was wide awake once more, for the place was filled with the sound of singing. This was something other than I had ever heard before and curiosity overcame my weariness and I slid from under the net and walked towards the singers.

They were seated round their chief. Each had his betel nut and lime gourd by his side and held in his hand a lighted *wiki,* a primitive candle made from a strip of resinous wood. In the darkness of the hall they formed a great circle of little flaming torches while just outside the circle a group of boys were preparing *gumada* for the men's use. They were chewing a root with water sipped from a coconut bowl and thus squeezing the juice from the root, the resulting liquid being squirted into a great wooden bowl round which they sat. Fermented, this becomes a mild intoxicant, the only intoxicating drink I have ever found among the Papuans, for most drank nothing stronger than water or coconut milk. I watched the boys, thankful that there was no need for me to drink with them, and then turned to the singers. Facing the chief, and within the circle, was a very old man who

seemed to be Master of Ceremonies. He would give out a line of
the chant which all took up, and as they sang, Chief Nania beat
time with his *wiki* and the men waved theirs gently to and fro.
As they came to the end of each stanza, they would unite in a
loud cry sounding like *Wai he* twice repeated, the *he* rising to a
shrill, drawn out, piercing note. It was fascinating to watch and
wonderful to hear. Never before had I listened to native songs so
musical. The deep, soft voices of the men blended together in
the chant and other voices from unseen singers joined in, shriller
and less pleasant, yet somehow harmonizing with the rest. The
women and girls, hidden in their own apartments, were taking
up the song, and the voices of all filled the building with strange
music that went on and on through the night. For just how long
I cannot tell, for I was very weary and left them singing, while
I lay down once more beneath my net. They sang me to sleep
and I slept deep and long, and when at last I awoke the song had
stopped and another day begun.

The more I saw of these people the deeper grew my respect
for them. Their houses were wonderful, their canoes and paddles
works of art, and that song one of the loveliest I had heard
among primitive Papuans. Outside, I noticed how beautifully
kept was the ground around the building. The approach was by
a broad road, straight and clean, with gardens on either side.
Down the entire length of both sides of the house crotons of
varying shape and colour had been planted bordering a broad
path fifteen to twenty feet wide which ran past gardens as neatly
arranged as those in front. Everywhere were signs of careful
planning and a sense of the beautiful that made us anxious to
learn more of these remarkable people.

We would have stayed on, but I had arranged for the *Pearl* to
go up the Bamu to pick us up should we be successful in finding
an overland route. The crew were to wait up the river until a
certain date and if we had not got through by then, to return to
Gaima and look for us. The date was already too near and very
reluctantly we made preparations to push on, and as we talked
to Nania and his men our hopes of reaching the Bamu rose, for
they spoke of a stream that led from the lake and eventually
reached a great river, and this we felt must be the one we sought.

We had no boat but there was the splendid canoe in which
we had travelled from Warigi; and if I could get that we could

go on. I had brought trade for such an eventuality and sent for the owner and sat down with him to talk things over. At first he would not contemplate a sale, but I had things his people seldom saw, things that would help in building other craft and I began to display them. Fish lines and hooks, a garden knife with a sixteen-inch blade, hatchets and a camp oven, fifty sticks of tobacco, thirty yards of cotton print. One by one these things were laid before him until a smile dawned on his face and he nodded. The price was right and the canoe was ours.

We were a small party, and were surprised and delighted when Nania came striding up to say he and two of his men would come with us. To have three able-bodied men ready to join our party seemed almost too good to be true, for not only did they bring our number up to eleven but they knew something of the first part of the way.

Nania with his belt, strip of cloth and woven armlets looked well dressed; Gumaroa, a fine well-built man, seemed content with a pair of plaited arm bands, whilst Garoa wore a cone-shaped hat which remained firmly attached to his head through all the vicissitudes of the long journey. All three brought their paddles and came to the canoe surrounded by hosts of friends, while their womenfolk brought a supply of food to help them and our crew upon their way. Everything was stowed as safely as possible and there was much waving of hands and some weeping as we set off.

The sunshine covered the lake with sparkling light and touched with fresh beauty the islets with their palms and tall, waving grass. We found ourselves going cautiously through shallow stretches where blue and white water-lilies seemed to rebuke us for trespassing on their loveliness and then came to where a very narrow stream led from the lake. Adventure was in the air. No white man had gone this way before. We were the pioneers and went gaily on, happily ignorant of all that lay between us and journey's end. Suddenly we swept from the narrow stream into a river about one hundred feet across, a shining pathway through the forest with the trees often festooned with rattan or the scarlet glory of the D'Albertis creeper. Hour after hour until the sun had set and hour after hour by the light of the moon we paddled downstream, shifting the strain of the paddle from one arm to the other as each in turn got tired.

We had decided to travel night and day while on the water, and had divided our company into two watches so that half might rest while the others pulled, though in the day we mostly worked together. It was night and I had completed my watch and was sleeping on the floor of the canoe until awakened by a sense of something wrong and found Gumaroa trembling with excitement and every voice hushed. Ahead were the fires of a village whose people were hostile to the men of Barimu and our helpers feared they would get some arrows into them if seen. There could, however, be no turning back and as it was night, we thought by keeping silent, we might get past unobserved. Garoa was at the stern with his steering paddle and the current was carrying us along, so leaving him to keep our craft well under the shadow of the far bank, we approached the place in silence. Men could be seen in the light of the fires and their voices came across the water as my crew crouched low in fear. They were anxious moments, but we slipped by unobserved much to the relief of all, and especially the Barimu men who had very unpleasant memories of that village.

In a country where there was so much inter-tribal fighting, and with the responsibility for my little crowd on my shoulders, my sleep was very broken for the rest of the journey as none knew what lay beyond each bend of the river. We had travelled with the current that had always helped us, but its speed gradually increased, and further on mud banks began to appear and we knew we were approaching tidal waters. After a slack period, the current turned against us and as it increased in strength we gave up paddling and made fast to a tree. Ashore, it was one vast swamp, so we slept on board. It was not easy to stow ourselves among the gear, but as all were very tired they were not long in settling down, and the floor of a canoe is quite a good place to sleep on provided one does not mind it being hard.

We were up early next morning with a strong current in our favour, and went down the river at increasing speed, but as great mud flats appeared to right and left of us we wondered if there would be a bore so far from the coast. The Bamu River had the reputation of having one of the worst in the world but we did not expect to meet it then. We were therefore taken by surprise when we heard the noise of one coming towards us and saw the first wave appear round a bend some distance downstream.

"My 'boys' panicked, but we managed to keep them by the canoe as we ran it on to the mud and tried to drag it to the bank. We sank deep in the black ooze as we pulled and strained, but at last had to give up with the bank still far away. The 'boys', now terror-stricken, waded to the bank and started climbing trees, leaving Landtman, Boidam and myself by our craft. There was some excuse for them, for the onrushing wave was a terrifying sight; but we were in country where the canoe was our only means of getting out and I did not dare to think of what might happen if we lost it. We accordingly hung on, though we soon realized we could do very little against the mighty force with which we had to battle. With a rush of tumbling water, the bore leaped upon us and we found ourselves struggling for our lives.

I was in the worst possible position to meet the danger. The whole weight of the canoe, backed by the terrific force of the raging waters, was being driven on top of me, and owing to the mud into which I had sunk, I was almost helpless and slowly forced down and under. Though it was a desperate chance, I knew that I had to let go while the canoe was being driven over me and then when clear, get a grip on the other side. If I failed I was a dead man. As I went under the muddy torrent, those who watched thought I had gone for ever, but I was vividly alive to everything, and though the weight of the canoe forced me beneath the slimy mud the rushing waters drove it over me and I felt the bottom of the hull grind across my face. Then with a mighty struggle I flung my arm up and just caught the edge of the canoe as it was driving past. Looking back I realize the seemingly impossible had happened, for humanly speaking I had not the ghost of a chance, caught as I was in the mud with the roaring torrent beating me down. My hair, eyes, ears and mouth were filled with filth; I was a dirty, grey, slime-covered object, but I was alive, gripping the edge of the canoe and being dragged after it.

As the raging waters cleared the mud from my eyes I looked round for the others. Boidam had been able to slip round the bows so that the bore was driving him on to the canoe. Landtman was in a less favourable position and struggling desperately, but I had no chance of getting to him, and fortunately he was able to hold on until we were swept with the canoe right up to the bank and the scared deserters came down from their trees and helped us from the river. Much that had been in the canoe was lost and the rest soaked, and we three looked in pretty bad condition. The 'boys' helped to pull our mud-filled garments off us and then cleaned us down by pouring water over us, after which we donned some wet clothes retrieved from our swags. They remained wet, for it started to rain and kept on for the rest of the day and night.

The tide was racing up the river and while we waited for it to turn, the 'boys', in spite of the rain, got a fire going under the shelter of a tree and cooked some sago. All felt much better by the time the tide turned, and with the current once more in our favour, we set off again. We had been travelling for some time when a wide stretch of water ahead of us appeared, and we swept out on to a river far broader than any we had seen since leaving the Fly and knew we had reached Bamu. No white man had ever come this way before but since that day others have entered and planted the Church among the peoples we met on that journey, and that has made hardship and danger more than worthwhile.

There was no sign of the *Pearl* but on the far bank was a village which gave us a clue to where we were. It had a bad reputation and we did not feel like visiting it just then. Its people some time before had sent an invitation to some coastal people to come and join them in a dance and feast. About thirty accepted the invitation but none returned. They missed the dance and provided the feast, being set upon by those who had invited them and killed in true cannibal style.

Tired and almost exhausted by our travels and wondering where the *Pearl* had got to, we pushed on downstream and about sunset sighted a large village. We could go no farther, so slowly paddled towards it, wondering what awaited us. We need have had no fear, for though a very wild-looking crowd, the villagers received us with native courtesy and turned out in force to drag our canoe on to the high bank, as they expected another big bore that night. We were at the mercy of these people, yet they gave us kind hospitality, offered us the shelter of their homes and lit fires before which we could dry our clothes and blankets, while the women cooked some food for us. We tried to thank them, though there is no word for thanks in their language, and after we had fed and were somewhat rested, we called them round us and told them of our journey and, after thanking God for bringing us through many perils, lay down on the rough mats they had brought for us listening for the bore. As we heard it roaring up the river and went out to watch it pass and saw it leaping and thundering along we realized still more how wonderful a deliverance had been ours.

Our hosts gave us news of the *Pearl*. She had been almost sunk by the bore of the night before, and wanting to avoid another, had returned down the river. We also learnt that news had somehow spread around that we had all been killed, and years later I met an old gold fossicker in New Guinea, who told me he had heard the rumour and was preparing to get a party together to make a search when the rumour was contradicted.

The *Pearl's* movements led us to feel she was making for Gaima and if we were to catch her we would have to be off as soon as the tide turned. It was dark when I woke my tired forces but early as it was, the villagers also turned out to put our canoe back into the water and then with renewed thanks to our kind but unwashed friends we embarked and set off down the river.

The weary work at the paddles went on hour after hour as we drove steadily through the darkness and on into the light of the morning. It was a cheerless dawn with the rain streaming down but as we rounded a bend, the 'boys' gave a shout of joy, for the *Pearl* was lying right ahead. The crew were already at the windlass hauling up the anchor, but stopped as they saw us and we were soon alongside and received a warm welcome from the men who had wondered if they would ever see us again. The *Pearl* had had her own adventure and the bore that had almost ended our existence had nearly ended hers. She had almost sunk under the weight of water that poured over her and flooded the cabin, and there was nothing dry on deck or down below.

We decided to get away to Wabuda, thinking we would make it in an hour or so, but it began to blow heavily and a wave caught the canoe broadside on and over it went, flinging the steersman and everything in it into the water. We dragged the steersman on board, retrieved everything that floated and lost all that sank, and towed our waterlogged canoe under the shelter of Wabuda where we baled it out, and finally reached our anchorage late in the afternoon.

By the end of the month we were back on Darnley Island

where the crew and those who had come overland with me had a wonderful reception, and many were the late nights spent with their friends recounting their adventures and telling stories that lost nothing in the telling.

10

NEW ADVENTURES

So much of my time was being spent on the water that my friend, Mrs. Robert Maynard, of Whittlesford, felt a motor vessel was needed if I were to get about without the long delays unfavourable winds and calm spells create for sailing craft. She won the interest of men like Sir Robert Baden-Powell and ultimately raised some £2,000 for the purchase of a small motor cruiser.

Meanwhile I went down to Australia for a short furlough and before it ended was engaged to be married to Miss Ena Davidson, only daughter of J. M. Davidson of the Bank of New South Wales.

A year later the promised cruiser, which had been built in England, arrived in Sydney and to bring her up the Australian coast to Thursday Island and Papua, Sali and Poi, two of my Island 'boys', volunteered to serve as crew. We went south by steamer and found our new craft waiting for us. She was a much finer boat than I had ever hoped to possess, forty-eight feet long, with good quarters for myself and crew, and had been named *Tamate* in memory of James Chalmers, who was known by that name throughout Papua. She proved a fine sea boat, serving us well in fair weather and foul. I was a bit staggered by the engine, however, for I knew I would have to be both captain and engineer, and the great fifty horse-power motor made me feel small and inadequate, especially as there were no instructions as to running and maintenance. To make matters worse it was a type new to Sydney folk and one of the main bearings persisted in running hot and the Sydney agents seemed unable to discover the cause.

We had a sea journey of two thousand miles ahead of us and my friends were much concerned at our attempting it in so small a vessel, but I was introduced to a younger man named Huntingdon, who though an amateur, had had a lot of experience with oil motors and small boats and was anxious to come with me in order to see something of Papua. We reckoned that with Sali and Poi as deck hands we could manage well but the powers that be insisted on our taking a master-mariner as far as Thursday Island. The agents also sent their engineer to watch the engine as far as Brisbane, but he knew so little of the oiling system that when near the Queensland border one of the main bearings seized and we had a bad breakdown. We were towed into Tweed Heads and later to Brisbane where the engine was dismantled and repaired.

Even then the bearing still gave trouble and no one seemed able to locate the cause until I discovered it in a wrong adjustment of the oiling system. I could never understand how the trained engineers had all failed and left it to a rank and file amateur to put things right.

Perhaps it was a blessing in disguise, for as I worked alongside the engineers I was constantly learning more and the knowledge thus gained enabled me later to do all our running repairs, install engines in motor boats, build up a machine shop and tackle fairly big engineering jobs. The *Tamate* provided my apprenticeship, and Brisbane just then was an attractive place in which to serve it, for after the day's work I could go to my fiancée's home while on occasions she would come to the boat and bring us a tasty lunch or make afternoon tea.

Once the cause of our troubles was located all went well and we eventually got under way again and ran down the river and across Morton Bay and out to sea travelling north. We had no more trouble with the engine and the *Tamate* proved herself a good sea boat, though on the small side for so long a journey, and we were not sorry to reach Thursday Island and feel we were at last close to the people the little ship had been built to serve. Here I was well known, for my adventures with small sailing craft had caused much comment, and the arrival of the *Tamate* created considerable interest.

Those who worked to secure the boat expected as I did that more than half my time would be spent on the open sea, but a new adventure was opening up, and in that the *Tamate* was to prove herself invaluable. From the day I reached Papua my thoughts had constantly turned to the tribes where Chalmers and his party had met their deaths. I had come out with the intention of getting among them, but my colleagues had been much against it; and when Sir Hubert Murray, then Governor of the territory,

heard what I was planning he sent me a personal letter urging
me not to attempt it for, he wrote, "those Goaribari men are as
wild as hawks". In spite of this I felt I had to go, and after long
discussions with the District Committee they reluctantly agreed
to my exploring the area.

A heaven sent opportunity to make contact with the people
presented itself in the person of an extremely dirty and di-
shevelled man. He had been entlced on to a boat that was looking
for plantation labourers, but had managed to escape and was
trying to get back to his village. Unfortunately for him, to reach
it he would have to pass through the territory of a hostile tribe
who were also cannibals, and he knew if he were caught he
would certainly be killed. Some of our folk found him both
frightened and desperate and brought him to me to see if I could
help. He could not have turned up at a more opportune time, for
I was preparing to go that way and now had one who could
introduce me to his people.

We were down the Papuan coast and taking our very unkempt
passenger on board, set off at once for the west. He went right
for'ard and seated himself by the windlass, and hour after hour
looked across the water to where somewhere over the horizon
lay his village. He seemed to be in dire trouble and every now
and then would wail aloud as if he feared my crew would suddenly turn on him and treat him as his people had the habit of
treating strangers, but he looked far from appetizing and we were
not all that hungry. We were hungry enough for a meal, however, and the crew set about preparing one and cooked their rice
and opened a tin of bully-beef. Then Sali went for'ard to Amuku-
mere, as he called himself, and led him to the feast spread upon
the deck and, seated among the rest, he lost his fears and at last
began to feel that all was well.

The coast was dangerous with sandbanks and shallows stretching for miles off the shore. We steered westward until the island
of Goaribari appeared and then felt our way into the channel
between it and Cape Blackwood. East, north and west of us was
low-lying, swampy land covered by the endless mangrove, but
far inland we could see a cone-shaped hill marked on the chart as
Aird Hill which I determined to explore as soon as possible.
Further up the channel a village came in sight on the eastern
side which Amuku-mere said was Gobai-bari, with another some

miles further on named Dubu-muba. Away to the north lay the entrance to the Kikori River and a creek west of it led up to a large village named Aimehai, though we had to take Amuku-mere's word for this, as, like most of the villages in the area, it was tucked away out of sight and well up the creek. There was soon, however, plenty of evidence, for out from the creeks up which the people had their homes, came swarms of canoes laden with arms and painted men.

It was a wonderful sight as they swung into view with ten or fifteen men in each canoe. They stood upright in their long dug-outs swinging their paddles in unison and stamping their feet on the floor as they drove their paddles into the water and came swiftly towards us. They were screaming with excitement and trying to cut us off but my boat was faster and we were soon leading the fleet with their amazing crews paddling furiously and strung out in long line astern.

We passed Dopima where Chalmers and Tomkins had been killed, and Kerawo, with an enormous house for the fighting men, built broadside on to the water. Some distance ahead near the mouth of the Omati River, another village came into sight, and as he saw it, Amuku-mere was overcome with emotion, for this was Muba-gowa he feared he would never see again. Long before we got near, the water shallowed and great mud flats reached out from the shore. So, running back to a better anchorage, we let go and swung to the current.

The canoes that had been following were rapidly approaching and men were dragging others across the mud, and soon we were overwhelmed by a wild shouting crowd of painted savages decorated in barbaric fashion and clambering on board. Amuku-mere was yelling at the top of his voice and the men were shouting back, and as all seemed to act as if the rest were deaf, the noise was terrific. Our passenger, without waiting to say good-bye, jumped into a canoe and made for the shore, and shrill cries of the women came to us across the water as they welcomed back the man they had given up as dead.

With their friend out of the way, the rest turned their attention to me and invited me to come ashore with them. It was toward evening and I looked at the village beyond the vast stretch of mud and saw the sun was near to setting and took stock of the wild looking men with their long bows and barb-

tipped arrows and shook my head. I felt I would rather face that
crowd in the daylight so signed to them that I was tired and
would sleep on board and come ashore in the morning.

I do not know what they thought, but they put a guard on my
boat. While some sat on the deck smoking or chewing betel nut,
others prowled round in their canoes or came on board to talk
with the rest. All through the night there was much coming and
going, those on the ship shouting to those ashore with answering
shouts from the village. Men would poke their heads down the
companion or look in through the port-holes and discuss my
appearance, others came into the cabin to get a closer look, and
what with one thing and another I had a very restless night.

It was with real relief that we noted the first signs of dawn and
I went on deck and found the crew looking rather weary and
very concerned. They were still more troubled when the dinghy
was lowered and I prepared to go ashore. Sali alone came with
me, and my heart still warms as I think of him. He was really
scared and knew he was running into danger and thought he
might be killed; yet in spite of all his fears, he would not let me
go alone. We were not alone for long, for as we left the *Tamate*,
canoes surrounded us, escorting us in barbaric state towards the
shore.

Though very early, Muba-gowa was wide awake and scores of
men in war-like trappings came wading through the mud, and as
the dinghy grounded caught my hands, arms and clothes and
pulled me out into the mud, dragging Sali after me and with much
shouting started marching us towards the village. Marching is
hardly the word, for no man could march in the filthy ooze
through which we were struggling. A man hovered nearby with
his hatchet in a very purposeful manner. I did not like the look
of him and kept my eye on that hatchet as best I could with the
wildly excited crowd plunging through the mud around us. To
add to my concern Sali started to call to me and there was fear
in his voice. "Buta," he cried, "they are going to kill us, I can
see it in their faces; I can hear what they are saying; they are
going to kill us." I fully agreed with his impression but was a bit
sceptical of his knowledge of the language, and in any case there
was nothing we could do but wait and see. We were at their
mercy and I turned to Sali and tried to cheer him up, though
things looked far from encouraging. We reached the village and

as the crowd grew, so did the uproar. Women and girls came out from the houses to look at us and seemed tremendously impressed by the whiteness of my skin; men were gesticulating and pointing to the *dubu-daimo* or men's house, in which were the skulls of scores of men they had killed and eaten. They were leading us to it and, as we reached the entrance platform six feet above us, they dragged me up and Sali after me. Wondering what the next act would be, I took a hasty glance around and saw something that put my mind at rest and explained the excitement. Lying near the entrance was the body of a dead pig and men were trying to tell me something in a language I did not understand, at the same time pointing to the pig and to me. I realized that the talk of killing which so disturbed Sali referred to the pig and not to us and that this was a welcome and not another kill. It was all plain. They had been so surprised at receiving back a man they had given up as dead, and that a man like those they had killed had brought him, that they felt they had to do something about it and had gone into the village and shot this pig to give me in token of their friendship. It was covered with mud and blood and had several arrow holes in it, but it struck me as one of the most beautiful things I had seen for a long time for it spoke of the success of my first contact with the people.

An eager crowd gathered round us beneath the overarching roof and a man, adorned in next to nothing, stood out from among them. He was their chief, and as he stood in front of me he gave an order, and men brought the pig and laid it at my feet. He then made an impassioned speech and by his looks and gestures I gathered that I was being welcomed. He said a lot I could not understand so I evened things up by saying a lot he could not understand and then did something they could all appreciate and brought out some sticks of trade tobacco and gave everyone a piece with an extra big allowance for the chief. Things quietened down after that, as all sat down and taking their *suku-dowea* or bamboo pipes, started to smoke. As we tried to understand each other and laughed together at our attempts, the feeling of friendship grew and I sensed the dawn of a new way of life for those who had slain my predecessor.

It was a good beginning, but I was to learn later that the receipt of such a gift carried certain responsibilities. Long after, when I had built my home in the heart of their country, I received a deputation. They came in grave procession up the hill and sat around me for a time without a word. They seemed to have a weighty matter to discuss but were not sure how to introduce it. Then one began with a question: "Do you know where we come from?" "Oh yes," I replied. "You are men of *Muba-gowa*." "Do you remember the first time you came to us?" the questioner went on, and the scene came back to me with its mud and crowds and wild shouting and maddening uncertainty. "Yes," I replied, "and I'm never likely to forget it." "Do you remember the pig we gave you?" Yes, I remember the pig all right, that gift of grateful men who had received back their long lost friend. "Then when," my questioner asked, coming to the point that had brought them all to see me, "when are you going to pay us for it?" I was rather taken aback, for up to that day I had been under the impression that I had more than paid for it by all that I had done, and by a very liberal distribution of tobacco. The Papuan has no word for "thank you" and the smokes I had given were a sign of friendship and ended in smoke, but the pig was a different matter. It was property, a tangible asset, and having given it to me they wanted something tangible in its place. That is as near as I could get to their reasoning and it led to the discovery that for these people presents always call for a return gift even when the presents given are for favours received.

At the time the pig was given these things were hidden from me and as we sat on the platform of the *dubu-daimo*, I tried to make them understand that though I could not stay just then, I hoped to return very soon and make my home not far from where they lived. All seemed well content and when at last I rose they accompanied me to the dinghy: our departure was much quieter than our coming.

11

AMONG THE HEADHUNTERS

WE had made our first contacts, and before going further I returned to Darnley to take leave of the people there. A new man had been appointed to take charge in Torres Strait, and this set me free to explore the delta and open up work among the tribes in that area.

The Islanders were very unhappy at my going, and had the call to this new task been less insistent I might have been content to settle down among these friendly people with whom I had spent such full and happy years. The Christian faith had become a very real thing to them. They were far from perfect, and domestic troubles, village rivalries and moral failures sometimes marred the life of the community, but, as a people, they knew this was God's world and had come to sense that it would only work in God's way. They had come to look to me for leadership and accept me as their friend and, when I left, they crowded down to the seashore and it was hard to get through the throng that pressed around to say good-bye.

We steered direct course to Papua, and in the exploration of the delta the *Tamate* proved herself invaluable. Once again we sighted Goaribari and dropped anchor off two big villages.

Our arrival created the usual excitement as many started dragging their canoes across the mud flats and then came across the water towards us. They were a fearsome lot as they tumbled over the rails, full of curiosity concerning us and our boat and everything we had. None showed any fear, and many were trying to make away with our gear, and I caught one trying to remove one of the ventilating cowls above the engine-room. We seemed to have landed in a den of thieves, and they needed very careful handling, as we did not want to antagonize them, but also did not want to lose the ship's fittings. Gradually we got them quietened and, to show we trusted them, decided to go ashore in one of their canoes. It was manned by a few wild-looking men and I took the precaution of telling my crew to come and look for us if we were not back by a certain time, although I had my doubts about their doing anything of the kind, for they were anything but happy at our going. They were also very dubious about the canoe, for it was a frail craft and we had to get through a good deal of rough water.

This did not seem to worry the villagers, who set off gaily. They seemed confident enough, but I found myself wondering how long it would be before we had to swim, for we were crossing a tide-rip, and as we entered the broken water the canoe lurched violently and waves came curling over the sides. Delta men, however, manage their canoes with amazing skill and, as the seas came in, they swept the water aft and out of the stern by strong swishes of their feet and steadied the canoe by holding the broad blades of their paddles against the waves and, though we were expecting every moment to be tipped out, it was fascinating to watch them. Our fears were lost in admiration of these wild men who, standing upright as they paddled, and balancing themselves and their canoe in a wonderful way, drove us through the tumbling seas until we reached the shelter of the land and approached the stunted mangroves that fringed the coast.

The village, like most in these parts, was in a swamp, with the houses built on the highest spots, and at low water the place was indescribably filthy. The main street and side paths consisted of the trunks of trees and saplings laid end to end and pegged down to keep them from being washed away.

Along these we had to walk, and it was no easy task, for they were wet and slimy, and occasionally I would slip off and go down to my knees in the slimy ooze. We were among people still in the stone age and when, a year or so later, I took my friend Frank Lenwood among them, he was greatly struck by their appearance and realized the truth of my remark that you can tell they are coming before you see them. As he put it: "When their canoes were twenty yards to windward, a strong whiff, as of high partridge, came down the breeze!"

In those days, before the white man had touched their villages, the delta carried a large population, and crowds surrounded us as we landed. I had not come as a complete stranger. My boat was linked with the story of *Amuku-mere*, which had been told and re-told throughout all the villages, and men, women and children gathered round to see the white man who had brought him to his home. I was therefore able to move among them freely and balanced my way along the logs towards a large house that had attracted my attention. On the platform were a number of boys and young men, as this was the *ohio-daimo*, or boys' house, and the village lads, as soon as they reached the age of puberty, were taken from their mothers' homes and lived here until married. It was a kind of primitive boarding school, where they were under the tutelage of senior men who instructed them in the rites, taboos and customs of the tribe, and taught them how to hunt and fight and fish and share in the work of men among whom they would one day have to take their place. They lived here for years, never returning to the homes of their childhood until the day came when they were fetched away to share in ceremonies that ended in their marriage. There was little to attract one in the great hall, which was dirty and ill kept, and the boys seemed very unsure of themselves as I tried to win their confidence.

Beyond their home was a line of rough-looking huts, each about fifty feet long. These were known as *moto* and were the homes of the women, girls and little children. As a rule there were several rooms in each *moto*, for the inmates, though of the same clan, might belong to several families, and a family might consist of several wives of one man, with their respective children. Like the *ohio-daimo*, these homes were far from clean and were cluttered up with fish traps and nets, garden implements and those for sago making, together with earthenware cooking pots, bundles of sago, and crabs with their claws bound with raffia, while from the smoke-blackened roof hung dried fish, articles of female attire and raffia bags of many sizes.

Few of these women could be called lazy and most found their days well filled with work of one kind or another. Much time had to be spent in fishing and digging crabs from the mud, with whole days spent in sago swamps beating and washing out the sago from the trunks of the palms. This provides them with their staple diet, and its extraction involves much labour. After the tree is felled, the bark on the upper side is stripped off, exposing the pith. The under half is left to form a trough. Then, with what looks something like flails, the women beat the pinkish looking pith, cutting and crushing it into pulp. Meanwhile troughs, made from the lower part of the midrib where it springs from the palm, are fastened to stakes, with the broad end uppermost and the smaller sloping down to a rectangular tray placed on the ground. This, and the buckets in which water is brought from the creek, are made from sago spathes, and often beautifully fashioned.

Having arranged their troughs, a strainer is pegged half-way down each of them. These are woven from soft raffia, each shaped like a narrow bag, something like a stocking, closed at the bottom but widening towards the mouth, and so strong and flexible that they can be squeezed and wrung out time after time without splitting. Here again one sees the artistic instinct at work, for various patterns are woven into the strainers, making them good to look at as well as use. It was interesting to note that practically everything required for the extraction of the sago came from the palm itself, whose fronds also provide a shelter for the workers. Between them the sago and coconut palms could provide the Papuan with food and drink, house and clothes, and with no income tax to worry about he was untroubled by finance. Once the troughs and strainers were in position, some of the crushed pith is put at the head of a trough and water from the buckets poured on to it. This carries the pith into a strainer, which is kneaded and wrung to squeeze out the sago which runs with the water in a milky stream into the deep tray-like receptacle on the ground. The sago looks something like wet cornflour and, being heavy, quickly sinks to the bottom, while the water runs off at the top, and as it collects it is scooped from the tray and put into holders made from the leaves of the palm and these, I used to reckon, had an average weight of about thirty pounds.

This work, carried through in the steaming swamps, was but a part of woman's work. Back in the village there was always the cooking and the care of babies and small children, while in addition they had to make their nets, traps and baskets and prepare the materials from which all these were made. Unlike the women of the east and central districts of Papua, they wore no skirts but a long whisp of soft fibre drawn between the legs, with the ends tucked into a belt of plaited raffia. It was a very scanty costume, but when I watched them wading through the mud as they searched for crabs, or working in the sago swamps,

I realized that their meagre attire was well suited to the life they had to live. On the whole they worked fairly well together, though at times wild fighting broke out and they attacked each other with sticks and various implements in a most ferocious manner and often did each other grevious harm. Polygamy was probably the most fruitful cause of strife, for it often led to much jealousy and bitterness between different wives of the same man.

Maybe that partly explains why the men lived apart from their wives and families in what was the most remarkable building in the village. It was usually separated from the *ohio-daimo* by the line of *moto* or family dwellings, so that the boys' house at one end of the village and the *dubo-daimo* or men's house at the other. After negotiating with indifferent success the greasy tree trunks that formed the road, I reached it and climbed to the entrance platform. The arching roof reached over and beyond the platform, and the wall that faced me was made from the midribs of sago palms lashed side by side to the framework of the house with thin strips of cane. Fastened to the walls were skulls of hornbills and crocodiles, the jawbones of many pigs and the bony saw of a great saw-fish, while from the outermost point of the arched roof hung a totem shield swaying in the wind. The platform creaked and groaned under the weight of the crowd that had gathered to welcome me, but when I essayed to get into the building I was reminded of the house at Gaima, for the entrance to so big a place was absurdly small and so narrow that one had to squeeze through it. On enquiry I was told that this was for protection, as an unwelcome visitor could easily be clubbed as he stooped. My head fortunately remained intact, but I had a very eerie feeling once I got inside.

We had come from the sunlight and at first could see little save a small patch of light beyond a doorway at the far end. Slowly our eyes got used to the gloom and, as I looked around, the length of the place amazed me, and to find out how long it was I started to walk, counting my steps as I went, while the crowd surrounded me wondering what I was doing. Actually I was doing what none of them had ever done, for they could not count as we do and had only two numerals: *na'u*, one; and *neewa*, two. They joined them together for three, *neewa na'u*, and *neewa neewa* was four. They could also get to nineteen by starting at the little finger of one hand and working through the digits, wrist, elbow, shoulder, breast, sternum and across the other side of the body to the little finger of the other hand. That seemed as far as they could get and beyond that they solved all their arithmetical problems with one word, *godogodo,* or plenty. There was no multiplying, subtracting or dividing. They could not do what I was doing as I counted my steps, but when I reached the far end I found they had done something we white folk would have found very difficult, for they had a built a house a thousand feet long, raised on piles high off the mud and thatched so well that tropical rains could not penetrate the roof, and had done it without nails, saw or tools other than stone axes and knives of flint, shell or bamboo.

The men were keen to show me through their building of which they were very proud. Each had as his own apartment one of the stalls built on either side of the hall, where the owner kept his drum, bow and arrows, spears and fishing nets, shell ornaments, feather head-dresses, and all the personal possessions of a Papuan who lived simply but did much with very little. At intervals down the building were side entrances and a space clear of cubicles where groups of men could sit together near to a fire burning on a hearth of baked mud and smoke and talk as they worked at their nets or carved strange figures on their totem shields or intricate patterns on their bamboo pipes. Above such a group the light was shining on a queer image, looking rather hideous with its carvings coloured red, white and black. Before it was a shelf on which were what I took to be offerings of coconuts, until a closer look revealed them as human skulls. Most had a loop of cane passed through the base, by which the skull could be carried or hung before the image which was called an *agibe.* Some had been split by an axe and others splintered as by a club, but all were the skulls of enemies on whose bodies my new friends had feasted, and they were treasured above all other possessions. In some tribes no man could hope to marry until he had first secured a head by killing its owner, and among the people who surrounded me, the man who could claim most skulls was the man most respected, and held a position of authority by reason of his prowess.

It was among such folk that I had come to live, and as we tried to talk together I discovered that their language had some relation to that spoken on Kiwai Island. As I knew a little of that we were able to learn something of the surrounding country and to let them know that we were looking for a place where we might settle. They were quite excited at the prospect and the day passed all too quickly, and when at last I had to leave, they helped me into a small canoe and slid it over the mud to the water's edge and took me back to my boat, and through all the years that followed they remained my friends.

12

EXPLORING THE DELTA

We had made our first contacts with the people and now had to find a centre from which to work among them. In those days the delta country, with its vast areas of forest covered swamp, was almost unknown. The people also were difficult to meet since they were suspicious of strangers and would make for the bush as soon as my boat was sighted. Again and again we reached a village only to find it deserted and would waste a great part of a day waiting around in the hope that curiosity would overcome their fear and bring the people back.

During our explorations we found ourselves on a stretch of water over a mile across, and on our right was a promising sand beach with a line of coconuts that spoke of a village, though we could see neither people nor houses. We landed and started to walk along the beach, but stopped suddenly, for dodging among the trees were armed men. None would come near, and when I moved towards them they made off so quickly that it seemed impossible to make contact. Then down a small stream came two canoes, whose occupants stopped paddling as soon as they saw us and began talking together in shrill voices. After a while they came on again, very slowly and with considerable hesitation. While on the water their way of escape was open, but when I tried to entice them ashore I met with no response. They stood in their canoes, wild, timid men watching me, but keeping a respectful distance. I held out a little present but they immediately sheered off, so I laid a bit of trade tobacco on a log near the water's edge and walked some distance and sat upon the sand.

There was still much hesitation, but their curiosity had been aroused and they slowly edged towards the bank, and while the rest kept an eye on me, one jumped ashore, snatched the tobacco, and was back to the canoe like a flash. I laid another piece on the log, with the same result, and then another, and slowly won their confidence, until at last they landed and surrounded me. They were very excited and talked ceaselessly, though I could

make little of what they had to say, but as they had lost their
fear, and I was feeling hungry, I motioned them to come with
me to the *Tamate* while I got some breakfast.

We were pulling across the water, thinking all was well, when
out from the creek poured a fleet of war canoes crowded with
men in their war paint, and we were entirely at their mercy. It
was a magnificent sight as canoe after canoe, laden with splendid fighting men in their barbaric trappings, came speeding towards us. But we did not stay to admire them; we pulled for the
Tamate and arrived just ahead of the crowd. I knew if they
meant mischief there was nothing we could do about it, but I
wanted to be with my 'boys' in case trouble was brewing. We
had barely time to climb on board before we were overwhelmed
by as wild a crowd as I had ever seen, and for a moment things
looked dangerous. The earlier contact, however, saved us, for
our first acquaintances gave a good report of us and we were
soon at ease.

Though we could see no sign of it, there was evidently a big
village nearby, and after a meal we set off to visit it. My dinghy
was at once surrounded by canoes, whose occupants almost
deafened us as they discussed us at the tops of their voices. The
journey proved a longer one than we had anticipated, and the
dinghy was slow and cumbersome compared with their canoes,
which would slip past with effortless ease, with the occupants
making disparaging remarks about our speed. I soon tired of this,
so signalled a canoe alongside and got into it with two of my
company, while the men shouted with delight and took us proudly
and speedily towards their home. As we rounded a bend we saw
the village right ahead with its great houses towering above the
rest. News of our coming had preceded us and crowds lined the
banks and I walked through the village surrounded by a noisy
throng discussing my appearance.

The chief, standing in the middle of the road, was waiting to
welcome us, and took me in his arms and gave me a fond em-
brace, and though he left his mark upon my shirt I returned his
greeting with equal warmth. He was a dignified old fellow, and
after our introduction he turned and led me into the great building where his fighting men foregathered.

This was quite different from the *dubu-daimo* we had seen
around Goaribari and more akin to the *eravo* at Orokolo.

Though not so long as the Kerawo homes, it was as gloomy and awesome, but more picturesque. Down its length, suspended from the roof, were the great dancing masks, so big that the men who wore them were hidden from the spectators. Like those in Orokolo, they were also made of cane frames covered with tapa cloth and, though shaped differently, were also adorned with grotesque figures. This was the home of a cannibal tribe, but amongst them I received nothing but kindness, and many were the presents of food they brought to us. As we wandered among them we tried to learn something of the surrounding peoples, but owing to our ignorance of their language could not get much of the information we wanted, though those hours with the villagers made our subsequent contacts much easier, for the news of our visit reached far and smoothed our way when entering many other places.

We were anchored near what seemed the mouth of a big river they called Paia, and across the water the land was low and uninviting, but we decided to have a look at it and early in the morning heaved anchor and set off. Nearing the shore we could see a break in the mangrove where a broad stream ran inland with a sand beach and coconut grove near its mouth, and where there were coconuts there were usually people, so we decided to go ashore.

As we left the dinghy and walked along the sand, the place seemed deserted, but very soon we were conscious of men watching us from among the trees and then saw a crowd collecting ahead of us. They appeared much the same as others we had met elsewhere and I was not surprised to find them armed and keeping their distance. We were strangers and therefore objects of suspicion. My 'boys' hung back while I tried to make contact with them. The great thing was to bide one's time, for a hasty action could easily startle them, and in their fear arrows might fly to keep us off. I stood still for a time and, when nothing happened, walked slowly towards them. Immediately they began to move back, and the further I went the further they kept moving. All my gestures of friendship were of no avail. They kept their distance and eyed me with suspicion, so I decided to try the tobacco trick again. Nearby, a coconut palm undermined by the sea was lying on the sand, so I sat upon it and waited, while they watched from afar, and no one seemed in a hurry. Then I got up and again walked slowly towards them and, putting a piece of tobacco on the ground, went back to my seat. After a good deal of animated discussion one of their number set out to investigate. Keeping an eye on me to see I did not move, he approached the thing, hurriedly picked it up and ran back at top speed to his friends, who passed it from hand to hand and found it good. As they talked I put a second piece not so far off, so near in fact that for a time none would make a further move. But tobacco was a thing they hungered for and desire overcame hesitation, and once again the same man came along and, sneaking up, grasped his prize and ran. We were obviously making progress, so while remaining seated I took a third piece, and holding it at arm's length offered it for him to come and take it. This was almost too much, for he evidently felt it was a very risky thing to come so near, but his friends were shouting encouragement, and the tobacco drew him like a magnet draws a piece of iron. He took a few steps and stopped while he calculated the risk, then came on a few steps more and stopped again and looked back at his friends who were urging him on; he came nearer still, with fear written on his face. He looked at me appealingly, and I smiled a welcome but did not move, so with a quick rush he snatched the tobacco and was off in a flash. It was like taming rabbits, but this kind ate men rather than grass and one never knew what they would be doing next. It was also very interesting to watch fear and suspicion giving place to interest in the stranger, and I felt we had really arrived when the whole crowd came slowly forward and surrounded us.

Once contact had been made we set off with our wild companions and soon reached their village, which differed greatly from the villages around Goaribari. On the entrance platform of the men's house, called a *mene*, very similar to the *ravi* of the Purari delta, a group of older men were seated watching our approach. Their impassive faces gave no sign of welcome, but they received us gravely and accepted small gifts I offered, though, as we knew nothing of their language, it was impossible to explain who we were and why we had come. The most we could hope to accomplish was to give them some assurance that we were there as friends and thus pave the way for closer relations later on.

I have always been a non-smoker but have often felt it might help a lot if I could join in when the bamboo pipes were lit and passed around, but had to content myself with supplying the wherewithal for their enjoyment. Their method of smoking intrigued me. The pipe was made from a piece of bamboo two or more feet in length and about two inches in diameter. Near its closed end a small hole was bored, and into this was fitted a cigarette made of tobacco enclosed in a piece of dry leaf. When lit from a fire stick, the owner drew the smoke through the bamboo from the open end, and when the bamboo was full, removed the cigarette and passed the pipe round to his friends, who each took a whiff and then passed it back to be filled again. It took quite a time to smoke one cigarette and even longer for each man to have a really good smoke.

As I sat among them I could scarcely take my eyes off an image suspended above my head. It fascinated me and nowhere else had I seen its like. It was fashioned as a warrior with a feather head-dress above a brick-red face, through the nose of which was thrust a nasal shell. It wore a belt into which a bone dagger had been thrust and held a bow and some arrows in its hands, and was fastened just above the entrance of the building. When making one's first contacts, it was never wise to exhibit too much curiosity, but I thought no harm could come from making a few enquiries and gathered that the name of the image was Iriwaki, and as the years passed I found that Iriwaki might be regarded as the God of War, before whom victims were sometimes slain. I was also surprised to discover that they felt he could be troubled by their evil ways, and learnt this when in one of their villages I noticed Iriwaki was not in his accustomed place. I was told that he had gone away, but just why and for how long they could not or would not tell me, though it seemed that he had been offended by something they had done, and I am still wondering if a taboo had been broken and the old men had removed him for a time. His name was held in reverence by the tribes through all the delta, and to many he appeared as the greatest power they had ever heard of.

As I saw him above my head I knew nothing of this, and was also unaware of the fact that we had made our first contact with one of the strongest and most difficult tribes in the delta, nor did I know that the broad stream off which we had anchored would have taken us right into a group of cannibal villages where anything might have happened. Even as we sat among that group beneath the fearsome image we were not feeling very secure, for there was a noticeable absence of real friendliness, and this made us anxious not to outstay our welcome. We had made our first contact, and that was enough for the time being, so without giving an appearance of undue haste we took our departure and made our way back to the *Tamate*.

The place we were especially interested in was a cluster of hills marked on the charts as Aird Hill, so named by Captain Blackwood of H.M.S. *Fly*, who sighted it when surveying the coast. As he saw it, it appeared as a single peak only visible from the coast when the weather was clear. Actually it is an island covered by precipitous hills and surrounded by rivers and swamp. Geologists say it is an extinct volcano, and when at various times we suffered severe earth tremors we used to wonder if it was as extinct as some folk thought. The highest hill rose to a thousand feet, and was known as Neuri, and separated from it by a narrow valley was the next highest, known as Dauri-bari. The place attracted me, as it seemed right in the heart of the delta, but when we eventually reached it we found the hills so precipitous that we almost despaired of finding a site for homes on it.

We had travelled all round the island looking for level ground and found none until we came to a place where the hills rose well back from the shore. Standing here we found a site that became more promising the further we explored it, and had I been free to do so I would have started right in to clear the ground, but we had first to find the native owners and then report to the Papuan District Committee at Port Moresby.

Two senior colleagues were appointed to examine the place, and on looking it over they felt there would be far more room for expansion on another site I took them to a mile or so further round the island. I very reluctantly bowed to their decision but have always felt the earlier choice would have been a better one. In fact it was so good that those who had been ready to let us have it decided to settle there themselves, and built a new village now known as Kumukumu. I knew the site my colleagues advised would be more difficult to develop and would involve the construction of a road across a swamp, but I was young and the difficulties were there to be overcome, so we set to work to clear the forest and prepare the ground for our first buildings. Again and again we thought regretfully of the earlier choice as various disadvantages in the one selected became obvious, but there was no turning back as people were already building their village on the other site.

We were facing a tremendous task with only unskilled labour to help me. My assistants were the crew of the *Tamate*, who had come with me from the Fly River, and Fitui and his wife, two Samoans who had previously been working on Wabuda. He was capable of hard work but was quite unskilled, so the direction of everything devolved upon me. As we cleared the bush, the possibilities of the place became clearer, and also the amount of work that lay ahead. The road across the swamp had to be built and the top of a low hill levelled for my house and other buildings. We were in the wilds and months would elapse before things urgently required could be secured, in fact in the early years the bulk of our goods came up in the *John Williams* once every twelve months. Fortunately we were not limited in the matter of building and roofing material, for we cut whatever timber we wanted, and the nipa palm provided us with thatch. Surveying, designing and planning all devolved upon me, and as I turned from one task to another I was rapidly developing into a Robinson Crusoe without his loneliness.

Men from surrounding villages often came along to see what we were doing and some would stay for a time and help us, and when they found we were ready to reward them for their work they came in greater numbers. Money had no attraction, as they did not understand its use. We consequently paid with fish lines and hooks, beads and looking-glasses, knives and hatchets, axes and cotton print. Tobacco was an easy first. Not only was the demand for it insatiable, but for us it was almost as easy to handle as money and soon had a fixed value.

There was so much to be done that we needed all the helpers we could get, but at first we found them very unreliable. They did what they liked when they liked, and what they didn't like was left undone. They could not understand being tied to a job and resented anything that interfered with the desire of the moment and, after a short stay with us, would be off to their villages again. Frequently we would find that all the workers had disappeared. Some visitor had probably called the night before and brought them news of a dance, and in the darkness while we slept they had all slipped away. It would not have been so trying had they merely left us. Work would have been delayed and our time-table upset, but we could be pretty sure that others would soon come along and take the place of those who had left. Our main trouble was that the defaulters often took our axes and other tools, and without these we were helpless.

Weather as well as labour troubles delayed us considerably, for we were unprepared for the conditions we had to face. In the west and around Port Moresby we could reckon on long, dry spells between April and October, but in the delta these months proved the wettest of the year and rain fell so constantly and copiously that everything was sodden. On one occasion our rain-gauges showed over fourteen inches in under fourteen hours and I have measured over 300 inches in a year. The air was heavy with moisture and tools and iron instruments quickly rusted, while boots and leather goods became green with mould. My books fell to pieces, and furniture that had been glued fell apart, and iron nails rusted away inside the wood into which they had been driven. We lived in an atmosphere similar to that of a tropical glass-house, and yet our health did not seem to suffer any ill effects.

Tools such as I was using were unknown among a people just emerging from the stone age. We taught them first to handle the adze and its keen cutting edge frightened them, for to men who had known the stone adze there was something uncanny in this new instrument that cut timber with such ease. I had to watch them carefully as there was always the risk of them doing themselves serious harm, and I saw one man literally swoon in terror when the adze slipped and nicked his foot. The wound was only slight, but the fact that it had been inflicted by the strange implement he had been learning to use frightened the senses out of him.

The ordinary hand saw amazed them. Men would leave their villages and travel for days that they might see it, and would gather round to watch me cutting through a plank. Never before had they seen anything that could do the sort of thing that I was doing. Their fathers, with great labour, had hacked through a piece of wood with blunt instruments, and shouts of wonder rose on every hand as they watched me do with ease what they had found so difficult.

The auger also delighted them. Among some tribes further east I had seen a simple hand drill with a flint point that was used in fashioning bone and shell ornaments. Here the hole was usually made by burning, and the size was difficult to control. Now they saw me make a hole swiftly and just the size required, and the ease with which it was done became a matter of excited talk in many a village. There was a special reason for this. Second only to the possession of a human skull ranked the possession of a drum, and the making of this from a log two or three feet long was a lengthy and laborious process. They put live charcoal on the end of the log and, with a blow-pipe made of bamboo, directed the flame downward, slowly burning out the wood they wanted to remove, and, if the fire tended to go too far into the sides, a dash of water stopped it. The work needed care and patience and took much time, and I have often wondered at the skill with which it was done and admired the way the drums were shaped and intricate figuring often carved into the woodwork.

Now their sons were experimenting with new tools that enabled them to do work on which their fathers spent many days in a fraction of the time. The saw cut the log neatly and speedily and just the length required, and the great auger drove a hole from end to end, making it easy to burn and widen to the width required. The new tools had speeded up an ancient craft, and if that were all we might be glad. What always troubled me was that the growing and inevitable contacts with the Western world were not merely speeding up but destroying the ancient craftsmanship. Old arts and crafts tend to die out as a younger generation discovers that money will buy better things than those their parents fashioned with so much pride and skill. They may be better things for the purpose required, as a galvanized bucket will last longer than an earthenware pot, but how much has gone from life if the art of the potter is lost? A metal spoon will be more convenient than the one carved and fashioned from the shell of the coconut, but what can make up for the loss of the craftsmanship that filled hours with delight for many a worker? We are so proud of our improvements and of the way we can make things bigger and faster than our fathers, but in this machine age we lose a lot that once enriched the lives of those who lived more leisurely, and having lost so much of the joy of the hand-worker we are unconsciously taking that joy from these other peoples into whose lands we penetrate. These primitive men were real craftsmen. Their bamboo pipes had wonderful patterns carved into the hard material from which they were fashioned, their armlets were woven with most intricate patterns, the feathers in their headdresses were arranged and secured in a wonderful way, and their fish-nets would compare favourably with our own. Their canoes were often works of art, fashioned with infinite care and patience, and often carved with remarkable artistry. I remember standing by when a young man came along in his canoe and carefully drew it on to the bank. I could see he was proud of it, and felt he had good reason for his pride. It was splendidly shaped and the carving down each side and at the bows was beautifully executed. I longed to secure it for one of our museums that our people might see what the Papuan could accomplish; but when I asked if he would sell it he turned away almost in scorn. Nothing I could offer was worth what this, his own creation, was worth to him.

Only those ignorant of the life they had to live would call them lazy, though it is probably true that when working for the white man on jobs that have no interest for them, many will not work harder than they have to; but in old Papua these people had to work if they were to live, for none could buy the labour of others. It was a Papuan, addressing another of his race, who remarked, "Do you think you are a white man that you sit there and do nothing?" We have divided life into many callings and professions; and one is a builder and another a farmer, and some make things which others distribute, and a thousand different tasks are performed by a thousand different men. The primitive man knew nothing of this. He was a self-supporting entity despite his tribal allegiance. Each was a farmer, house-builder, artisan and fisherman, for all had to rely on their own exertions to supply their needs and thus learn self-reliance and become expert in using the material nature provided. They started with nothing but their hands, making or securing by their own exertions, tools and string, paints and dyes, all the clothes, articles and weapons they used, the house in which they lived and the canoe which was their means of transport. As with us, there were experts in various forms of work, and the advice and guidance of such were sought by others, but in the long run every man had to be able to tackle every job on his own. The women in their own domain were as talented as the men and, to my mind, worked harder, but they were also more conservative and clung to old customs more tenaciously than the men.

Such were the people who were helping us to cut and shape the timber from the forest, make roads and build our houses, and my thoughts go back to those early days when a new way of life was opening up before these men and women. Even if we had not come, they would have had to face it, for the white man was already in the country, and our being with them enabled us to offer them a way of life based on the Christian faith that could enrich all that was good in the old and strengthen them to resist that which was bad in the new. Let us not imagine, however, that all we bring is an improvement on the things that were, nor that better things necessarily mean a better life. We were the heralds of a new age but, as I look back, I can sympathize with those who met us with suspicion and hostility, and can enter into the feelings of the older folk who resented our intrusion and clung to the ways of their fathers. Of that hostility we were often conscious during our first years among them.

Though very fully occupied at Aird Hill, I would sometimes leave Fitui in charge and go off in the *Tamate* to seek new villages, and frequently our coming would create an uproar. One such occasion stands out vividly. We had set off to visit a big village known as Dubumuba, and ran down the river where crocodiles were basking on the mud banks and the dense forest closed us in on either side. Leaving the Kikori, we entered the broad waters of the estuary and saw the village some distance off. As we made for it, we sensed our approach was creating a tremendous disturbance. Women and girls were rushing to the bank of a creek, dragging the smaller children after them. There they jumped into canoes and paddled furiously into the forest. We seemed to have stirred up a hornets' nest for from the great *dubu-daimo* hundreds of dark-skinned men were pouring, their bodies streaked with white and yellow, while above the brick-red of their painted faces the fighting head-dresses of cassowary feathers waved in the wind. Shouting fiercely, they lined the shore, and as we came near and prepared to land, suddenly raised their bows and drew their arrows to the head. It looked as if all the pictures of Red Indians I had revelled in as a boy had suddenly come to life. They yelled defiance and threatened to kill us if we dared to come ashore, and nothing was to be gained by accepting the challenge. To have done so would not only have been foolhardy, but against our policy, for we were out to win their friendship and not to force ourselves upon them.

It was often like that. These men lived in a world of enemies, and most strangers could be reckoned as foes, and it took time for them to realize that our coming meant no harm. We made our contacts warily and never forced our way into places where there was no welcome. In the end it was the quickest method, for it soon became known that we could be trusted, the news being passed from place to place, until the time came when, instead of being repelled, we were receiving invitations to visit villages we had never seen.

13

PARTNERS IN ADVENTURE

After weeks in villages among the swamps it was refreshing to get clear of the mud and back to Aird Hill or Neuri, as our people called it. Though we had only made a beginning, much had been accomplished. The main site had been cleared and a rough road cut through the swamp and up the hill. We had built homes for our helpers and a store had been put up for our tools, trade goods and food. Then we started on the home for myself and the wife I hoped would join me there. Work was often slowed down by the rains, and I was constantly being called away from one task to another, for I was by turn architect and surveyor, carpenter and builder, master of my boat, engineer, doctor, teacher and parson. As a result, my home was far from completion when, towards the end of 1912, I had to run down to the coast and on to Orokolo to await the *John Williams,* which was to take me to Australia. The framework of the house was complete and most of our roof thatched, but the flooring had to be laid and the walls planked up and finished off. I left Fitui instructions as to what had to be done and eventually reached Brisbane, where I was married to Miss Ena Davidson. The wedding aroused much local interest, for my wife was well known and linked with two of the oldest Queensland families. Her father was greatly respected, a man of sterling character and a fine Christian gentleman, and her elder brother, Alfred, who followed his father into the Bank of New South Wales, rose to be General Manager and later received a knighthood in recognition of outstanding services he rendered Australia during the great depression of 1933.

Early in 1913 the *John Williams* took us back to Papua, and darkness was falling when we anchored off Samarai. As we looked across to Kwato we saw the hills lit up by lines of flaming torches held above the heads of marching Papuans, whose song of welcome came to us over the water. It was a very lovely greeting, and as my wife and I stood together we watched the lights go out one by one, and silence came as the sound of singing died away and the warm darkness of the night closed round about us. Over the water the mountain ranges reached on and on for over a thousand miles, hiding in their valleys multitudes of men and women still living in a stone age and utterly unaware of the Western peoples who were breaking in upon their land.

We stood there side by side, and our hearts were awed by the thought of all that lay ahead, but in the early morning everything took on new beauty as the sun lit up the scene. Canoes were coming from the islands, some so frail that one wondered how they could support the occupants, and on one that looked like three bits of wood tied together sat a young Papuan, carefree and gay, though there seemed every prospect of his suddenly being tipped into the sea. In contrast was another, with bow and stern well raised and beautifully fashioned, and close to it one carrying three very small boys who were bringing baskets of limes for sale, the baskets being made from plaited coconut leaves.

The Papuan District Committee was to meet at Kwato, and while we waited for the *John Williams* to bring our colleagues from their various stations, Abel planned a visit to the villages around Milne Bay. It was a delightful experience, for the coastline is very beautiful with thickly wooded hills rising from water so deep that our boat could often tie up to trees. Here and there we would catch sight of a waterfall foaming down some precipice, while sea and sky were lit up by most glorious sunsets.

We were sitting together delighting in all the loveliness around us, when suddenly our peace was ruined by loud squawking. Two fowls that had been presented to us at one of the villages were being despatched and prepared for our dinner that night. Sitting at the stern, the cooks plucked them, and our track was plain to see by the trail of feathers that stretched far astern. My wife had never seen so quick a transition from the live fowl to the cooking pot, though I had grown used to it, for when anchoring off islands in Torres Strait, I often saw a crowd of youngsters chasing some unfortunate bird, and soon after landing found a boiled fowl awaiting me.

Talk of Milne Bay still brings back memories of sandy beaches where the palm trees came close to the water's edge, of evenings when sea and sky were full of glory, and of villages where crowds of brown-skinned men and women almost overwhelmed

us with the warmth of their welcome, and where we listened
with wonder to the singing of Papuans and joined together in
evening prayer. If someone had even hinted that those forest-
covered hills would re-echo to the noise of guns and wild fighting, and that Australians and Japanese be locked in deadly
combat amidst all the quiet beauty, we would have deemed him
mad. And yet it happened and the loveliness of that bay will
never be the same again, nor the Papuan ever return to the simple
life we saw him living in those villages by the sea.

The *John Williams* arrived soon after we returned to Kwato
and we settled down to strenuous work, enlivened by cricket,
where the Papuans, trained by Abel, proved to be more than a
match for us. The days passed quickly and soon we were joining
the steamer again with those of our company who were travelling west, and to whom we said our good-bye as one by one they
were landed at their various stations. We left the ship at Orokolo
and later set off in the *Tamate* through the maze of waterways
linking the various outlets of the Purari River, and after crossing
a wide estuary entered a stream we thought would take us
through a deep but narrow waterway to a river leading towards
Aird Hill. It was a mistake, for this stream wound its way into
the forest and then began to shallow, and I slipped down into
the engine-room to go astern, but was too late, for the *Tamate*
slid up on to a mud bank and stuck, and though I put the engine
hard astern there was no shifting her. The tide was running out
and I knew we would have to stay put until it came in again. It
was a steamy hot morning and the boat commenced to heel over
as the waters fell and long stretches of black mud appeared.
We sat on the sloping deck watching some queer crabs, each
with a single multi-coloured claw folded in front, and were also
interested in the mud fish which scientists regard as a link between fish and reptiles. They sported amid the ooze and moved
with surprising speed as they chased each other. From the forest
came the noise of many birds and insects, and as the sun rose
above the trees that had shaded us we sweltered in the heat.

Then one of our crew, with a scared look on his face, whispered that we were being watched. He had seen faces among
the trees, and as we also caught sight of them we heard a high-
pitched cry and, looking up stream, saw a canoe laden with
dark skinned men. They stopped paddling and began to shout to

others, and answering cries, growing ever louder, could be heard. A second canoe joined the first, and then another and another, until a fleet of large and small dugouts had assembled. Having collected their forces they started to approach us, and we were surrounded, with no chance of escape. These were the wildest lot of men my wife had ever seen, and though I was used to such crowds I was anything but happy at seeing them just then, for my explorations had taken me into some of their villages and I knew they were headhunters. We were at their mercy, with no chance of doing anything save wait for the tide to set us free.

There was tremendous excitement as they saw my wife, the first white woman they had ever met, and the men crowded in to get a closer look, and discussed her hair and dress, her skin and blue eyes, at the tops of their voices. To keep them in good temper I slipped into the cabin and seized some sticks of tobacco and an old newspaper, and was back on deck as quickly as possible. As I distributed the tobacco I asked my wife to give each a piece of paper for their cigarettes and to keep smiling. The situation was not helping her, for these men looked so dreadful and were making such a noise that her heart went cold with fear, but she did her best and set about daintily handing small bits of paper to the crowd of naked savages and meeting their questioning looks with a smile. It was not as bright as many of the smiles she had given me, and she later confessed that it was the hardest she had ever produced, but she did her best and won their confidence, while I kept one eye on them with their bows and arrows and one eye on the tide now slowly coming in. Somehow it felt as if never in the world's history had a tide come in so slowly, but at long last the *Tamate* was on an even keel and then afloat and we were no longer helpless prisoners.

Meanwhile the sullen suspicion of the men had given place to looks of friendship. They again started calling, their voices raised in strange, high notes, and we wondered how many more of these painted warriors were coming along. But this time the canoes were laden with women who, unlike the men, sat on the floor of their craft as they paddled. For a time they kept well away but, encouraged by their men, they came slowly nearer, and soon were chattering with amazement as they looked upon this other woman with a skin so white and eyes so strangely blue.

Our hearts felt lighter, for women do not come when trouble

is brewing, and their presence added to our confidence. We were being treated as friends and I did not want to mar that friendship by starting the engine, as it created a shattering noise and I had seen men jumping into the water and yelling in fear when, without sufficient warning, I had done this. To them it sounded like an angry spirit, and as we did not want to leave a bad impression we warped the boat round and poled her into mid-stream, while an old warrior went ahead sounding the waters with his long paddle to show us where the channel lay. Then, after many warnings and exhortations not to be afraid, we started the engine and were soon away, leaving behind a crowd of friends who waved to us as long as we remained in sight. Those hours of waiting had proved a good thing and the friendships formed smoothed our way in the years that followed when trying to make contact with adjacent tribes. The rest of the journey was uneventful, but the bride's homecoming proved far from that of the story books.

We entered the creek that at high water would take us to a solid landing place, but once again the tide was falling, and in those parts it can fall about twenty feet. We were soon grounded and took to the dinghy, but the dinghy also stuck. There was nothing for it but to get into the deep, stinking ooze and drag the dinghy over the various sunken logs, with the wife sitting on the thwarts wondering what would happen next. We got through at last, and Fitui and his wife, with their helpers, were at the landing place waiting to receive the bride, and though the rest of us were very muddy I was glad to see her able to greet them looking clean and presentable.

I was most anxious that her first impressions of the house she was to live in would be encouraging, but I had had to leave the laying of the floor and the planking up of the walls to Fitui and the 'boys', and they had used so many nails on the floor and other things that they had none left over for the walls. We did not know this and went up the hill in high expectation, until what was to be our home came into sight, looking something like an aviary. It had a roof and a floor, but was open all the way round, and though this made for coolness it deprived us of any privacy. Something had to be done about it before we turned in for the night, so I tacked some matting to the stanchions and made the place a bit more secluded. For some months we had to live very roughly, and the change from the lovely home at Kwato, with its well-trained Papuan helpers, was very marked.

Life was full of shocks for one who had lived a somewhat sheltered life in a very good home. Cockroaches were her pet aversion and abounded in cases that had lain for long in the holds of coastal vessels. They are disgusting anywhere but in the tropics can be a nightmare. Scorpions and centipedes also disturbed my wife's peace of mind, and after finding a big one under her pillow she was never sure where the next would turn up. Snakes were plentiful, and, on hearing an excited cry, I would run along to find one on a journey of exploration through the house. Aird Hill seemed the home of these reptiles, large and small, harmless and dangerous. Now and then someone would be bitten and we had to act promptly to save their lives, and we always kept lancets and drugs handy, but sometimes we were not informed until it was too late and then the sufferer died.

Once, when conducting a service, I was impressed by the unusual stillness of the congregation. The crowd seemed to be much more attentive than usual, though I sensed something peculiar in the way they were looking towards me. All the same, the stillness was so unusual that I felt I was really getting somewhere and it was the most encouraging service I had ever conducted until, as it ended, a young man came cautiously towards me and whispered that a very bad snake was above my head. I shifted hurriedly and saw a red-skinned reptile, one of the deadliest known in those parts. We shot it down, to the delight of all, who evidently felt it was the best part of that morning's worship, but I was left rather disillusioned and wondered what my hearers would have done had it dropped on me during my discourse.

Some varieties of constrictors were constantly attacking our fowls. They would crush and swallow a fowl whole and then lie comatose while they digested it. Often one found a hole in the wire netting that protected the roosting place. It would get in when empty, but with a fowl inside could not get out, and thus we caught and killed it. One I shot had just swallowed part of a setting of eggs. We cut it open and recovered the eggs, still intact, and popped them back under the fowl amongst the eggs that had escaped. I have always been sorry I did not mark them, for some hatched and some were duds, and I've never been sure if those lively chickens had had the unique experience of being for a time in a snake's inside.

Life at Aird Hill in those days was neither comfortable nor very safe, but my wife faced it cheerfully and usually found something to laugh at, even when things happened that many would have found nerve shattering. Her presence had a fine influence on surrounding peoples and brought her a name that she retained for the rest of her life. Mamu was their name for mother, and young as my wife was she became Mamu to them all. I had become known as Buta, but also as Abea, or father, and later as Copu-abea, or father of the villages, which name I prized, as it made me one of themselves. Mamu's presence brought many visitors, and among these was Kerawaia, the chief of a nearby tribe. He was one of my early acquaintances and a firm friend, and once persuaded me to give him a nose that was the envy of all his people. I was on the Tamate, painting the mouths of the ventilating cowls a brilliant vermilion. Red was the favourite colour of all these people, though the only red they could get in those days was made from a clay or from certain seeds they crushed. Neither could compare with my enamel, and Kerawaia, who happened to come along in his canoe, came on board to talk, and after admiring the colour of my cowls, looked at my paint with envy and pleaded for some of it. We talked of many things, but he always returned to the paint until, to satisfy him, I carefully applied it to his nasal organ. It was a broad and prominent feature and I took some pains with it, and when at last the task was complete, Kerawaia had a nose the like of which the tribes around had never seen. He was filled with pride at the result, and as he paddled towards his village, proud to think how his tribe would admire and envy him, his face was one great smile of happiness, and every now and then he stopped and turned to wave to me in sheer delight, and that nose shone in the sun like a beacon-light.

Kerawaia was greatly intrigued by my wife and could not understand her being the only one. Deeply concerned about the matter, he came to talk it over. "Buta," he asked, "how many wives have you got?" He seemed to think I had a harem stowed away somewhere, and when I modestly confessed to having no other than the one who was with me, he considered I was not living up to my position. He had two or three, and other chiefs had more, and I was rather a poor sort of fellow, for a man with only one wife must have been unfortunate when the bidding took place. He turned up one morning with two of his ménage, both very unwashed and under-dressed. Each brought a present of crabs, for which we were expected to pay, and while my one wife was doing this he was trying to impress me with the fact of how much better off he was with the two to work for him.

Soon we were getting deputations of women from more distant villages. The news that the man whose white skin had caused so much interest now had a woman whose skin was even whiter sounded preposterous, but the men affirmed it to be true and so they would set off to see for themselves. Sometimes it meant a long journey, and they would travel up the rivers by day and sleep in rude humpies by night, and be two or three days on the way. Their canoes would enter the creek at the foot of the hill and later we would see a line of visitors coming up the steep path in single file, each wearing nothing but a woven girdle and a wisp of fibres. They would stand shyly and silently before the house and then, when Mamu appeared, come on to the verandah and gather round her. They would look her up and down, speechless with wonder, and then break into excited gossip as they discussed her appearance. The whiteness of her face and arms, the softness of her hair, and most of all the blueness of her eyes, were matters of tremendous interest, and they were very intrigued by her strange garments which hid most of her person. One would reach out and feel the white arms and leave her mark upon them, while another might edge behind to have a closer look at the dress and pinch it to see if my wife was there, and she was there every time. When at last curiosity was satisfied, they would open their raffia bags and display the crabs caught on the journey up. Mamu would lay a bit of tobacco beside each in payment, after which the women would take their departure to boast in the villages of what they had seen.

Woman had always been a chattel, the property of some man. He bought and owned her, would beat her when he felt like it, and if he killed her no one, save perhaps her relatives, would bring him to book. He was the dominant partner, or thought he was, and the woman seemed to accept her position of inferiority, but I soon discovered that she had her own ways of getting what she wanted. In reality she often ruled, while her husband was under the delusion that he was lord and master. Behind his blustering it was the woman who pulled the strings. Even among the wildest tribes one would find women of outstanding character and husbands who gave heed to them, though, as I have already had occasion to remark, they were probably the most conservative force in tribal life. It was tribal custom that led them to submit to things we would consider an outrage, and now they were seeing a way of life they had never known. Men and women alike noted the fact that the white woman stood beside her man as his equal, husband and wife living and working together in happy companionship, and they began to sense something richer than their own tribal custom, and caught their first glimpse of a Christian home.

We had only the beginnings of a station when my wife arrived, and as we worked she shared in the planning. It is not given to many white folk in these days to carve out a home from the primeval forest, and we have always been thankful that it fell to our lot, though the work involved was very heavy. The mere clearing of the bush was a tremendous task in itself, for the felling of the trees was only a beginning, and the disposal of the fallen giants a much more exacting bit of work. Many of the trunks were sawn into eight or nine feet lengths and were used as piles beneath the house, which was built well off the ground, the space below providing a splendid drying ground during our abnormally wet season, while I utilized a portion of it as my personal workshop. The great roots had to be grubbed up and all over the area fires were glowing night and day as these, together with useless timber, were being burnt.

I had no skilled helpers and was teaching the boys as I worked beside them, and some of them were very difficult to handle. They had never felt the need for self-restraint and passions flared up at the slightest provocation. There were fights among the workers and threats against ourselves, and sometimes more than threats. I was directing a gang on one occasion when two of them suddenly came for me with flashing eyes and lifted axes. They were out to brain me, and had I run would probably have done so, for they could run faster. Fortunately they were not very stout-hearted and when I seized a chunk of wood and rushed at them with a yell, they were so startled that they turned and ran, as I chased them down the hill. I might add that I took care not to overtake them.

Stories of inter-tribal fighting often reached us, and in one case a canoe-load of men and women a mile or so away from us were set upon and killed and their bodies eaten by the murderers, who took the skulls to hang in their *dubu-daimo*. Life was held very cheaply, and a young man who was helping us seemed quite proud of the fact that he had killed a man, for the killing had won him the respect of his fellow tribesmen. Others would come to us telling of fights near their homes and would give us gruesome descriptions of the feast that followed and of the way portions of the bodies were shared out.

Life in such surroundings could hardly be described as dull, but there was also much around us full of interest and beauty. We would sometimes wander into the bush looking for new ferns and flowers. The former abounded in plentiful variety, but flowers were not so numerous, though every now and then we would discover a lovely orchid, and once came upon a flower-ing creeper that brought us wondering delight. Glorious blossoms sprang in profusion from a leafless vine whose stem, about three inches in diameter, wound its way, snake-like, up a great tree. Each blossom was two or three inches across, with its four petals bifurcated and glistening white as if shaped in wax; stamens and pistil were about four inches long, and from the rough vine sprung bunches of green nodules looking like clusters of nuts, each a bud. We had never seen anything like it before and I often wished I were a botanist, for Aird Hill would have been a happy hunting ground.

We were constantly coming across strange and sometimes dis-agreeable things such as, for instance, the stick insect. This can be up to six or eight inches long and on the trunk of a tree looks like a dry branch. There were spiders of tremendous size and sometimes very poisonous, and once I watched a collection of small twigs and bits of bark moving along and found it to be a caterpillar using this strange camouflage to protect itself from birds. When observed, it stopped dead and looked like a bit of debris, but as soon as it felt safe, on it went, carrying its pro-tective load along with it. There were beetles of vivid colouring and others of surprising size and shape, and one fairly small which we named the push beetle. It had remarkable strength and, instead of going round an obstacle, seemed to enjoy pushing it forward. Often when one alighted on our table we would put a book in its path and it would push it right off the table. Lizards abounded, and some species made their homes within our house and often ran across the ceiling catching flies or insects. Now and then they lost their grip and fell on to the table or floor and would lie as if stunned for a time, and then go off seeming none the worse. I found if I caught them by their tails they would run off leaving their tails behind them, and it was a nasty sensation to find oneself left with only a wriggling tail between one's fingers. They seem able to part with them on the least provocation and then start to grow another.

It seems strange to talk of spring in a land of eternal summer, yet each year about October many of the trees shed their leaves and clothe themselves anew with fresh foliage of every shade of pink, green and brown, and the leaves of one tree were such a glorious red that when we first saw it at a distance we thought it was in flower. Early in the morning the song of many birds would come to us from all the hills around, and those who could not sing atoned for the harshness of their voices by the beauty of their plumage. From our verandah we would look out across the forest with here and there a glimpse of rivers that wound their way to the coast, now lost among the trees and then shining in the sunlight, while away to the north in clear weather could be seen the distant mountains.

There is a widespread idea that tropical lands are store-houses of food, but many an unfortunate lost in the bush has found that far from the truth. It is easy to starve in a tropical forest. In the early days we relied largely upon imported food, ordering our stores once a year and grateful that so much we needed could be had in tins. Later we introduced goats and fowls. The goats throve and multiplied but seemed possessed of demons, for they ate our shrubs, broke down our fences, destroyed our gardens and did so much damage that we felt we would be better off without them. Fowls were more amenable, and with eggs and an occasional bird our diet was considerably improved. Neither fowls nor goats had ever been seen by the people until we brought them in, but before very long we began to find an occasional fowl in some village, for fowls had a habit of disappearing and we became more and more careful to lock them up at night. We were also growing various vegetables and had introduced good strains of bananas and pineapples as well as oranges and limes. The newly cleared ground yielded splendid crops of sweet potatoes and the villagers soon learnt that our large clearings were full of good food.

I was new to their habits, but when we seemed to be receiving an abnormal number of visitors I began to wonder what had brought them. Some had come from afar and one day, as I was setting off to visit sundry villages, they asked me to help them on their way by giving them and their canoes a tow. I noticed they were heavily laden and warned them that the boat travelled very quickly and the canoes would yaw and overturn unless the oarsmen were very careful. I also suggested that they would travel more safely if they went on their own, but this did not appeal to them. It seemed foolish to paddle when they could travel without effort behind my launch. They accordingly made fast to the ropes we put astern and we were soon under way. They seemed without a care in the world, a happy crowd surrounded by numbers of covered baskets and sitting comfortably in their canoes with nothing to do but enjoy the sensation of not having to work their passage. As the *Tamate* gathered speed they found themselves travelling faster than they had ever done in their lives, but though they seemed at ease I was far from sharing their confidence and my fears were soon confirmed. Maybe they grew careless or made a false move with the steering oars, but suddenly the canoes yawed, swung broadside on and capsized. At once the air was filled with yells of men and screams of women and children swimming in the river or clinging to their overturned craft. We came round to pick up the swimmers, and as we did so received a considerable shock. The reason for the influx of visitors was before me, for the crowd was struggling in water covered by large quantities of my best potatoes. More than half our crop disappeared and none of the people I rescued had any sense of shame—only a deep regret at being caught. It was no use talking of the wrong they had done, for their ideas of right and wrong differed vastly from ours, as did their whole outlook on life, and we had to try to understand them before we could help them. I suppose justice demanded that I should confiscate their cargo, which really belonged to me, but at that stage I felt it wiser to let them collect the floating spoils and then share it all between us.

14

THE PAPUANS' SPIRIT WORLD

QUITE early in my missionary career I sensed that if I were to get anywhere with the Papuan, I had to begin where I found the people and with what they believed, and from there try to lead them on to that larger conception of God Jesus brought to men.

The casual observer never suspected how big a part religion played in the life of the tribe and the individual. He looks in vain for temples and idols and people performing acts of worship, yet all the time the primitive Papuan was so aware of an unseen world about him that no part of his life was unaffected by it. I never felt I was among an irreligious people. On the contrary, I was conscious of the fact that these wild folk were more alive to things of the spirit than many of my own countrymen. They were dominated by strange superstitions, and some of their ceremonies savoured of sexual debauchery, but I never mocked at their crude beliefs or approached their sacred places lightly. I recognized that though they might be unconscious of what they were doing they were nevertheless feeling after God, and realized that if I wanted to help them it was up to me to learn all I could of their beliefs.

In my student days the study of anthropology had little or no place in our theological colleges and we had to do it on the field with little but our own native wit to help us. We were in danger of thinking the wild man knew little while we had much to teach, but one gets further when one is humbler and aware of how much we also have to learn.

The nearer I came to the Papuan the more I realized how for him religion and life were so closely interwoven that the one could not be touched without affecting the other. They had their sacred objects and places, but religion was not something for the temple or for special days; it was something they could never get away from and affected every thing and every occupation. It had its place in the building of the house, the making of the garden and construction of the canoe. Their journeys often commenced with a religious ceremony, and the queer customs associated with birth, marriage and death all had religious significance, and their dance festivals that appeared to many of us little more than bestial orgies, were for them a reaching out towards a life-giving spirit. Their lives were lived with the consciousness of being surrounded by unseen forces on whom, or which, they were dependent. Recognition of that was seen in simple acts, such as when the women brought the evening meal to their menfolk in the *dubu-daimo*, one of them before they ate would lift a stick of roasted sago towards the *agibe* in front of which the skulls of enemies were piled. It was a recognition of their debt to a power beyond themselves, almost a grace before meat.

I was never able to discover a belief in one supreme Being, though Iriwaki was held in high honour in many places. When I set out to learn about him they told me that he had a brother with him whose name was Meriwaki, but when I sought the name of their father no one could tell me; no one, strangely enough, had ever heard of Iriwaki's father. It was too good a chance to miss, so I told him I knew his Father, and as they looked at me, surprised that I should know something about their Iriwaki, I told them of the God and Father of us all, and at once God was not just a white man's story but one who belonged to them and was part of the life they knew.

Among other spirits are shadowy beings concerning whom endless stories are told, legends of mighty ancestors and unseen powers, which have been handed down from generation to generation. These were the powers that made the hills and rivers, the trees and birds, the fish and fire. The stories may appear to us grotesque and often foolish, but they represent the Papuan's attempt to explain the world in which he finds himself and account for the things that happen to him.

The study of his beliefs not only enabled me to know and help him better, but threw light on customs still practised by my own people. Arthur Chignell, in his delightful book, *An Outpost in Papua*, speaks of two flint razors so alike that they might have been made by the same hand, but one had been picked up in England, fashioned maybe two thousand years ago by a Briton in the stone age; while the other had recently been used by a Papuan. These flints suggested that our ancestors lived a life not so very different from these others, and as we watch them, we catch glimpses of the way our ancestors also thought and acted. We find ourselves looking back from the wild creature who confronts us with his barbaric weapons to the days when our fathers roamed wild and untamed through the primeval forest, and it is as if a veil had been lifted and we can catch a glimpse of the way which we have come.

As I think of this, my mind turns to the Papuan. For him the night has been spent in dancing. The drums began to beat before sundown and continued until sunrise. Often I have gone to sleep with their rhythmic throbbing in my ears and awakened in the early morning with the sound of them still rolling across the water. Since the night has been given to dancing the day must be given to sleep, and our friend who was so gay last evening now lies wrapped in slumber. The feathers look bedraggled, and the paint is streaked by perspiration, for the dance was strenuous and it lasted long. His head rests on a wooden pillow, and his body twitches as he sleeps, for he is dreaming. He is out in the forest, hunting the wild pig, or in his canoe by the mud flats where crocodiles lie basking in the sun, or maybe dodging among the trees as he seeks to elude his enemy. All dreams, we say, are the result of too much pig the night before, but he won't believe that, nor will his friends. Rather, when he awakes, he will tell to eager listeners how he has been away in a spirit-world where all things are possible. That his body never moved presents no difficulty. His friends have had similar experiences and are convinced that there is a part of him that can go where the body can never travel, for the spirit is other than the body which it can leave and does leave every time he goes off to do those wonderful things we can all do in the land of Nod. That is why, when he sleeps, his friends hesitate to wake him, for it is considered a bad thing to recall the spirit too hastily from its wanderings, and more than once when I sent someone to fetch a 'boy' I wanted, the excuse for not bringing him was considered unanswerable—he couldn't come, for he was sleeping. In other words, his spirit was away on other business.

Believing things like this makes it easy for a man to think of himself as of more than flesh and blood. He feels he is a living spirit within a mortal body and able to go on living when the body decays. Moreover, he also believes that things as well as men have spirits, for in his dreams he has recognized places and seen trees and houses, fish and animals. He saw them because they, too, had spirits, and thus we find a belief common to all Papuans that everything has a soul, or something we might possibly describe as life force, that makes existence possible, and here the savage comes remarkably close to the modern scientist in his conception of matter as something quite other than what we see. He makes small distinction between things and persons, as for him everything is personal. His outlook is something akin to that of the man who damns his engine when it will not start.

With such thoughts as these, the Papuan found no difficulty in explaining the fact of death and never thought of it as the end of everything. I have moved among many tribes and been where no white man has been before, but I have never found a people who believed that when a man was dead he was finished; always there was an assurance that somewhere the dead still live. To the primitive man, death is a form of sleep, and when asleep the spirit often leaves the body. He has known it to do so when he himself marched out into dreamland. This time the one who has died has probably gone further, or some strange thing has happened and he will never come back to his body again.

Death is not always so permanent, and before I realized that, I got a shock when showing my lantern slide pictures and people cried out that one of the audience had died. It seemed a tragic end to what had been a jolly evening, and I sadly made my way to where the crowd had gathered round the body, only to find the corpse had fainted, and to learn that a person can either be dead or very dead. A swoon, faint or trance are all forms of death, but in these cases the dead will come to life again, while in other cases they never come back; they are very dead. But they are not finished with life, and many are the stories of the lands to which they have gone, and of the ways by which they reach them.

When in France during the first World War, I was intrigued by the fact that the phrase of a fallen comrade, "He's gone west", expressed exactly the idea of the Papuan. The belief in tribe after tribe is that the dead go west towards the setting sun, and always they are thought of as enjoying a life similar to that of the living, and requiring the things they used when among their fellows. Where our people place flowers upon the graves of their friends, the Papuan might put weapons and pipes or other things the dead man prized. I have often wondered if this custom, expressed in different ways by them and us, is not linked with the primitive belief so beautifully expressed in Maeterlinck's *Blue Bird,* that the lives of the departed are richer and happier when remembered by their friends.

This thought or something akin to it led to very gruesome practices. I was standing in a village talking to the old chief as he sat cross-legged looking down on me from the entrance platform of the *dubu-daimo.* A change of wind brought with it a horrible stench and looking round, I saw a platform raised six or eight feet above the ground on crooked posts, with a long object, covered by a native mat, upon it. "That is my son," said the old man, "he died some time ago"; and I could well believe it. He was much less disturbed by the proximity of the body than I was and gave me to understand that he was keeping him near to hold him in remembrance, and I have never forgotten him. This practice of exposing the body was common among the Kerawo tribes, and frequently a widow would have to sit beneath the platform of her deceased husband while the flesh decayed, after which the skull was carefully cleaned and painted and kept within the home. The whole process appeared to us very loathsome, but behind it all was the fact of remembrance, and all that it might mean to the departed.

The Papuan also shared with many white folk a belief in ghosts and reckoned that the dead haunted the village where once they lived, though this might only be for a time. The villagers had an uncomfortable feeling that being able to get around unseen, the dead can revenge themselves for any unkindness received when living. Various precautions were therefore taken as soon as a death occurred, and the openings into all the houses carefully shuttered to prevent the entrance of the spirit. Seeing the homes thus shuttered made me think of the darkened windows I had seen as a boy in England when the blinds were all drawn as soon as a death took place. Probably few asked themselves how the custom originated but I wondered if our forefathers had the same fears as the Papuans.

Similar thoughts have come to me concerning the very substantial meal provided for mourners in some parts of England when I was a boy. Our ancestors probably made this feast for reasons similar to those of the Papuan, who thinks of his friend as having started on a long journey, and thus provides the feast to sustain his spirit on the way. Though the mourners enjoy the food the nourishment is supposed to strengthen the departed. The Papuan, like ourselves, has forgotten the origin of many of his customs, but I have a suspicion that he remembers some things that we have long since lost track of.

The belief in a far-off world where the spirits of the departed foregather is accompanied by a belief in an unseen world, lying close at hand, full of the spirits of men and things and mysterious powers. Yet with this vivid awareness of strange powers there was little conception of what we call prayer, though in a sense they lived in an atmosphere of converse with the unseen. There were times when a man would go out alone and build a rude shelter on a hill or by the river and watch and wait until a spirit revealed itself to him. I never succeeded in discovering just how the revelation came, but I have no doubt that it meant much to him and to his people.

Most of their ceremonies were of religious significance, especially those connected with marriage, the planting of gardens and the ingathering of the fruits. In such there was much that we would consider obscene and revolting, yet through all, like a golden thread, ran a sense of dependence upon mighty powers outside themselves. At the heart of what appeared to be a sensual carnival was the germ of something beautiful, and the day comes at last when the heathen ceremony is tansformed into a Christian marriage or a Harvest festival.

Side by side with all this, emerges a figure that brings more fear than joy: the Sorcerer, or man who stands between the common people and the spirit world. He is supposed to know more than others about the unseen and can tell why spirits are angry and why trouble has come to the village. He can detect the wrongdoer and bring death to those who offend him, and in primitive life there is no figure as powerful as he is and no one more feared. He carries strange charms and practises secret rites, and we must not think of him as a fraud, for he deals in things that are real to him. He believes he has seen the spirits of whom he speaks and he and others have known men die when he said they would. We may put it down to imagination and the power of suggestion, but he knows nothing of psychology, and the things he has seen and known to happen are such that it is not surprising that he believes in himself and is a power to be reckoned with. In my time, the government recognized this and placed every convicted sorcerer in gaol for longer or shorter periods in much the same way as our fathers punished witches, for the sorcerer was often a menace in the community. The Papuan seldom imagined that a man died what we would call a natural death. Some evilly disposed person or power had had a hand in it, and the sorcerer would be called in to discover the culprit. After various incantations and use of charms the chances were that he would name someone he had a grudge against as the cause of the trouble, or mention another tribe. The friends of the dead would then seek revenge, and the man named be murdered, or an attack made on the tribe supposed to be implicated. The sorcerer sometimes used poison to bring about the death of his victim, but the power of suggestion was often enough, with the result that he was able to extort what he wanted from the people who feared him.

Papua has many different tribes, languages and customs, but all alike had one thing in common, and that was fear of the unseen that overshadowed life and was to them the cause of all their troubles. I have seen ulcers so terrible that I wondered how the sufferer lived, ulcers that were never cleansed, in which worms had bred, and whose stench nauseated me. The sufferer knew nothing of the connection between dirt and disease and blamed all on the spirits who tortured him. Contagious diseases were also considered to be the work of an evil power moving among them and inescapable, and this attitude of mind bred a kind of fatalism or hopeless acquiescence which persisted long after they came in contact with civilization and often interfered with our efforts to help them.

I was with a colleague in Port Moresby when a mother brought her child for treatment. She had had ordinary conjunctivitis and a simple lotion would have saved the girl endless suffering had it been used in time, but the complaint had been neglected and then left to the sorcerer. Who, they argued, could outwit the evil spirit that was tormenting the girl, who, unless it was the sorcerer? They had gone to him and his treatment had intensified her needless suffering and when at last they brought her to us, her sight had been destroyed. Such tragedies were common, but the story of that girl had a happier ending. She was no use to her people and they left her at the mission where she was cared for, and the horror where her eyes had been, cleansed and healed. She was trained in our school and later sent to Sydney where, in an institution for the blind, she was instructed in useful arts and crafts and learned to read Braille. Trained thus, she returned to be a teacher of her people, and when I was last in Port Moresby I saw how her life had been enriched by all she had learnt and softened by the love with which she had been surrounded. She was a happy young woman finding richness of life in the service of others.

For years I never came across twins in any delta village. They were born, of course, but never allowed to live, for the people believed the father of one or the other must have been an evil spirit and so both were killed. The same fate met the infant of a mother who died in childbirth. When she was buried the living babe was buried with her, the argument being that she would have nursed it had she lived, so now let her take the child with her.

It is not surprising that the early missionaries coming up against the cruelty and bestiality associated with primitive religion saw nothing good in it, yet with all its crudities it brought direction to these simple folk, and gave meaning to the world in which they lived. However much it failed them, it helped them to meet the mysteries of life and death and shed some light upon their way, and with all its contradictions it kept tribal life from falling to pieces. With its clans, totems and family laws it prevented inter-marriage between those closely related, and with its taboos it made for protection of women and property. Their ceremonies, charged with religious and social significance, gave meaning and colour to their life and the legends of their race, repeated by the old men as they sat around the fires at night, linked them with the past and made them proud of their inheritance. All this should never be forgotten, and as I recall what I have seen and what the years have taught me, I sense with Longfellow's *Hiawatha*

That in even savage bosoms
There are longings, yearnings, strivings,
For the good they comprehend not,
That the feeble hands and helpless,
Groping blindly in the darkness
Touch God's right hand in that darkness
And are lifted up and strengthened.

The tragedy of the new day that has come to Papua is that the religious foundations of tribal life are being broken up and the people robbed of much that gave them guidance and direction. I saw that happening all around me and knew a strange twist was being given to old customs that made them definitely evil, while the faith that once supported them was falling into ruin.

15

HIDO

WE had not been long on Aird Hill or Neuri before we discovered that we were living in a place associated with many of their legendary heroes, among whom Hido was the greastest. I first heard of him when among the people of the Fly River, where he was known as Sido, and though the stories were very similar, Neuri seemed to be associated with his adventures in a special way. In these primitive stories there are always many differences and it is difficult to get the whole tale linked up in orderly fashion and there is still much I do not know.

Hido was both a man and a spirit. It is possible that he was thought of as the first man to rise from the dead and he was always returning to life. His origin is uncertain and the earliest story I could get still left the question of whence he came unanswered.

It is the story of a man who had two wives. One day the women went fishing and found a body on the water and took it ashore. There they made a grid of light poles upon which they laid the cold body, and lit fires beneath it. As the warmth entered the body they saw it move and the spirit came into it and Hido came alive.

The women then made sago for him and when he asked for water, brought it from the sea, for salt water was the only water they had ever known. So Hido took a wooden spade and dug a well and brought the water from it to his foster parents and they drank and cried aloud with wonder and delight. "All our days," they said, "we have drunk water that was salt and now you bring us fresh, sweet water and make glad our lives."

Hido not only taught the people how to dig wells, but seems to have introduced the coconut to different tribes and his ways were the ways of the people who tell the story.

For some reason Hido became angry with the two women who

had first found him and went off and shot fish, and with poison obtained from it, poisoned the well.

Then he travelled away to where people were getting ready for a dance. He came across two small boys who wanted to go to it, but had no drum and were trying to fashion one from a log of wood. Hido at once sat down and completed the task and made the drum beautiful with carving, and in gratitude the boys told him of their sister, Hiura, who would be at the dance. Hiura came from Dudi, which is the home of departed spirits, but she was to be at the festival, and Hido went to meet her and with her or near her, he danced through the night and on until the sun rose. The people welcomed him and brought him food and made him one of themselves, and so he stayed with them and married Hiura.

All might have gone happily, but one day the women went fishing, and Hiura caught a fine fish and, after cooking it, gave part to a youth named Baru, a sure sign that she favoured him. Hido was angry, and went to the house to give his wife a beating, but Hiura had fled in fear far out into the forest.

Hido turned to the women of the tribe and asked where she had gone, and they sought to deceive him by saying she had gone to the fishing grounds again. But she was not there.

So Hido called Orura, the brother of his wife, and sent him to look for her, and Orura climbed a tree and found Hiura hiding there. Quickly she slipped away from him, and from tree to tree she went, always hiding and always being found, until at last she climbed a tree known as Nabea. It was a small tree, but Hiura spoke to it and it grew quickly and carried her high up out of reach of those she feared.

Hido, still seeking her, travelled far, tracing her from tree to tree without result, until the two small boys for whom he had made the drum came to him and told him where Hiura lay. Quickly he came to the Nabea tree and called to her time and again, but she would not answer. Then he called a snake named Oa, and got inside it and the two tried to climb the tree, but Oa was not able to get among the branches. So Hido called the bird Warie and paid her to fly to where Hiura hid, and Warie found her but could not bring her down. Then Hido sent for the snake Dumani, and told him to fetch her, but Dumani was no better climber than Oa, and gave up the task. So Hido called another snake named Poro; he was a tree climber and went up without much trouble and there among the branches found Hiura. She refused to move and was very heavy, and Poro struggled hard but could not lift her, and so came down to earth again. "Brother," he said to Hido, "I found her but I could not bring her. She is there among the branches but I cannot lift her off."

Then Hido was angry and fetched his stone axe and started to fell the Nabea tree in which Hiura hid and as he cut, the chips that flew in all directions turned into fish of many kinds, but still the tree stood firm against the blows. Then Hiura called from among the leaves that hid her, and beguiled Hido, seeking to mislead him. "Put your axe in the fire, O foolish one," she said, "and it will become keen and strong to cut through my tree." Hido obeyed her voice and after casting it into the flames, drew the axe out and struck the tree again. And the stone axe splintered with the blow and the tree still stood. And Hido took another axe and still listening to the deceitful voice, thrust it into the fire and with the red-hot stone blade hit the tree and saw the axe-head splinter once again. Five axes he took and each time with the same result, until all the axes lay in fragments, and Nabea, the tree, still stood.

Then Hido was exceeding wrath and called to the wind, to Konobo, the great west wind, called it to blow Nabea down. And Konobo blew with a mighty roar and still Nabea stood; and Konobo blew with ever wilder gusts and Nabea swayed and bent, but still remained unbroken. Then Konobo gathered all his force and with a roar that split the heavens, rushed upon the tree and with a splintering crash it fell, and fell towards the hill Neuri, and as it fell Hiura was flung right to the summit of the hill, and far beyond the reach of Hido, who saw her go.

On Neuri, at the summit, she met Aibaro living in a house he had built there, and with him was his wife Meuri, and there Hiura dwelt as second wife to Aibaro.

But Hido could not rest. His heart yearned for his wayward woman and he longed to get her back, but could find no road up the steep slopes through the dense forest, and in anger sent birds and beasts and reptiles to pester her, but all in vain. Hiura still remained the wife of Aibaro.

Then, from a piece of wood, Hido made a crocodile and told it to bite him, and it came alive and bit him fiercely. And Hido

took it and made a hole in its snout and placed a croton branch
in the hole so that when the crocodile submerged, the croton
branch would show its whereabouts. He found the creature
could stay beneath the water for long hours at a time and decided
to travel in it under the water to Neuri. He took his bag with his
betel nut, lime gourd and shells, and entered the crocodile whom
he named Imiuma, and Imiuma set off travelling up the rivers
until at last he brought Hido to Neuri. There was a rough wooden
jetty alongside which the crododile lay and on to which Hido
got, and by it he built himself a house and later set off to climb
the hill.

It was a steep ascent but at long last he reached the summit
and saw the place where Aibaro lived with his two wives. Aibaro
was lying sick and his abdomen was terribly distended, so Hido
sharpened a stake and thrust it into Aibaro's stomach and from
it fell all kinds of fishes. Thus was Aibaro cured of his sickness
and the two men became friends.

The women were absent; they had gone into the forest to look
for food, and Hido and Aibaro painted their bodies and adorned
themselves with feather head-dresses and shell ornaments, and in
the splendour of their barbaric trimmings, awaited the return of
the two women. Meuri entered first and found the two men
there, and knew that Hido had come to claim his wife, and going
out, came in again bringing Hiura with her. Thus after her flight
and all her wanderings she came face to face with the husband
she had wronged.

Next morning Aibaro sent Hido and Hiura away and they
clambered down through the forest until they reached the house
by the wooden jetty. Hido was glad but the heart of Hiura was
heavy. She had no care for the man who had claimed her; her
desire was for Aibaro and she sought a way of escape that she
might return to him. Her quick mind soon evolved a plan and
she came to Hido with a story that she had forgotten her *kisau*,
the garment of grass or fibre that every woman wears. She told
him she had left it to bleach on the roof of Aibaro's house and
must return to get it. All unsuspecting, Hido let her go and
waited long for her return. Hiura had no intention of coming
back and Aibaro, having learnt why she had come, shut her in
his house to keep her for himself.

Meanwhile Hido waited on, wondering at the long delay, and

then set off to seek her once again. There at the top of the hill he learnt the truth, and his anger rose against her and against the man to whom she had gone. They talked together, Hido and Aibaro, and fierce were the words they spoke, until friendship turned to hate, and as his anger blazed, Hido raised his bow and drew an arrow to the head and shot Aibaro dead. Thus did Hido overthrow his enemy and, having revenged himself, claim his wife again.

But Aibaro had a brother, Kobai, and when the news reached him, Kobai wept. Then, as he stood mourning at the summit of Dauri-bari, he looked across the valley to Neuri, where his brother had once lived, and saw Hido standing there in triumph, near the house of his dead rival. And hatred greater even than his sorrow woke within him and he took his bow and one straight arrow and drew taut the string and let the arrow fly. It sped across the valley to where Hido stood proudly and triumphant, and so true was the aim, that the arrow smote him, and pierced his eye, and Hido the great, with a mighty crash, fell dead on the mountain top.

Then all the people who had looked to him for leadership gathered round their fallen hero, and there was a great mourning. They sought to bear him away for burial, but he was so big and tall that they could not lift his body from the ground, and because they could not carry him, they started to roll his body down the hill, singing sadly as they went. The song they sang was a song of remembrance and in my day it was still sung for the dead. They called it the *uba-gido* and I have heard its mournful chanting in the darkness of the night as the people took farewell of one who, like Hido, had passed away. Slowly as they sang their plaintive song, the body was rolled on and on down the hill, while Hiura followed weeping as she went. Beyond and below them was the river and they sought to roll Hido to the bank and carry him in one of their great canoes, but the body was heavy and they could not stay the rolling of it, and then a strange thing happened and the dead hand clutched at a croton bush and ever since, the marks of Hido's fingers can be seen on the yellow and green leaves of its descendants, curled and twisted as if a hand had grasped them. But the dead hand could not stay the rolling, and gathering speed the body outstripped the mourners and with a resounding splash fell into the water and was lost from sight.

Yet Hido could not die. Up from the river he rose again and as he looked around he cried aloud, "Where are my people? Let them come to me." And as he cried, they came to him, their hearts touched with wonder and their spirits much afraid. And Hido changed them all, made them tall, taller than all the peoples of the rivers, so that they are known unto this day; they can never be hid, for all the tall people are Hido-mere, or sons of Hido, and all the short folk are Aibaro-mere, or sons of Aibaro. Then, having wrought this miracle, Hido plunged into the river again and travelled beneath the surface to the place the white men call Cape Blackwood, and there he made his home.

I do not know if the story has an end. Hido is always returning. He found a canoe, filled it with coconuts and brought these as gifts to the Wera people and thus the first coconuts came to their land. He went to Kerawo and there found another wife, named Otoa, and to her people also he brought the coconut, that is for them both food and drink. Nor had he done with their tribe, but made them all his own. He made them a good people, though goodness with them is something other than it is with us.

He travelled far, meeting many tribes as he went from place to place, until at last he reached the village of the Iamu-iamu tribe. Wild they were and great fighters, who raided the villages of other tribes, and adorned their temples with the skulls of the slain, and feasted on their bodies. Finding Hido in their midst, a stranger to their tribe, they slew him there and shared his body among their people as food for all. Yet Hido still lived on and his spirit walked beneath the ground, travelling under the rivers and the forests until he came again to his Kerawo people.

He was growing weary of his travels and adventuring but he must still go on, for his spirit cried for Hiura, in spite of all her faithlessness, and it drove him forth in search of her again. Up the rivers he went until he reached Neuri, and climbed the hill down which his people had once rolled his body. Among the trees he saw the house that long before Aibaro built; he saw the place where they had fought and he had slain his enemy; he stood where he had stood before the arrow smote him to his death, and looked across to Dauri-bari where Kobai had stood, drawing his bow so mightily. Then in the silence of that place of many memories he went towards the house, and entering, found Hiura once again and all alone. No longer did she seek to run away, but came to him, her lord and master, ready to follow where he chose to lead, and together they set off, leaving the hill with all its tragic memories, and travelling far, until at length Hido brought Hiura back to Dudi from where, long before, she had come, and there among the spirits of the dead who live again, the two found rest.

So runs the legend, passed on from one generation to another, as in the great house when night fell the young folk listened while the old men told the oft repeated tale; and if one forgot, another took the story up carrying it on, each helping the other in the telling. This may explain why the story has so many different versions, for they had no books or writing and only in oft repeated telling could the tale survive and spread. Hiro's fame reached far along the coast, and the story, with all its variations, is still the story of the one man, whom death could never hold.

This great legend explains why Neuri was regarded as a sacred place. We did not know it in the early days, but long before we had pieced together Hido's story, there would sometimes come to us the sound of men's voices singing their songs throughout the night. High above us, on the summit of Neuri, they were gathered, and one day we set out to explore the mountain and find the spot from which the singing came. We crossed a creek and pushed on through the forest to where a stream some fifteen or twenty feet above us fell over the rocks into a deep pool at our feet. Mosses covered the rocks and ferns flourished luxuriantly in their crevices and we lingered for a time by the waterfall. Rested and refreshed, we set off again and soon were climbing the mountain. It rose so sharply that in places we had to pull ourselves upwards by the roots of trees above us. Loose rocks sometimes gave as we stood on them and went hurtling down, while we clung to roots or branches lest we followed them. Everywhere the ground was sodden by the tropical storm of the night before, and the air was heavy with moist heat and no cooling breezes reached us as we struggled through dense undergrowth. So we climbed, until we came upon a path worn by the unshod feet of men who had often passed that way. They had come from the farther side of Neuri and we wondered why they had come and

whither the path would lead. Following it, we came at length to
a place from which all the undergrowth had been cleared and,
under the shade of the trees, saw numbers of tiny homes, replicas
of village homes, but far too small for men to dwell in. Here and
there were others, strange little places where the roof rose to a
point, like a Red Indian's wigwam. We stood for a time in
silence, filled with wonder at the care bestowed upon the place,
and as we looked around we sensed the meaning of the songs
heard in the night.

These were the homes the tribe built for the spirits of their
ancestors, that to these little places the friends of long ago might
come. So in the night, the tribe would gather in the place where
its unseen members also met, and in that glade of memory they
would sit and sing the *uba-gido,* the song that linked them with
those who had once lived and worked and fought with them and
had passed on into new scenes where they still lived and moved
among their kind. We, who heard those songs in the night, found
new kinship with those who sometimes appeared wild creatures,
but whom we knew were men and women like ourselves, feeling
after the meaning behind the mystery of life, and knowing amid
all the dread fates that threaten man, that he can never die. It was
not surprising that those houses should have been built on Neuri,
under the shadow of great trees, nor that the tribe should meet
there to remember; for this was the place their great hero knew
so well and from which at last, after long journeyings and much
travail, Hido went on with his wife Hiura, to Dudi where the
spirits of old friends live again.

Now, as I tell that story, the thought of later happenings comes
back to me, shedding a fierce light upon what is happening to a
simple people and to the faith that once sustained them on their
way. It was after we were fairly well established, that the
Western world began to take an increasing interest in the commercial possibilities of the land, and the search for oil began.
Often the oilmen travelled with armed patrols where no white
man had been before, and one day such a party came our way
and climbed the hill to make some observations in a survey of the
country they were exploring. The sound of crashing trees came
to us as they cleared a site from which to look across the land,
and we wondered what was happening to the sacred place we
knew so well. For two or three days the surveying party stayed,

making their observations from the top of Neuri. They were a good bunch of men, but much more interested in oil than in the people of the land; for us the sacred place of our friends stood for something great and we hoped that it had been preserved.

We determined to find out, and after a struggle, reached the narrow path we had found on our first visit, but could scarcely make our way along it, for it was blocked by fallen trees. Clambering under and over the wreckage, we came at last to the sacred place, beautiful no longer, but a scene of desolation with the little homes now trampled on and smashed and the sacred spot defiled by careless men to whom these symbols of a people's faith counted for nothing. Never again did we hear the sound of men's voices singing in the night. There are no songs now upon the mountain top, and the wonder and beauty of it all have gone. It is a symbol of what is happening to the old life of Papua, and not of Papua alone but of Africa and the islands and of races scattered round the world. Our Western commerce and ways of life are shattering the faith and ancient traditions of the people and no longer can they tread the road their fathers loved.

16

A HOME IN THE WILDS

Our thoughts on the forces transforming Papua have taken us far beyond the time when we stood on Neuri among the ruins of that sacred place where primitive men had held communion with a spirit world that seemed both real and near to them. Before it was destroyed, Mamu had left to be with her mother and when she returned she placed in my arms our first child. I had met her at the steamer, making the three hundred mile journey in the *Tamate* and was anxious to return as soon as possible, as the south-east monsoon had broken and the seas were nasty and likely to get worse.

The first stage was not so bad as we were under the shelter of a reef for much of the way to Delena, where we spent a week-end with my old friend Dauncey.

While there, Phyllis Neuri, as we named her, was baptized by him, and the day following we renewed our voyage. The weather was bad and a beam sea made travelling most uncomfortable and we made for Kukipi as I wanted Mamu and Neuri to have some rest after two days of ceaseless tossing. The entrance was difficult but a native of the place had joined us at Delena and we were assured that he could pilot us in.

The coast was low and sand-bars made navigation dangerous and as we neared the river mouth the waves were breaking all around us. I did not like the look of things, but the pilot seemed sure of his marks and I could see quiet waters well ahead, so hoped for the best. We were running in amid tumbling seas when I felt a sickening bump and knew we had struck the bar. The *Tamate* lifted to the waves and drove on again, but struck a second time and a third and went aground with the waters roaring round us. The breakers seemed bent on our destruction and the waves smashed on to our deck, or lifted the launch and bumped her so heavily that I feared she would break her back. The crew were terrified as our boat rolled from side to side with the water pouring over her. We put out our kedge anchor and tried to heave her off, but the hawser broke and we lost the anchor. Our dinghy was so small that I did not dare to send my precious passengers away in it, but kept it astern as a forlorn hope should the *Tamate* show signs of breaking up.

Then to our great relief we saw a whale-boat coming from the river with a white man in the stern sheets. He proved to be a trader named Brahm who, seeing we were in a dangerous plight, had set out to our assistance. With the aid of his crew we got our main anchor into his boat and they took it well across the bar and dropped it in deepish water so that we could haul on it. The whale-boat had taken on a lot of water, but feeling it would be better for Mamu to take the baby ashore and leave us free to try to save the *Tamate*, Brahm brought his craft near enough for the wife to jump, and though she landed safely with the little one in her arms, the water was swirling round her knees. It was a relief to see them safely ashore as we turned our attention to our boat.

The tide was rising and, as larger seas came over the bar, the bumping increased, but we knew if only our ship would hold together we would soon be free; so while the 'boys' hauled on the windlass, I started up the engine, and after some moments of suspense, we felt the *Tamate* begin to move. With a shout of joy the 'boys' redoubled their efforts and soon after we cleared the bar and reached smooth water. Our stout little craft had not suffered as much as we feared, but amid the breakers our dinghy had been torn away, and we never saw her again.

We anchored off the trader's house. He sent the whale-boat to fetch me ashore and I shall never forget that landing, for the sand flies rose in millions as we crossed the beach until we seemed to be literally pushing through them. In all my experience I had never come across anything like it, and felt very sorry for Brahm, living among a crowd of Papuans who showed little friendliness and gave little help. He was a man of education and did everything to help us, even getting a bath ready for the baby and giving us of his best, though I must confess to being glad to get my family away from the very squalid surroundings and back at last to a clean ship.

I often wondered what had brought men like him to live in such places. They were not infrequently men of education who had been brought low by some unhappy events, though here and there were others who had deliberately chosen such a life. They were a strange assortment. One had been a lawyer; another was still reading his Greek classics while living in a humpy with a native woman; another a member of a fine English family; while yet another was the father of a famous Arctic explorer. They had once known all the amenities of civilization and I found them living in rough chanties among the natives, surrounded by few comforts and much dirt and yet still possessing some of the marks a cultured life had left upon them.

Brahm died, possibly from blackwater fever, soon after we left his place; dying in a shack in a benighted, fever haunted spot; one of the many who began life with great hopes and ended in defeat.

Once clear of Kukipi, we were free of further misadventures and there was great excitement when we reached Neuri with the first white baby the people had ever looked upon. Her blue eyes and fair skin were a never ending source of wonder to our dark-skinned visitors, who crowded round to see her and discussed her every movement. Yet in our minds, tragedy rather than joy is associated with those first weeks.

We were not the only white folk in the delta. The government was also making its influence felt, for soon after my first visit to Goarihari, they started to establish a station on the Kikori River about fifteen miles from where we had settled. Their buildings and ours were going up at the same time, and as we were all amateurs, we would occasionally meet and compare notes, and after one or two of their houses had collapsed, I was glad to be able to suggest methods of strutting the framework that enabled them to avoid further misadventures of that nature. As I was the only man with medical training I was also able to serve their community as well as our own and we kept in fairly close touch with each other.

With a much larger labour force, they were able to develop their station more quickly, but we found we were making more intimate contacts with the people. This was understandable, for the government was there to enforce law and order, while we could enforce nothing but had to win our way by friendship. The delta tribes quickly distinguished us from others and soon learnt that we had come to live among them as friends; while the government was regarded with deep suspicion.

Frequently I would reach a village that a patrol officer had found deserted and be met by crowds who had fled to the bush as soon as they saw the police approaching. This constantly happened and was easy to account for. The government had to enforce the law and when the police came to the villages it was usually on account of some trouble they were investigating or some custom they were suppressing, such as leaving dead bodies to decay on platforms in or near the village. In those days murders were common and crimes of violence and theft still commoner and the people were beginning to discover that such things brought retribution from a source they had never known before. They resented the interference and could not understand the reason for it. These armed police, brown men like themselves but directed by white leaders, took as prisoners the very men the village held in honour for killing their enemies, and the District Magistrate acted most outrageously by putting some of their very highly respected leaders into gaol. The delta crowd found it hard to understand this government with its queer ideas, and impossible to argue with its officers, so as soon as a government vessel was seen approaching, innocent and guilty alike fled precipitously lest evil come upon them. Consequently, when seeking to make arrests, the authorities sometimes sought to take a village by surprise and this led to a very ugly affray which made the people feel the government had become a raiding party akin to those with which they were familiar but infinitely stronger.

I have already mentioned the village of Kumukumu, built where we had wanted to settle and of which Kerawaia was one of the chiefs. His young men often worked with us and on the day of our return with Phyllis Neuri, they had turned out in force to help unload the boat and carry up the cargo. They were an interesting people, but the tribe was restless, and resented the presence of the government with its regulations and insistence on law and order. Unfortunately for them, just after our arrival a launch passed their village with some native constabulary on board, and as a gesture of defiance the Kumukumu crowd had let fly a number of arrows at them. No damage was done but this was something no government could overlook.

One morning soon after, as I was setting off in the *Tamate* to visit some villages, we saw two launches approaching, one of which was towing a whale-boat, and found they were carrying the District Magistrate, with three other white men and a company of armed constabulary from the station on the Kikori River. Coming alongside, the magistrate told me there had been a fight at Kumu- kumu the night before and he was on his way to investigate.

It was a sad story. The people had asked for trouble when they let fly their arrows and the authorities had to act promptly, but unfortunately a young and inexperienced officer was sent to deal with the offenders. Coming at night while the people slept, he placed a party of armed police outside one end of the great build- ing where most of the tribesmen lived, and with another group entered from the other. At once there was pandemonium and a rush to escape. Helter skelter the villagers made for the end they thought was free, but as they came through the door the police fired into the crowd, killing six men, a woman, two girls and a boy, while a number of others were wounded. It is possible that the screaming and wild terror was such that the police lost their heads, but there seems no doubt that they got out of hand and caused the Kumukumu people to pay very dearly for their earlier defiance.

Visiting the village after the government party had left, and taking bandages and dressings in case there were any we could help, we found the place deserted but could see how most had died while trying to escape. The platform on to which they had crowded was in places covered by the blood of the slain and all around were evidences of terror-stricken flight. At the entrance to one of the smaller houses we found the body of a girl who had been stabbed through the abdomen and soon after, one of my lads found a baby girl. As we did not know if the mother was among the slain we took the baby back to our station where the women- folk cared for it and gave it a bath and a feed, both of which it badly needed.

We thought, as we looked round the village, that we were alone, but later learnt that men were watching us from the trees and debating whether to kill us in revenge for the death of their people. Something restrained them, however, and we never knew of it until Kerawaia told us some time after.

That night the sky was lit up with a great red glow. Survivors had crept back and set fire to their home, for the great house they had built with so much labour had become for them a place of tragic memories to which they felt they could never return.

The days following were full of concern for all on the station.

The magistrate expected more trouble and we knew our lives were in some danger, for we belonged to the race that had brought wounds and death to the tribe and were the nearest upon whom they might wreak their revenge. Day and night we were kept on the alert as disturbing rumours reached us, but though we had some anxious times, the rough handling the men had received probably deterred them from any further adventures.

The magistrate, who regretted the affair as much as I did, asked me to come over and fix up one of the prisoners whose femur had been shattered by a bullet, but it was too late to do much for him and he died soon after. We tried to meet the villagers but for a long time we could not get near them until we met a group in a canoe. Imumere, a chief with whom I had always been friendly, was among them, while on the floor of the canoe a man was seated with a horrible wound in his thigh. They told us ten had been killed, including the chief Iobo, and this did not include the man who died at Kikori. They were very resentful and inclined to view us with suspicion but at last realized that we were as troubled as they were. This led to a renewal of contacts and one day our old friend Kerawaia arrived and I took him up the hill to our house and he saw the baby we had rescued.

The little one, looking so well and happy, convinced them all of our good intentions and later, visitors told us that the mother of the child still lived. She had left the little one when she fled in terror on that awful night never expecting to see her again. We were inclined to doubt the story as for weeks the mother herself never put in an appearance. Then one day some men came up the hill and with them the parents of the child. They were covered in mud as a sign of mourning for their dead, but as they stood in their filth they claimed their little one. We knew we could not hold her against her parents' wishes but it seemed to me all wrong when I took the little one so clean and sweet and laid her in the unclean arms of the mother who, without a single word or look of gratitude, clasped her to her mud-stained breast and turned and walked away. It hurt to see the child go back to the dirt and ignorance of village life for we had longed to give her a chance such as had come to none other of her people; and it hurt the more as we thought of Phyllis Neuri, just about the same age, but surrounded by love and care such as the other could never hope for.

Our own child gave us much concern for we were far from help when things went wrong. In those days before radio or aeroplanes, communications were so poor that we never knew when the goods ordered would reach us and were in real trouble when a ship carrying our stores and a supply of infants' food was wrecked and all her cargo lost. Fortunately we had some tins of arrowroot biscuits, and by baking and pounding them, we made an improvised baby food on which the infant seemed to thrive and which solved an awkward problem.

Meanwhile we were learning to talk to the people in their own language with increasing fluency. There were no books of any kind to help us, for the language was unknown to white folk and we were the first to learn it. It was a fascinating but far from easy task and we had to begin like children, listening, watching and connecting sounds with things. The people were our teachers and though we found many words could be learnt by pointing at the different objects, we also discovered it could not carry one very far, in fact it frequently led one astray. The learner points at an object, and his informant thinks he is pointing at something else; for if he pointed at a woman just as a pig passed, he would probably get the wrong word, and the woman got insulted. Mistakes like that are frequent, and words had to be checked and rechecked and the vocabulary constantly revised. Moreover, one cannot point at verbs, adjectives, prepositions and such like, and knowledge of these only comes by listening and use. It was difficult for our helpers to realize what we were after. We would try to get a word and instead get a sentence, for these people had had no need to consider words apart from their context. They had never had a written language, so had never seen words as we see them, strung together in sentences and yet separated or spaced out. They expressed their thoughts in sounds which all had their definite place in conveying the thought they wished to express, but they had never seen those sounds as words. What we call nouns, adjectives, verbs, etc., are for them sounds that express their thoughts, and are seldom if ever considered apart from their context. Gradually, however, we helped them to separate nouns from adjectives and both from verbs, and here and there would find a word that took on sundry changes at different times and thus we came to learn the grammar of the language, for these changes were due to affixes, suffixes, or infixes which brought new shades of meaning or transformed a singular into a plural.

While their methods of expressing numbers were more complicated than ours, their numeration was most primitive, for they had, as we have already noted, only two numerals, *na'u* and *neewa* for one and two. To arrive at a certain number or date they used a tally, cutting notches into a palm leaf or piece of soft wood up to the required total, or using a bundle of small sticks to achieve the same result. In this manner they recorded the number of days a journey would take, or fixed the date when a dance would be held. In spite of this crude method, their language was in some ways more precise than ours when indicating number, for in addition to changes expressing plural, they used affixes and suffixes to show that one, two, three or many were being referred to and other changes that indicated everyone or everything or only a limited number. As these changes affected both verb and pronoun and sometimes the adjective, we found the grammar at times very difficult to master.

Those unacquainted with primitive tribes often think their languages must be uncouth, but as you live among them you soon discover that they are quick to note what we would call grammatical errors. They may lack a large vocabulary because their range of interests is much smaller than ours, though I doubt if the spoken language of many of our own people is much more extensive; but I am quite sure the primitive Papuan was more insistent on proper grammatical forms.

All this was discovered as time went on, and while learning to talk with them we were at the same time engaged upon a task that had brought revolutionary changes to peoples and nations throughout the world; for we were putting their language into writing. Wherever I went, I kept a piece of paper and a pencil handy so as to add words to my vocabulary, and they were rather mystified about the white stuff I called "paper" and the queer marks I made upon it. I might be seated on the floor of a *dubu-daimo* talking to a crowd of men, and each time I caught some new word out would come my paper and down it would go. Some of the crowd would then get up and look over my shoulder and see the strange markings I had made, and unable to make any sense of them, return to their comrades to discuss the matter. I sometimes had the feeling that they thought I must be a little mad, for they could not understand what I was doing, and none could realize that the most wonderful thing that had ever happened in their history was taking place before their eyes.

Later I was to see a whole group suddenly grasp what it all might mean, and in their lives and mine that was a red letter day, the day in which a people began to sense the wonder of the written word. We were building a house and a number of men had come from some distant villages to see us. They were a dirty, but rather picturesque lot and were bent on getting as many nails as they could secure without our noticing it. These, especially the long ones, aroused their cupidity. They fingered them lovingly, sensing that a five or six inch nail, well sharpened on a stone, would furnish them with a wonderful instrument with which to carve the figures on their drums. We had retrieved most of the nails and were getting on with the job when I found I needed a tool from my workshop on the hill. To give one of the visitors a job, I picked up a slither of wood just adzed from a log one of my men was squaring. With my carpenter's pencil I wrote on it what I wanted, and calling one who was near me, I asked him to take it up the hill to my wife. This, he evidently felt, was senseless, for what could anyone want with a slither of wood, and when I explained that it would tell Mamu what I wanted, he was more mystified than ever. He looked at the wood and the markings on it, turned it over and round, and for a time refused to budge. Doubtless he thought me a bit mad, though I did my best to reassure him. Finally, after much hesitation, he set off with the chip in his hand and a self-conscious look on his face, which increased as his friends laughed at him for setting out on so useless an errand. He did not hurry, but with slow reluctance climbed the hill while I waited for his return. Then he suddenly reappeared, running and leaping as he came down the steep slopes, and as he drew near we could see the look of amazement on his face. He had the tool but was bringing the chip as well, and he looked at me as if I were a worker of miracles. Breathlessly he handed over the tool, then rushed off to his friends waving the slither of wood as he ran. "Look what the white man has done," he shouted. "See this wood: he made it talk. I took it up the hill and it told his woman everything. It talked!"

To us who have grown up with the written word, it seems strange that so small a thing could cause so much commotion, yet that small piece of wood held one of the most wonderful things in the world: the written word that links man to his brother across the seas, and defies time so that the man of ancient days still speaks to us, and the wisdom of the ages, its poetry and romance, its joys and sorrows, all are ours. That written word, with its untold possibilities, had at last come to a people who knew no alphabet, and these wild men had glimpsed the miracle.

17

TEACHING AND HEALING

ONCE the Papuan had seen what the strange marks we call writing could do, the next thing was to teach him how to recognize and form those same marks and figures so that he himself could read and write. As there were no school books in the language, we made wall sheets, printing them with large rubber type we imported from Sydney. Each sheet took them a stage further than the previous one, and with blackboard and slate we taught them to form the letters for themselves.

Those who first came had the greatest difficulty in forming the simplest words, but this was largely because they were dealing with that which seemed to have no relation to anything they had known. The younger folk were much quicker, and some learned to read and write in a surprisingly short time and began to use their knowledge in writing to each other. Once they began to sense what it was all about the school became a popular institution, though they soon wearied of the mental effort it required.

We would be up at sunrise and commence the day with an act of worship, followed by an hour or so tackling the mysteries of reading and writing, and finishing off with physical drill which helped to instil a bit of discipline and became very popular. After the morning meal, all save the children shared in the work of a developing station, felling trees, planting gardens, preparing building material, or learning the use of tools, and assisting in building operations. Always we tried to cease work in time for a game of cricket or football, and in these ways life had variety, and the discipline of regular hours was not too irksome.

The most popular days were Friday, which was given up to work in the food gardens, and Saturday, when most would be away fishing and hunting and return with the queerest assortment of things deemed eatable.

There was great rejoicing when rats proved more abundant than usual, and I shuddered when told that one of my 'boys' had eaten three and another four at a sitting. Snakes also provided a change of diet for some, but when Fitui killed one over thirteen feet long, I noticed that while it provided a feast for one group, members of another would seldom touch it, probably because the snake in question was a totem of their clan. They soon discovered what we liked and would bring us fish, crabs and prawns, the latter known as *gaisi*, which provided a welcome change from tinned stuff. They loved fishing and occasionally caught a saw fish which, measuring up to twelve feet in length, would take a dozen men to haul on to the bank. The capture of a crocodile also filled their hearts with joy and there was always the chance of finding a nest of crocodile's eggs which meant a splendid feast, for these reptiles will lay sixty to eighty at a time. Our people seemed immune to ptomaine poisoning and much of their food was so high that, when on the boat, I saw that it was kept on deck and as far aft as possible; yet when I gave some of them a piece of plum cake they examined it with deep suspicion and after smelling it and taking the smallest of bites left the rest severely alone. They evidently considered our cake was not to be compared with a hunk of putrefying pig.

During the early years, our biggest difficulty in running the school and training the young was that very few would stay with us for any lengthy period. They had never been used to steady work, for in their villages what was not done today could be left until tomorrow or next month and they would drop everything at the desire of the minute to go fishing, hunting or away to another village for a dance. At times this completely upset our plans, but after a while we managed to get some good out of it. It was no use fighting against a way of life they had inherited and which was interwoven with their whole upbringing. Some day discipline would take the place of this irresponsible and haphazard existence, but it would take time, so meanwhile, by getting a crowd to stay a few weeks and then seeking others to take their place, we were able to widen our influence and the circle of our friends. Our personnel was always changing and each change brought much rejoicing among those leaving us when they received payment for the work they had done, such payment consisting of knives, axes, fish-lines and hooks, loin cloths and tobacco. Laden with this wealth they would crowd on to the *Tamate*, and when they reached the villages others would come to us waiting to take their places and share in their good fortune.

It was on one such occasion that we found, on reaching Kerawo, preparations for a great dance were in full swing. From all directions people were bringing in food for the feast. They had been busy in the gardens for months, and hunting and fishing expeditions had been organized, and the result was seen in the bundles of sugar cane, yams, taro, and sweet potatoes, vast quantities of sago, numbers of pigs and baskets full of fish, crabs and grubs.

Women and girls were busy at the fires and it was evident that quantity meant more than quality, and when I saw the way the food was being prepared I was very glad I was not one of the guests. I watched some women preparing a dish that all seemed to regard as the choicest of all. Each would take a leaf from a sago frond, and bending it into the form of a gutter, half fill it with moist sago. Then from a basket each had beside her, they took numbers of thick, white, wriggling sago grubs and pushed them into the sago like so many plums, and deftly pinned the edges of the leaf together with small splinters of midrib, and roasted the whole on the embers. When cooked, the sago formed a glutinous-looking stick with the grubs inside and I have been told they are most tasty though I could never bring myself to sample them.

All through the afternoon, canoes, laden with men, women and children, were arriving and the shore was lined with their craft, each fastened to a stake or paddle driven well into the mud.

Inside the *dubu-daimo* men were preparing for the dance, painting their faces a fine brick red on which fantastic patterns were picked out in white, black and yellow. Shell ornaments of various kinds were hung round their necks or worn on their legs and arms, while clusters of gay leaves were fastened in their belts, and a bunch at the end of a lengthy sprig with plenty of spring in it tucked in at the back so that it would rise and fall behind them as they danced. Through the septum of each man's nose the nasal shell stick was thrust and shell ornaments suspended from his pierced ears, the whole ensemble being completed with a feather head-dress that added enormously to his appearance. Most of their dances had a special significance and this was called the *hawa-gama*, and as we sat watching the men at their preparations, we tried to learn what it was all about. They were not very informative but it was evident that it had something to do with tribal warfare, and as they did not seem anxious to tell us much, we left them for a time and returned to the *Tamate* for our evening meal.

Meanwhile, the feast had started, but was soon over as most of the food after being well displayed, was carried away in baskets to be eaten at leisure. The dance was of greater importance, and for this the people scattered to make ready for the night.

The murmur of many voices came to us across the water, and as darkness fell, people carrying torches of dried palm leaves began to make their way to the great house. We could hear the sound of the drums as they tuned them, tightening the dried snake skin over the fire by drawing the edges through the plaited cane hoops that secured it to the wooden body. So, amid the chatter of the crowd, could be heard the spasmodic tapping on the drums until there was a hush, and then the drums began to beat in unison and the air was filled with their rhythmic throbbing. The dance was on.

We pulled across the water and landed by the light of a hurricane lamp and walked to the *dubu-daimo,* now filled with the sound of many voices and hundreds of drums. Climbing up to the entrance platform, we were faced by armed warriors standing on either side of the doorway with their long bows in their hands. They stood silent and motionless as we approached, and I wondered if we were in for trouble, but as no one turned us back we went on past the sentries to the low doorway, and stooping to get through, entered the great hall.

It was no longer dark, but far more awesome than when we saw it in the daylight. The long building was full of flickering light from torches of dried leaves held by old men and women high above their heads, the smoke from which, rising to the roof, hung there in blue clouds. A great procession was advancing towards us, each member of it intent on his or her part in this great occasion. Their seriousness appeared strange for it was almost as if they were engaged in a solemn rite and I looked in vain for a smiling face. At the head of the procession came a line of men adorned in barbaric finery, each holding his drum by one hand and beating with the other, while performing the movements of the dance. Following the drummers was a group of women and girls arrayed in skirts of coloured fibres and decked with necklaces and chains of small white shells. Into their armlets and skirt bands bunches of shining croton leaves were tucked and scarlet hibiscus flowers decked their hair. Some of the women were holding a pole, to the top of which had been fastened a human skull that had formerly lain before the *agibe*, and from it were suspended numbers of yellow streamers held by the rest, so that it looked something like a hideous may-pole. A warrior wonderfully adorned and dancing in solitary estate was leading the group which was followed by another looking very fierce and proud in his warpaint. The first was the *epia-duba*, or killer, the second the *tawa-dubu* or accomplice, and the thing held above them was the skull of the man they had slain, while these were their womenfolk sharing in the prowess of their men. All down the long building the order was repeated; lines of drummers followed by groups of females with their warrior men leading and following and the skulls held in triumph high above them.

About midway in the procession were those for whom the ceremony had particular significance and was probably part of their initiation, for here the lads from the *ohio-daimo* were grouped together in a ferocious looking company. These had yet to prove themselves, but were adorned as fighting men, with feather head-dresses, painted faces and nasal shells showing white against the red. Each carried his long bow and man-killing arrows, and gravely performed the steps of the dance while surrounding the great chief of the tribe. As I watched I heard him give out the line of a chant and the lads took it up and a wild song broke out, sounding harsh and cruel, as the whole company joined in. The singing was so full of menace that the place seemed charged with the horror of unreasoning hate.

All through the night the dance went on and as I listened to the cruel song and watched the passing of these fearsome figures and the skulls rising and falling above the heads of the dancers, I sensed something of the fascination this wild life held for these people and saw how they gloried in it. Neither they nor I suspected how swiftly it would all be swept away, though I know the impact of our Western world must ultimately destroy it and much also that gave meaning and colour to the life they lived. We had come to help them find something better, though anxious to retain all that was good in the old tribal life; but each year saw the people drifting ever further from the ways of their fathers. The changes gave added meaning to our work, for even as their old ways were tumbling into ruin we were bringing to the people a faith that could help them meet the changes, and find a life giving more than all the old days had to offer.

Our interest in their village life and tribal ceremonies led to a constant widening of the circle of our friends and as time went on an increasing number were ready to stay with us for longer periods, with the result that work in the school became more encouraging and from among those who stayed, we found some who became useful helpers. They began to get a vested interest in the place, for I encouraged them to have their own gardens and later a young man brought his wife, and we built a house for them, and other couples followed, and we began to get children around us, and the school counted for more and more.

Medical work was making increasing demands upon our time and we were hard put to it to know what to do with patients who were walking cases, so I looked round for ways of keeping them usefully employed. We had a number of men with great ulcers on their legs, and while they remained for treatment, I set them to work making cane or bamboo sun blinds. It was an art with which they were familiar, as they themselves used a type of fish-net or trap made of thin strips of bamboo, six to ten feet long and fastened like sun-blinds with fibre or thin lengths of split cane. These, when the tide was at the full, would be stretched across the mouth of a creek, and as the tide fell the fish were trapped and though some would jump the net, men on the other side were ready for this with their spears and hand nets. I improved on the manufacture so that the binding was evenly spaced and suitable for sun-blinds, and also got them making a special set for fishing, and with it we made some fine hauls. We soon discovered that fish usually visited the same creeks and found, after several successive fishings, we had to seek another stream. The big rise and fall which at Springs amounted to nineteen feet, made this kind of fishing very suitable, as creeks carrying considerable water at high tide would be dry at low.

We needed all the food we could get for our rapidly growing family and I was often hard put to it to supply their needs. We had planted coconuts, oranges, mangoes and limes and introduced new varieties of bananas, pineapples and other fruits to improve the native diet and then commenced to develop the cultivation of sago palms to supplement those which grew wild in the swamps. Sago was still the staple diet and I used to watch the women making it and felt their primitive methods could be vastly improved, so invented a simple extractor that enabled my 'boys' to get five or ten times as much sago as could be obtained in the same time by the methods their people had used for generations. It was amusing to see their scepticism when I introduced them to the thing I had made. Of course it was quite useless for no one had ever seen or heard of such a thing and it was plain silly to expect a white man to know anything about sago making. Very reluctantly they agreed to try it out and the result amazed them. When they saw how much they had secured by one day's labour they were filled with admiration.

The main reason so many patients were on the station for long periods was the prevalence of ulcers, the like of which are seldom seen now since modern drugs have revolutionized their treatment. Looking back gives us a feeling that we were living in the dark ages, and yet most who have read *The Century of the Surgeon* by Jürgen Thorwald must have learnt with shocked amazement that only one hundred years ago the relation between dirt and disease and the causes of contagion were so little realized by our own medical fraternity that they stoutly opposed those who were feeling their way towards the truth. Even when we began our work, little was known of the cause of tropical ulcers and the way to treat them, but faced with horrible suppurating sores we had to do something, and were always experimenting. Some of our best results were obtained by putting the lead foil from our tea packets over the ulcers and keeping it in position by bandaging. Unfortunately the bandages constantly disappeared, for most patients felt they were wasted on a sore leg and looked much more attractive when worn round the waist or tied round the head with the ends streaming behind. Even if dressings and bandages stayed where we put them, the healing processes were so slow that the people who believed their troubles came from evil spirits, often left us and turned to the sorcerer, thinking he would do a quicker job, and the results were sometimes disastrous.

Many were suffering from a disease known as yaws which

affected quite a large proportion of the population and took various forms. Sometimes it attacked the soles of the feet and made walking a misery; sometimes it covered the body with a mass of suppurating sores. It attacked the uvula of one of my best helpers, and speech became so difficult that he had to give up his work. For years we could do little to relieve these sufferers but about that time medical science made a discovery that so revolutionized the treatment that millions of people have been saved from endless misery. Intramuscular or intravenous injections of bismuth and arsenic derivatives worked like magic, and as soon as the government was able to supply us with the drugs we became regarded as workers of miracles.

No sorcerer could hope to compete with one who worked such wonders, the news of which spread like wild-fire. As soon as I entered a village the people would bring along all who were suffering. There might be twenty or more, and after we had lined them up, one of my helpers would go along, cleaning a patch on the buttock of each. Another followed to sterilize the skin and a third accompanied me, carrying my syringe, needles and drugs. An interested and admiring crowd would surround us as we worked, and grunt in sympathy or horror as I pushed the needle in, but the result was amazing. In a week the sores were clearing up and in a fortnight the evil thing had gone, and the fame of this wonder-working medicine spread far and wide. These discoveries won us a welcome in many a village and hundreds came to Aird Hill for treatment.

There the people found us busy on another project. The excitement and unrest caused by the killings at Kumukumu was still at its height when we set to work to erect a building such as the people had never known. It was a very simple affair constructed of rough timbers with a palm-thatched roof, but it was the first Christian church they had ever seen and it was a great day when we called the villagers to the opening ceremony. Invitations had been sent to the surrounding tribes, and our folk had been fishing and hunting, collecting crabs and bringing in plentiful supplies from the gardens, for without a feast no ceremony would be complete. Canoes had come from many villages and at the appointed hour, a procession led by Fitui and his wife came up the hill. As they drew nearer, I heard a strange noise, for some seemed to be groaning and others chanting a dirge. I discovered later that they were trying to sing a hymn Fitui had composed for the occasion. The uninformed would never have suspected it, but they were doing their best, and all seemed pleased with the effort. My wife and I, with one of the girls holding little Neuri, met them near the entrance across which a length of white tape was stretched, for this was a church without doors or windows, cool to sit in and well ventilated withal. Mamu cut the tape and the dedication prayer in their language was simple and short—"We have finished the building of Thy House, O Lord; now as we open it do Thou come in with us." The words were few, but as we remembered the wild days we had lived through, it was a great experience to see the fighting men file in and seat themselves on the mats which covered the floor, and join in the service as best they could. We spoke of the way of life we wanted to share with them so that the divided tribes could meet as one family and in this place feel they were all in the house of their Father. They listened well, and from the church went to feast and dance and make the day and night a gladsome time, and we joined in and shared their happiness, though for us it had a deeper content, for it promised a new and richer life for all.

Next day the Resident Magistrate, together with his police, came across and shared in the first Sunday service and spoke to the people while I interpreted. It was a gesture we all appreciated and made for reconciliation between the Kumukumu tribe and the authorities. Though our approach was different we were very sensible of the fact that government and mission were both working for the good of the people, and during my time there was a growing appreciation of the work each was doing.

Papua owes a great debt to its early administrators and it was my privilege to meet them all, though the first two had completed their terms of office in Papua when I went out. Sir William MacGregor was Governor in Queensland when we first met in Torres Strait and I met his successor Sir George Le Hunt in London during the first World War. Captain Barton, who succeeded him, was holding office when I reached the country and Sir Hubert Murray took office in 1907. He was followed on his death by his nephew Leonard Murray, who continued the great tradition until the military took over after the Japanese invasion. All gave of their best but the two who played the greatest part in shaping the administration were Sir William MacGregor and Sir Hubert Murray.

Sir William was charged with the task of administering what was then British New Guinea as a Protectorate, in which the rights of the natives were to have first consideration, and he steadily adhered to the pledge given at the time of the annexation —"Your lands will be secured to you; your wives and children will be protected." It was a pledge scrupulously kept and up to the beginning of the Japanese invasion the government had little to be ashamed of in its record in Papua. Sir William laid the foundations of an administration that regarded the rights of the native population as its prime concern and consistently worked for their protection and advancement.

His successors followed the same path, but none did more for the country than Sir Hubert Murray. Few understood the Papuan better and there was never any doubt in his mind that the rights of the indigenous races were the government's paramount concern. His name will stand among the great administrators of the British Empire and it meant much to me to be honoured with the friendship of so great a man. He took an understanding interest in what we were doing and when travelling through the country, would spend hours making a special trip from Kikori to pay us a visit. We were appointed to Papua in the same year, he as Chief Judicial Officer and myself as a missionary, and he died a year after I left the country. Never had there been such mourning in the land as when he passed, for white men and brown were united in a common sorrow. We had lost a great friend and the people of Papua more than a Governor, for he was to them as a father who really cared for them and understood their ways, and they felt they would never see his like again.

18

WAR

OUR work in the delta seemed full of promise. We were on friendly terms with the tribes surrounding us and full of plans for the future, when a rumour reached us that made the tragedy at Kumukumu fade into insignificance. Today all the world is linked by radio, but at that time we would live for months shut off from all knowledge of what was happening outside our borders. We were therefore quite unprepared when a white man stopped at our station to tell us he had heard that England was involved in a European war. He had only caught a few sentences shouted from a passing boat, and we found it hard to credit, and hoped he was mistaken. With increasing anxiety we waited for more definite news, and it was long in coming, for events of which we knew nothing had led to the disruption of all shipping. When at last we learned the truth and sensed its horror, we had to recast all our plans. We had expected to take our English furlough, which was already overdue, but decided to wait until the war was over, thinking that Christmas would probably see its end. We never dreamed of years of strife and of how tremendously our lives and the lives of all the peoples of the world were going to be affected. As far as we could see at that time, our first duty was to stay with our people and it was well for us that there was so much to do. Men from tribes we had never before heard of were urging us to come and see them, and as we learnt of great villages hidden up streams we had never explored we would set off to find them. These journeys took me far from home, and it was not easy to leave Mamu and her baby surrounded by many who were still cannibals, though she faced such times with cheerful courage, but it was always a relief when we returned from our wanderings and found all well.

Among the swamps to the east were the Urama tribes whose people used to raid the Kerawo villages, and during my early explorations I had met some of them, but on my journeys we seldom saw either man or canoe in that part of the country, so doubted all the stories we heard of large villages and many people in that area. Actually the sound of our engine gave warning in time for every canoe on the route to hide up the numerous small creeks, and many had watched us pass while we were quite unaware of their nearness. All this country, once thought to be a great area of land between two big rivers, consisted of innumerable islets separated by many waterways, some of which were wide and deep enough to take large boats, with others so narrow that only tiny canoes could pass through them. There was no solid ground and mangrove and nipa palm flourished everywhere, yet in this repellent country we found numbers of villages and a large population. The mass of waterways gave the people a sense of security, since should an attack be made on them, there were many avenues of escape. Still more important was the fact that ample food could be secured with a minimum of effort. Fish of all kinds could be caught in the creeks, millions of crabs made their homes in the all-pervading mud, and sago flourished in the swamps. In addition, the mangrove forests gave them the timber for their buildings and the nipa palm provided them with thatch. Here they lived a self-sufficient life, and though the available water was brackish, they seemed to flourish on what we would find very hard to drink.

Entering one village, after our struggle through a sea of mud, we were surprised to find ourselves on ground that was really solid. It stood well above the highest tides, and the whole area had been raised artifically. During many years, all the timber and thatching from old houses, and all the shells, garbage, etc., had been retained and trodden underfoot until an area large enough for all their homes had been reclaimed from the mud.

This village of Kinomere had been longer established than most; with the result that land reclamation had gone further, but as we visited others, we saw how low stockades were built around each site to keep the refuse from being washed away, with the result that long established villages were much easier to get around in. The people were shy and many were in hiding, but as I walked among them and gave a smoke to one and another we were soon on good terms. I found their language was a far removed dialect of Kerawo but near enough for them to understand me. Surrounded by a talkative crowd, we made our way to a great *mene*, where several chiefs, on the entrance platform, were waiting to receive me. They were fine looking men, each with a dagger made from the thigh bone of a man they had killed stuck in his belt, and wearing the usual head-dress and nasal stick. They received me with native dignity and accepted my presents, but the crowd that was collecting looked wild enough for any adventure, while the great house or *mene* bore eloquent testimony to the life of the tribe

Above my head was the fierce looking figure of Iriwaki, similar to the one we had seen during our early explorations. Beneath Iriwaki was a veil of raffia-like fibres hiding the interior of the *mene*, whose roof sloped down from the platform which it overhung at a height of about fifty feet, until at the back it was scarcely high enough for one to stand beneath it. As soon as the excitement had subsided I asked if I might enter their home, and one of their head men conducted me through the veil into the great hall. Here we were confronted by two strange structures which evidently held a place of high importance. They stood to right and left of us as we entered and at the base of each were a number of totem shields. With these were other sacred objects such as canoe totems or images fashioned in human form out of the wood from which the canoe had been hewn. Incidentally, when on a journey, the canoe totem was often stuck into a lump of mud at the back of the canoe to which it belonged to keep watch astern while the paddlers looked ahead. Here, however, they stood with the shields possibly because the canoes to which they had originally belonged had been broken up. In front of the shields and images were the skulls of pigs and crocodiles, while above the shields rows of pigeon holes had been constructed fashioned largely from the midrib of sago palms. In each of these was a human skull. Most had been painted and worked up with clay or bees-wax and given eyes of cowrie shells so that they looked like hideous faces. They were the trophies of raids on other tribes or of murders perpetrated when members of these tribes had been caught away from the protection of their friends. Here their skulls were displayed and no possessions were more greatly prized, for these symbolized the prowess of the killers and added to the glory of the tribe of which they were members. As I stood looking at the gruesome objects, I knew that the men who surrounded me had no feelings of regret or shame and no desire for a life less cruel; this was the way of their people and they followed it gladly to the end. On either side of the building beyond the *awai,* as these structures were called, numbers of great dancing masks were suspended from the rafters. These were not as attractive as those in Orokolo but were constructed in the same way and each was large enough to hide the man who wore it. At the far end where it was very dark, was a sacred room of which I shall have more to say later on, but on this first visit I did not pry around too much, as I was not too sure of the attitude of those around me; so after seeing all I could, I came back to the platform and standing beneath Iriwaki began to talk to the crowd who filled the platform and the ground beyond.

I tried to make it clear why I had come, though I doubt if many appreciated my presence, but I got their interest when I talked of Iriwaki and what he stood for and then spoke of a Spirit greater than Iriwaki who was not far from any one of us and would have us living as one people instead of fighting each other. It was not possible to get far just then but they understood enough to assure me, as I looked at the rows of skulls, that those fighting days were past, an assurance I received with mental reservations, suspecting that if an opportunity presented itself they would not let it slip.

My suspicions proved correct and some months later, a rather raw government officer went into that same place to arrest some of them who had been doing a bit of headhunting. Such was their temper at the time, that instead of the culprits fleeing, the whole village rose against the intruders, and men came rushing from the houses armed and ready for the fray. The white officer had not met this sort of thing before, and as the arrows began to fly, he sensed possible disaster for his small company and cleared out, leaving the Urama crowd victors on the field. For a time the tribe was full of rejoicing and the villages filled with stories of a great victory that grew ever greater with the telling and the men of Kinomere walked proudly. Had they not met the government and driven those unwelcome visitors away in fear? It was a very short-lived triumph, for in a week or so another party from that same government returned and this time in such force that resistance was impossible.

This all happened more than a year after my first visit, since when I had visited them once or twice and travelled through

many of their waterways without any serious trouble, though on
our second visit we had some anxious hours that had nothing to
do with their warlike habits.

We had come in the *Tamate* and reaching Kinomere, prepared
to anchor, but instead of going astern, the engine began to race
and I knew something must have happened to the propeller. For
the time being we were marooned among a very uncertain crowd
capable of much mischief, so thought it wise not to let the wild
men ashore suspect that there was anything amiss. I got into a
canoe and went ashore to have a talk with them but for some
reason I could not discover, they were not very friendly, and I
was not sorry to get back to the boat where I found my crew in
a state of jitters and afraid they would never get away.

We had to wait for the fall of the tide, which we were thankful
would be well after dark when our plight would not be observed,
and meanwhile worked the *Tamate* towards the shallows, and
slipped into the water to investigate. We found, as I had suspected, that the big nut at the end of the tail shaft had somehow
worked adrift and the propeller had pulled itself off when we
went astern. It was very heavy and we feared it might have sunk
beneath the deep mud and been lost, but to our immense relief
we found it lodged between the rudder and the keel

Crocodiles abounded in those waterways and we did not feel
too comfortable, as in the darkness when the tide was at its
lowest, we went over the side into the deep mud and after a
struggle hoisted the propeller back and locked it securely with a
nut we carried among our spares. After that, and a great wash to
get the mud off, we all felt happier, for we were no longer
stranded and could get away when we wanted.

We could hear the murmur of many voices across the water
and knew we were being well discussed, but as I listened, I looked
ahead to a time when the wild days would give place to a richer
way of life, and these divided tribes work together to build a kind-
lier land. It was a day that lay far ahead and for a long time they
remained the most feared of all the delta tribes. Often I had cause
to rue the feuds that divided these people, as in their eyes the fact
that I was the friend of one tribe meant I was the enemy of others
who had fought with them, and only as time went by did they
come to realize that I was the friend of all and enemy of none.

As we moved among them we were oppressed by the horror of

what was happening in Europe and tortured by suspense as we waited long weeks for the next bit of news. Sometimes months would pass before it came, while thoughts of dread happenings in which our friends and near relatives were involved were with us day and night. The cruel waste of life and wealth filled us with hatred of all war, and reading over my journals of those days I am reminded of a day dream, part of which actually happened in France later on.

I was travelling back to Aird Hill. It was a perfect day and the river a place of peace and loveliness, but my thoughts turned to all that Europe was enduring. "Almost as in a dream I saw the opposing armies agreeing to a truce on Christmas Day and meeting on neutral ground, and I wondered how things would go if they then realized how near they were to each other and how strong is that brotherhood that unites all nations. I seemed to see the soldiers refusing to fight and saying to their rulers, 'We have done with our guns; you must settle your differences without sacrificing our lives.' What a queer revolution it would be if the whole quarrel came to a stop through the armies refusing to take or sacrifice another life. The rulers would have to settle, and the only settlement possible would have to be along the lines of a Parliament of Man." I wrote the above in my diary in November 1914 and was recently reminded that at Christmas in that same year, the soldiers on both sides did make their truce and the rulers were so frightened of its possibilities that such a thing was never allowed again.

1914 gave place to 1915 with the war showing no signs of ending and we learnt that the Directors of our Society were sending their Foreign Secretary to Papua in company with the Secretary in Australia and New Zealand to advise on the position. They would be spending several months in the country, and as it promised to be very difficult to get them from place to place I volunteered to take them right along the coast in the *Tamate*, and after that leave for my English furlough.

With Mamu and Phyllis on board, the *Tamate* left Neuri in December 1915 and crossing the Fly, made for Daru to meet the *John Williams* which was bringing my passengers and taking my wife and child to Brisbane where I was to join them later. After seeing them on board the steamer, I set off with my new passengers, Frank Lenwood, our Foreign Secretary, A. J. Viner, a member of the London Board of Directors, and G. J. Williams, our Secretary from Melbourne. They were grand travelling companions and the story of their journey is well told in Frank Lenwood's *Pastels from the Pacific*, so there is no need to write much about it here.

The journey gave me a wonderful opportunity of getting to know a very remarkable man and marked the beginning of a friendship that grew in richness until Lenwood met his death in a mountaineering accident in September 1934. He was a brilliant scholar and fearless thinker and had been President of the Oxford Union when among his contemporaries were men like Hilarie Belloc, F. E. Smith and J. A. Simon; the last two known later as Lord Birkenhead and Sir John Simon. He was most unorthodox both in the ordering of his life and in the expression of his faith but one of the grandest Christians I have known. I never cease to be grateful for the high privilege of having had such close fellowship with him during those months in Papua and as we travelled from Australia to England.

My passengers soon found adventure, for crossing the mouth of the Fly River, we ran hard up on a hidden sandbank when the spring tide was at the full. I was anxious, as we stood a chance of being stranded there until the next springs, or battered to pieces if a squall blew up, but fortunately the night tide proved still higher and we got clear.

Two days later we reached Aird Hill where all praised the situation of the station and reckoned our pineapples the most delicious they had ever tasted. Here again, they had another glimpse of wild Papua for at night a badly battered woman was brought to the mission house with a terrible cut across her head. As I dressed her wounds, I learnt that her husband had gone off to work on a distant plantation and his father wanted to take her for a second wife. The wife objected and a fight ensued with this result.

From Aird Hill we set out to visit the rest of the mission stations along the coast. I expected to be back the following year, but was not happy at leaving Fitui and all on the station just then, though things seemed to be quietening down in the villages. On the way to the coast I took our party to Kinomere in order to give them a glimpse of the Urama cannibals. They were tremendously interested in the great *mone* and in *Iriwaki* and the *awai* with its rows of skulls, but were less careful than I would have been as they explored the place, and I sensed rising resentment among the men. I also saw a crowd of young warriors gathering in the village and reckoned it was time to move, so shepherded my companions towards the *Tamate* while keeping a watchful eye on the armed and sullen group whose looks were most unfriendly. It was with much relief that I saw my friends safely aboard, and in the light of the attack made on the police a little later, we may have been much nearer a nasty incident than any of us realized.

Kaimari, looking like a stone age Venice, with its great houses and many buildings along the banks of numerous waterways, fascinated the travellers, who wanted to stay and explore the place, but J. H. Holmes, whose district adjoined mine, was waiting for them, so early next morning we were on our way again, and by the time we reached Kwato our journey had taken us best part of a thousand miles.

At Kwato we spent a full week in conference and having done all I could to see the *Tamate* would be well cared for during my absence, we joined the *John Williams* and a week later reached Brisbane where I was welcomed by my wife and little daughter.

Australia was sending her sons to battle and shipping was difficult; but we eventually secured berths on an Orient Liner and soon after left for England.

I had left my homeland nearly twelve years before and was returning to a very different and war torn world. Numbers of ships had been torpedoed and owing to the many lost in the Mediterranean, the *Ortona,* also sunk on a later voyage, was diverted, and we steamed far south and them up to Africa, calling at Durban, Cape Town and Dakar. From then on we were in the danger zone and steamed with lights blacked out at night and ceaseless watch against submarine attack by day. In response to a call for volunteers I took my turn with others, scanning the ocean for any signs of enemy submarines. The bridge gave us a splendid view of all that was happening, though when on watch, one did not dare to take one's eyes from off the water.

We reached Plymouth in safety and I was presented with a long list of engagements that took me all over the country, but as with millions of others the war brought unexpected tasks and I soon found myself at work in France. The story has been

told in books and periodicals dealing with the war years and need
not be repeated here, save to say that right on to the end of the
war I was lecturing and speaking to tens of thousands of men
from Great Britain, America, Canada, Australia, India and New
Zealand, dealing with the emergence of a world that was no
longer that of the white man, and in the shaping of which the
coloured races were to have an ever-increasing share.

While in France, I was serving with the British, but at the
end of the fighting was offered work among the thousands of
Australians waiting for ships to take them back to their country.
The change was doubly welcome as it provided opportunities for
further service and also opened the way for return to Papua.
Civilian passages were almost unobtainable and even the Forces
had to wait months before boats were available, and meanwhile
my headquarters were in London.

It was a wonderful time to be there when so much was happening. I saw the American President, Woodrow Wilson, arriving
at the Mansion House with Lloyd George and most of the great
war leaders, and stood with the crowds watching the victory procession in which all the Dominion troops participated.

Another event had a more personal interest. A big Medical
Missions Exhibition was being held in the crypt of St. Martins,
and while there Her Majesty Queen Mary came in, followed by
the Princess Royal, and to my surprise I was brought along and
presented. All those around were struck by the interest the Queen
displayed in the Papuan exhibits and the number of questions Her
Majesty asked about the marine villages and customs of the
people. The Princess Royal was also greatly interested, and hearing that an object she was examining had belonged to James
Chalmers, at once replied, "Oh yes, I remember, he was killed at
Dopima by the natives of Goaribari." It was a revelation of the
wide range of information possessed by members of our Royal
Family, for not one in ten thousand of our people would have
known what the Princess knew of *Tamate*.

A month or two later we were on the troopship *Wahehe*
which in addition to men was carrying the wives and families of
many who had married during the war years. My family consisted of two girls, Neuri and Hilary, and Ralph, then a baby, and
we who had endured what many thought was a war that would
end war, little dreamed that Hilary, Ralph and his brother David,

then unborn, would be caught up in another, and be returning to Australia as we were then. There was no doubt about our being there, for when we arrived, a shipping strike was on, but fortunately *John Williams IV* was unaffected and I was able to sail in her early in the New Year.

I had left Papua in 1916 expecting to be back in about twelve months, but the war had disrupted my plans as they had those of multitudes, and four years had passed before I got back to Aird Hill.

19

BACK TO PAPUA

AFTER so long an absence, there was no telling what our Papuan home would be like, and we felt it wiser for my wife to remain in Brisbane with the children until I found out, though when we said good-bye neither of us thought that it would be more than a year before we saw each other again.

Sickness and war conditions had led to such a shortage of staff that on my return I was charged with the supervision of the Orokolo and Urika districts in addition to my work at Aird Hill.

The *Tamate* had been so badly neglected that repairs promised to be almost as costly as a new boat. It was therefore decided to dispose of her, and I was left to carry on with the aid of the Urika launch, which also needed a lot of attention. The *John Williams* put me ashore at Orokolo and that evening I stood alone on the beach watching the ship steam over the horizon.

Darkness fell and found me alone, almost overwhelmed by the magnitude of the task awaiting me. For three hundred miles of coastline and in all the hinterland there was no other European missionary; strung out eastward various villages with Samoan or Papuan pastors or teachers looked to me for help and guidance, and westward were many villages and tribes I had yet to visit. This would mean tramping for days along the sand beaches, or travelling hundreds of miles through creeks and rivers with the knowledge that until the *Purari* was repaired, all the delta work would have to be done by canoe.

To add to my difficulties the people around Orokolo were suffering from a form of hysteria that became known as Vailala madness, as it first made its appearance in the vicinity of the Vailala River; though since the second World War, it has appeared elsewhere and is named "the cargo cult". It had spread through the villages between Arihava and Vailala and was associated with a belief that the spirits of their ancestors would soon return, looking like white men and arriving in a big ship laden with good things. In various villages along the coast preparations were being made to give them a fitting welcome. Flag poles, gaily painted, were erected, and roughly made tables and seats arranged near them, the tables being decorated with flowers stuck in empty beer bottles. They evidently expected their returning ancestors to have adopted the customs they had noted among traders and planters. Consequently, once a day the men of the village would come together and sit at the tables, as they partook of a common meal after the manner of white men. At night they would wander up and down the beach, looking expectantly out to sea, until someone imagined a ship was approaching and would awaken the whole community with cries of "Sail oh!", whereupon pandemonium would break loose as crowds rushed to the shore, carrying torches of flaming palm leaves and shouting at the tops of their voices as they worked themselves into a fever of excitement. Many developed nervous symptoms akin to St. Vitus's dance, jerking their heads rapidly from side to side, while legs and arms twitched violently until they fell trembling to the ground. Gardens were neglected and village life disrupted, and there was wholesale abandonment of the old festivals and customs which led to the discarding of the shell ornaments and head-dresses that were once their most treasured possessions. As a result, a trader on the beach reaped a rich harvest by securing for next to nothing valuable curios which were formerly unobtainable, for until this madness swept through the villages, the Papuan would never part with such treasures, though now he almost threw them away. On the other hand the trader's legitimate traffic in coconuts and copra came to an abrupt end, since the villagers, instead of selling them, were stacking the coconuts in preparation for a feast to welcome the expected spirits, or for loading on to their ship.

The movement disrupted village life so greatly that the District Magistrate decided to treat those most affected as disturbers of the peace, and putting some of the worst sufferers in gaol helped to stop the infection spreading. It was months before the disturbance died down, and its effects remain to this day, since much of the old life with its festivals and dances has never been revived.

The unrest was largely due to the impact of our Western world, but among the people of the delta some forms of hysteria were accepted as normal and at times spread like a contagious disease. A boy would become sulky and start walking about the place with a blank look on his face. If armed, he could be dangerous and create a reign of terror as others joined him and began to threaten the rest with knife or tomahawk. Sometimes they roamed aimlessly about the station or disappeared into the bush, and once when downstream, one such suddenly appeared on the bank and let fly an arrow which shot over my head. The direction was excellent and if it had been a bit lower I would have been in a bad way, but I have a suspicion that mad as he seemed he was not out to kill.

I felt that much of this hysteria was due to auto-suggestion, and at times it seemed remarkably like the devil possession mentioned in Scripture; so like it, in fact, that during a bad outbreak I had the sufferers captured and brought to me. They squatted on my verandah with madness written on their faces, yet listened and seemed to understand when I talked of others like themselves, who had been caught by evil spirits and set free by Jesus Christ. Then I told them I was going to ask the same Jesus to set them free, and they were quite silent as I prayed aloud. After that I laid my hands of each in turn and in the name of Jesus commanded the spirit to come out. In practically every case the reaction was the same. They seemed to blink and pull themselves together, while a change came over their dull faces, and as I asked if the bad spirit had left them, they nodded, then quietly got up and went away, and I had little trouble after that. We may explain it in psychological or religious terms, or both, but the thing that mattered was that they were healed.

At Orokolo the trouble was vastly different and whole villages had adopted a new cult full of fantastic imaginings. I was to learn more about it later, but my first task was to see how matters stood at Urika and Aird Hill, both of which had had little supervision during the war years. Accordingly I set off for the delta, tramping for miles along the sandy beach and through swampy country until we reached a creek and boarded a canoe. We paddled through the waterways passing the great village of Maipua, with its sacred houses and many smaller buildings standing in the filthy swamp in which they were built. Almost naked women, surrounded by evil smelling refuse, were beating sago from the trunks of palms drawn on to the low banks of creeks that intersected the place. Nowhere have I seen women looking more degraded and yet nowhere in Papua have I heard girls with sweeter voices than some of their daughters whom Mrs. Holmes had taught to sing. Here and there men were fashioning canoes out of great logs with crude instruments and spending long hours carving intricate patterns along their sides to add to the beauty of their work.

As evening fell we reached Urika where Homu, as J. H. Holmes was called by the people, had built his settlement on land largely reclaimed by drainage, though there were still large areas of swamp, and the mosquitoes were numerous. Both malaria and blackwater fever were prevalent and I never felt the place could be called a health resort. It was neutral territory, on which warring peoples sometimes met for tribal talks near sacred places where, according to the natives, spirits both good and bad dwelt among the trees. I caused considerable ill feeling by setting my Goaribari 'boys' to cut down a great tree that was darkening the house and shutting off the breeze, for I found, too late, that it was the home of sundry unseen powers and its destruction made me very unpopular, though it greatly improved our living conditions.

An inspection of the launch *Purari* was not encouraging. The hull required extensive repairs and parts of the engine needed replacing and there was no telling how long it would be before we could get the necessary fittings. It would take at least a month of hard work to get the boat into running order, and meanwhile I had to get to Aird Hill.

Fitui and his wife had returned to Samoa more than two years before and Williamu's health had broken down and the place had been left to the care of three Goaribari helpers. I did not like to think what I would find or not find when I reached the station, for in the early days the Goaribaris were inveterate pilferers and would make away with anything they could lay their hands on.

We set out in one of the local dug-outs. These were slow, heavy craft constructed for use in quiet rivers, but unfortunately we had to negotiate some miles of open water, for which such canoes were ill constructed.

All went well as far as Kaimari, from which place a wide stream led to the sea. The tide was running out and unfortunately for us the wind was rising as we left the shelter of a big sandbank and we soon found ourselves in very troubled waters. As waves started to break over us, the 'boys' became terror-stricken, for there was a good prospect of the canoe being capsized. Every now and then a breaker would come curling over the side and we were kept busy baling out, and though our crew were pulling hard, Vaimura Point which offered shelter seemed as far away as ever. Some doubted if we would ever make it, and when a wave came over the side and landed on top of me, a lad close by gave up in despair and, crouching down, waited for the end. Others were crying or muttering to themselves, and then, to my surprise, I heard one of them using the name of Jesus as he sought for help and courage. These were young men whose fathers had been cannibals, but as I heard that cry I sensed something of the change taking place among them. Their people for centuries had lived under the domination of a spirit world that brought them all manner of hurt but now, in the minds of some, there was dawning the sense of an unseen Presence who cared for them, and as I heard the name of "Iesu" on the lips of this man, I knew he had hold on things his father had never known. So taking a hand with a paddle to encourage them, we went on through the tumbling waters, and early in the evening reached the shelter of the point and soon after entered the mouth of a quiet stream. We had been pulling for hours with nothing to eat, so stopped for a meal, and then set off up a creek hoping to get through to the other side of Vaimura in time to catch the incoming tide which would sweep us towards Aird Hill. Instead, we stuck in the mud and became an easy prey to mosquitoes and sand flies. The mangrove forest closed us in and the darkness was full of strange whispering among the trees, but as the 'boys' sang together during our evening prayers there came to us the sense of another Presence, to whom the darkness and the light are both alike and we knew that all was well. Later, when freed by the rising tide, we got lost in a tangle of waterways. We paddled through streams overhung by trees and full of snags, feeling our way for hours until the moon rose and made the going easier. Left to myself I would have been completely bushed, but these delta lads have an uncanny sense of direction and eventually reached the village of Vaimura. The great *ravis* had a weird grandeur about them in the moonlight, and it seemed as if all save a crying baby were asleep, until men heard us paddling and called to us. Some were friends of members of my crew so we stayed for a short time and then reluctantly pushed on to make what use we could

of the current that was then in our favour. It swept us right up
Era Bay to Iviri Island when, as the tide turned against us, we
made fast to a tree and tried to get some sleep. The crew did
quite well but with eighteen in that dug-out it was somewhat
overcrowded and I was glad when, long before daylight, the
current again turned in our favour and we set off and eventually
reached the home I had left four years earlier, never dreaming I
would be away so long.

What cheered and surprised me most was the way things had
been cared for during my absence. When I remembered the old
days and the utter inability of the Goaribari to distinguish between mine and thine, it amazed me to find not a thing in the
house was missing. Since Williamu's breakdown these Goaribari
men had had sole charge of everything, and only those who had
known the old ways could appreciate the transformation that had
taken place in their outlook. Of the three who had been in charge,
Dauwa was easily the most outstanding. All three had come from
the old days of fighting and cannibalism and Dauwa was at
Dopima when Chalmers, Tomkins, and their eleven companions
had been killed. He was a quiet, steady worker, one of nature's
gentlemen who met you fearlessly and never tried to take advantage of you. He was a great hunter and expert canoe maker,
whose advice was sought by others when hewing and shaping
their dug-outs. His prowess as a hunter led me to get him a shooting permit so that he could add to our food supplies by bringing
in an occasional pig, cassowary or pigeon. The latter were at
times so plentiful that I have known him creep beneath a tree
and bring down six or seven with one cartridge. He would have
horrified the English sportsman, for he never believed in shooting
a bird on the wing but stalked them and waited for a sitting shot.

He found the gaura or crested pigeon a sore temptation. It is a
splendid bird about the size of a barnyard fowl, and a very
welcome addition to the table. It was also very tame and would
let one get quite close before flying off, and such a glorious sitting
shot was almost impossible to resist. Unfortunately for Dauwa,
the government had issued regulations to protect it, although in
our part it was plentiful. Knowing something of the bird's habits
as well as those of Dauwa, I was not surprised when he arrived
with one he had shot for our Sunday dinner. I must confess to
feeling rather pleased; for we were weary of tinned food, but

being a law abiding citizen, I felt it necessary to tell Dauwa that he must never shoot another as there was a law against it. He nodded gravely, though I had a suspicion that he thought the law was very foolish and Dauwa doubtless knew, as I did, that these same pigeons occasionally found their places on the table of the government officer, whose shooting boy had probably made the same mistake as mine. All the same, when a second one arrived I felt I must not presume on this and gave Dauwa a serious warning against further errors. He seemed somewhat impressed and left me feeling that owing to my loyalty to the forces of law and order, this would be the last I would enjoy. In that I was mistaken for a week or two later another arrived and this time I read the riot act and described the dreadful penalties that must follow such transgression. "Don't you understand?" I asked. "These birds are government taboos, and we must not kill them, and if we do we will have to go to gaol." "Yes, Buta, I understand," replied the culprit, "but when I went shooting, that pigeon came and sat on a tree in front of me and I didn't shoot it. I looked and looked and then said to it, 'Why don't you go away?' But he wouldn't go. He sat and sat and sat and so I shot him." He evidently thought the bird had had fair warning, and knowing Dauwa I realized the temptation must have been irresistible. Like many another Papuan, he often found the ways of the government incomprehensible, but the way of Christ had captured his heart and he was the first of his tribe to become a Christian. He had stood by Williamu until the latter had to leave, and then himself took charge and I was deeply touched by the way he and his helpers had acquitted themselves.

It did not take long to discover that there were many things needing attention, for white ants and the excessive rainfall had done great damage. A lot of building repair work lay ahead of us, and the first job was to get the *Purari* in running order, for without a boat it was practically impossible to get round my three districts. We accordingly returned to Urika, where a fuller examination of the launch almost filled me with despair. Here was work for fully qualified boat-builders and engineers and neither were available, so with a minimum of tools and in sheer desperation we started on it ourselves. It was a heavy task and we were held up waiting for parts of the engine that needed replacing, but once they arrived we soon had it running, and in the meantime repairs on the hull had been completed and I was once more in charge of a ship in which I could get around.

A full month had passed, but in addition to being a shipwright and engineer, I had organized the work on Urika and paid another visit to Orokolo. It was a district that always interested me and as I walked along the sand beach I was reminded of the early days when I had one of the first gramophones ever brought into the country. On one of my journeys I started it up on the Orokolo beach. A dense crowd gathered round, amazed to hear voices coming from the trumpet, and many shrank away, terrified by the mystery. When no strange visitor appeared they came closer, and I have a delightful photograph of a very scantily clad woman looking down the trumpet to see if she could find the man inside. Our music puzzled them and they were sometimes frightened by men speaking, but laughing records set them off in paroxyms of delight, and they would shriek and roar and roll on the ground in utter abandon and beseech me to play the record again and again.

Orokolo was foreign territory for my Goaribari 'boys' and their first visit was made in much trepidation for none had ever before ventured so far from their tribal lands, but once the first adventurers had returned safely with stories of other people and places they had seen, there were always more wanting to come than I could take.

On various occasions I had to tramp many miles along the coast visiting the teachers and inspecting the schools and the lads found the long walks very trying. They were familiar with canoes, and people have remarked that you could tell they were delta boys by the way they walked, as they were used to wading through mud from which they had to drag their feet, and the lift of the foot was unmistakable when they came to walk on hard ground. A trip along the beach after days on the boat was for me an invigorating change but not for the delta lads. They would start off gaily but soon be far behind and when after a week's hard tramping we got back to Orokolo they would be utterly weary and seemed full of wonder at the way I could outwalk them. Said Ani, as he talked a journey over with his pals, "If Buta wanted to, he could walk to Samarai in a day." As Samarai is about six hundred miles on from Orokolo, I felt flattered, but not disposed to make the attempt.

Time never dragged in Orokolo for there was not only much to be done but much to see and learn. The Kovave dancers who paraded the beach, the tall masks with their fantastic figuring, the young men in seclusion, going through their initiation, were all parts of a wonderful tribal organization, whose ceremonies culminated in the amazing and colourful *semese,* when the tall masks were brought from the *eravos* and the whole population joined in a processional dance which linked the past with the present and bound the living with the dead, who still lived beyond the sight of mortal eyes. I'm glad I saw so much for no one will see it again.

Entering the *eravo* one day, I passed down between the great Semese masks and to my amazement came upon a white man seated on the floor making a sketch of one of them. He was the government anthropologist, later killed in an air crash. Until we met in that strange house I had no idea he was in the locality, but he had come along in order to see the Semese dances. Later we stood together watching a phase of the festival, impressed and delighted by the colour and action of it all. He turned to me insisting that whatever happened, this must be encouraged and preserved, and seemed shocked when I replied, "You cannot preserve it and nothing that you and I can do can save it." He began to argue the matter but I pointed out that the white man and his ways had come to Papua and ceremonies such as we were watching were doomed, and nothing we could do could save them. They belonged to a way of life that was being shattered by the new forces pressing into the land. Influences were at work that would eventually make it impossible for the people to carry them through. In the old days the preparations alone kept the young men fully occupied for months and without them the ceremonies would lose much of their meaning. Yet more and more of the strength of the villages was being used in the service of the white people. Soon there would not be enough men left to build the great *eravos* or construct the sacred masks that were housed in them, and the old men who loved these things, would find that the younger generation who were growing up in a world so different from that of their fathers, would set little store on the rites and customs that once held the tribe together. As we talked and the dancing went on around us, that day seemed far away, but it has come with startling speed. The second World War took no account of tribal rites and customs and there is little left of all we had found so fascinating.

The life and customs of the people in the Purari delta differed greatly from those of Orokolo and the Gulf, where cannibalism seems to have had no place, though practised throughout the villages in the vicinity of Urika when Homu started work. He had done a fine piece of pioneering and had translated the New Testament into the Toaripi and Namau languages in addition to preparing hymn and prayer books. He found the Purari villagers very unresponsive, but had gathered a goodly number of the younger folk around him when ill health compelled him and Mrs. Holmes to return to England.

Two Rarotongan islanders were helping him but left to themselves had become very discouraged, and, though they still had some young people round them, their teaching methods were most primitive. Although painfully conscious of my limitations as an educationist, I was able to suggest ways by which their school could be run more efficiently and also drew up a plan by which each in turn could get around the district, travelling by canoe with some of the scholars. It was what they needed, and soon there was a new spirit on the station and a more intimate association with the villagers.

Homu had established a coconut plantation and the proceeds from the sale of copra enabled them to add to the number of young men on the station and children in the school while at the same time giving useful training in an industry their people could engage in. Two methods of copra-making were being followed; the one by opening the coconut and exposing the kernel to the sun; the other by removing the kernels and putting them in a long shed on racks, beneath which slow fires were kept burning day and night. The trouble with the first was that rainy or sunless days slowed the drying and caused the nuts to mildew, while the smoke-dried copra was often dirty and fetched a lower price. I had seen a drier that kept smoke from the nuts and could be used in all weathers and accordingly set to work to construct one. It was a fairly big undertaking and there was as much scepticism among the natives as when I was working on a sago extractor, for Papuans are born conservatives and love the old ways; but when the new drier was completed and a trial batch of copra came from the racks, beautifully white and dry, they had to admit the

new was far better than the old. In fact it worked so well that the
teacher found he was drying the copra more quickly than the
boys were collecting the nuts.

With so much on my hands at Aird Hill, I was very glad when
Homu's successor was appointed a couple of years later and Moir
Smith took charge. At Aird Hill, several married couples had
made their homes on the station and an increasing number of
young people from the villages were staying with us, giving the
school greater opportunity for effective work, since it was no use
teaching young people to read unless we gave them books. Fortunately Williamu had recovered sufficiently to return with his
wife, and a new head teacher arrived from Samoa, who was able
to relieve me of much of the school work.

The damage done by white ants and the abnormally wet
climate was so extensive that we were faced with a big rebuilding
programme made the greater by the need for housing the rapidly
increasing numbers from the villages.

The days seemed too short for the seemingly endless tasks that
faced us. School required infinite patience and its theme song
might well have been, "Tell me the story often, for I forget so
soon". That was hardly surprising since paper and books, reading and writing, had absolutely no relation to the life the children
and their fathers had lived. On the other hand they took to
drill like ducks to water and were always eager for more and I
found it very strenuous exercise. They loved the rhythm which
had some association with the dancing, but the session had to be
kept within close limits as when they went off to breakfast, I
had to get to the hospital to attend the sick.

As a change from school and hospital I would turn to translation
as I sought to give the people the Gospel of Mark in their own
tongue, and in this Williamu's wife, Annie, proved a tremendous
assistance. She was a Kiwai girl of remarkable ability and had
been educated at Daru, when Baxter Riley was in charge, and
could speak English, Kerawo and her own Kiwai language with remarkable fluency. Some of the Goaribaris helped us when search-
ing for new words or the grammatical construction of sentences
and their help was greatly needed, for only those who have had
experience of translating the Bible into the language of a primitive race can appreciate the difficulties we were constantly
meeting.

Though they were very conscious of an unseen world and of spirits who touched their lives at every point, they had no words to express many ideas common among us. Even the word God brought us up against the fact that there was no word in their language for a Supreme Being. There were many great spirits, most of whom we would consider very ungodlike; there were also many creators, for their folk lore abounded in stories concerning the creation of fish and birds, coconuts and trees; but there was no thought in their stories of one creator spirit. Our word God was unsuitable, for the people had no closed syllables in their language, so we used the Hebrew name Iehova and also two words signifying Spirit Father or Father of Spirits. Grace brings to our minds a quality which we find difficult to express by any other word but I have come across translations where the translator has used the native word for help to express it. We tried to express it by two words meaning loving help though we knew it was inadequate, but as in the case of the word for God, we had to trust to growing experience of His love to give the words richer meaning.

On the other hand we were sometimes surprised to find words better than our own in the expression of an idea, as, for instance, their word for forgiveness. We had some difficulty in finding it but at last discovered that for them, to forgive meant to forget and that for the Papuan forgiveness means forgetting, or putting the wrong received right out of mind. That is real forgiveness, for you don't let the wrong keep rankling and the sentence, "I'll forgive but I can't forget" would not make sense to the Kerawo men, whose thought comes nearer that of the Psalmist through whom God speaks, saying, "Their sins and iniquities I will remember no more."

So in our translation we went on word by word and verse by verse at first slowly and painfully and then more quickly, revising and typing, and retyping and revising, until the task was completed and the work ready to take to England on our next furlough for the British and Foreign Bible Society to print and publish; one more language reduced to writing and one more in which the same Gospel had been printed and published; and such translations now number about twelve hundred. Work such as this could easily be a lifetime job, but in our case it had to be carried through at odd times, when able to turn from school and hospital, boats and building, and all that was involved in the oversight of a rapidly growing centre.

We were trying to help the people towards a richer life and there was so much we could teach them. When visiting the villages or looking for timber along the rivers I had seen cane festooning the trees and often wondered if we could use it in basket-making. Our people made baskets or bags of raffia but I had never seen them using cane, and I had had little experience of it save a painful one when I was a boy. I therefore obtained some books from Sydney, and set myself to learn basketry. We collected cane from the forest, dried and split it, and after a good deal of experimenting made a basket. The 'boys' watched my efforts with interest and some were ready to learn all that I could teach them. They found basketry easier to master then writing and before long became quite adept. A small ketch dropped anchor off our place one day and the captain came to the workshop to see what we were doing and when he reached Port Moresby he spread the news, with the result that the next mail brought a request for a number of large and very strong cane baskets for unloading coal shipped up from Sydney. The order helped us out of a difficulty, for with so many young people on the station, the problem of feeding and clothing them was getting beyond our financial resources. With a market for our baskets, the 'boys' could earn their living and this meant we had no need to limit the number of those who wished to join the school.

Soon there came another request, this time for cane furniture. Whenever I had had to tackle a new job I had been able to find books that gave me the necessary instructions; but I could find no books about cane furniture. Fortunately I had a cane chair, bought in Australia, and after studying it from all angles, I pulled it to pieces and put it together again. The operation taught me a lot, but rather spoilt the chair. After that we set to work with native cane, cutting and steaming, bending and fastening, with interest steadily increasing, as our first purely Papuan chair took shape. It was far from perfect but we were learning as we went along until at last we were turning out chairs that would compare well with the commercial article. From then on we could hardly keep pace with the orders that came to us and we were supplying chairs, tables and lounges to traders, planters, officials and missionaries all down the Papuan coast. Later our 'boys' introduced the craft into their villages and the day came when on entering a *dubu-daimo* I would be offered a cane chair beside the *agibe* with its cluster of skulls, the new and the old in strange juxtaposition. Basketry became very popular and this led to the foundation of the technical school which came to occupy a very important place in the training of our young people.

Our search for timber had led to the discovery of a fine piece of land on the Kikori River, known as Veiru, and later we were granted a hundred acres of it for agricultural purposes. A planter I knew did not consider a heavy soil good for coconuts, so after consulting various agricultural pamphlets, I obtained a consignment of African oil palm nuts from what was then the Dutch East Indies, which did extremely well. My main purpose in opening up Veiru was to extend our work to the west, and two young men and their wives from the Daru mission came over to help us and built their homes there and gathered a number of young folk from the villages into a school.

Looking back, I marvel at how much we crowded into those days, but towards the end of the year my health began to suffer, and a sharp attack of malaria and crop of boils made it hard to keep going and it was with much relief that I heard that Mamu and the children would be joining me in a few months.

They returned in the *John Williams* and we decided to go ashore at Urika, though I would never have consented to this if the weather had been other than very calm, for we were anchored miles off the coast.

From the steamer nothing could be seen save the mangrove forest fringing the low-lying shore, but after a long wait, we sighted a double canoe slowly approaching. It was well over an hour before it was near enough for us to recognize Tumupu, the Rarotongan teacher, with his crew of mission 'boys', and about another half hour before they drew alongside. We lost no time in getting our baggage and ourselves on board. Ralph and Hilary were tiny tots but Phyllis Neuri was seven years old and rather apprehensive as they settled themselves with their mother among the miscellaneous collection of boxes and packages.

We left the steamer with mingled feelings. It was good to have wife and family with me but it hurt to think of all it meant or might mean to them, so far from other children of their race and so out of touch with help if help were needed. I've never felt I made a sacrifice when I gave myself to the work that claimed my life, for it was full of all I had sought, but these children were leaving playmates and the good things of a civilized land, for a wild, untamed country, and as we slowly pulled towards it, I wondered what it held for them. Had I seen what lay ahead, I would have turned back and put them on the ship again, but we travel through life a step at a time and it is a wise and loving providence that hides the future from us.

The children seemed rather frightened to find themselves on so crazy a craft, while I watched the weather anxiously, for in those shallow waters a nasty sea can get up very quickly and we had to cross a sand bar before we reached the coast. Fortunately it remained calm and we got ashore without a wetting, though the two hours spent on the canoe had seemed much longer to Mamu in her anxiety for the little ones. Once on land there was plenty to interest them. They had few cares and soon got used to the dark-faced children who greeted them happily and were always doing odd things for them.

After a day or so, we set off in the *Purari*, whose engine this time behaved itself, and the family found endless interest in the journey up the rivers and had great fun spending a night on the boat, and when at last we reached our home, they were almost overwhelmed by the warmth of the welcome they received. The house became a real home, with the three little ones playing around it and Mamu looking after us all, and training at the same time a group of Papuan girls. We were a happy family and a very busy one, for the station work was growing into something really big. Before the family returned, I had drawn out plans for the first section of the main workshop for our technical school and the erection of it was well under way, while at the same time we were constructing a slipway and carriage to take the *Purari* or any other mission launch.

My new Samoan assistant, Tofiga, and his wife Seepa proved themselves very capable workers. He had a flair for cane work and his wife worked so well with mine that I felt much happier when I set out on journeys that kept me away for days and weeks. All the same, thoughts of the family on Neuri were always with me and it was a great relief when returning to see the house on the hill and small figures waving a welcome from its verandah.

All seemed well and happy until one day after the children had come down the hill to see how the work was progressing. Phyllis looked so unwell that we had her carried back and put to bed. Almost immediately signs of kidney trouble manifested themselves and we had no means of telling whether it was a return of that from which she had suffered in Brisbane, or if it was the dreaded blackwater fever. We were cut off from help and in spite of all we could do, she rapidly grew worse and died four days later. She was our eldest child, and for her and us the seven years of her life had been packed with adventure in Papua, Australia and war-time England. So many hopes centred on our little daughter, and now they were shattered and my heart went out to my weeping wife who, in that dark hour, had no friends or neighbours to help or comfort her. We were suffering as so many others in the lonely outposts of the world and our hearts were full of heaviness. Yet neither of us came near despair, and though those days were very dark we still cherished a great hope. For our Phyllis it was going on to a larger life.

It was about nine in the evening when she left us and later I went to the workshop with one of my lads to set about making the casket that was to hold her little body. We worked far into the night and when our task was completed, carried it to the house and in it laid the still form that had once been so full of life and laughter. Then when all was in order I went to my wife that she might take a last look on the face of our little daughter. At first she shook her head and then with much reluctance came and stood and looked for just a moment before she turned away again, crying in a broken voice, "It isn't Phyllis". She was right, for Phyllis Neuri had gone on, and in my sorrow there came to me the words which we later carved upon the little cross that marked her grave: "The face of death is toward the gate of Life."

Hilary and Ralph never entered into out great sorrow, nor did they see the sad procession when all on the station wended their way to the grave on the hill, or hear the weeping of the dark skinned boys and girls with whom their friend Neuri would play no more. Early in the morning they noticed her bed was empty and asked where she was and when told she had gone to be with Jesus, they were quite satisfied and even cheerful, as Hilary remarked, "That's good, and now she won't be sick any more."

They never thought of her as dead, neither did we, for I have never thought of death as an end but as a going on, and the years have confirmed me in my faith that we are among the deathless ones who will some day cast aside these earthly garments and go on in newness of life into the glorious liberty of the children of God. I have never really ceased to believe in the presence of the living Christ, for I have talked with Him so often and felt His touch upon my life; but I am still mystified about that mangled frame they took from the cross, for the Lord had left it and they never laid Him in the grave. What men call death had set Him free, let loose in all the world, and no longer would He need that earth-bound, torn, and mortal garment, with which for a time He had been clothed. We know so little of the great adventure we all some day must meet, but I have never forgotten the feeling of wonder that came to me when a day or so after we said good-bye to our little daughter, my wife quietly remarked, as if it were the most natural thing in the world, "I saw Phyllis today." I looked at her in amazement. "What did you say?" I asked and she replied, "I saw Phyllis. She was coming down the hill, carrying some flowers and looking at the house, and then it seemed as if she turned sadly away and went back and I saw her no more."

There was no sign of hysteria, and she spoke with a strange assurance, and just before her own death in 1955 recalled what she had seen, and spoke of it as something that actually happened just as she had described it. Maybe our dear ones are nearer than we suspect and less than a single step divides us.

20

THE *BUGURU*

For a time we moved among the shadows for we were constantly missing the laughter and chatter of our little girl, but there was much to keep us occupied and we were glad of the work that helped to fill the hours that she had left so empty.

We made contact with many new tribes and from these a group of Poromi boys came to live with us. The Poromi and Kerawo tribes had been deadly enemies and it was a great thing to have representatives from both living and working together, and to watch the old hatreds giving place to friendliness.

Then came a great day on which we celebrated the first Christian wedding and this created no end of a stir, for it was the first break in one of the most amazing and, in part, disgusting ceremonies of their tribal life. I had known of it for years and on two occasions had been driven from villages where it was being celebrated, since no strangers were allowed to look upon these rites. I had, however, learnt enough from those who shared in them to realize that their whole future was being threatened by the promiscuity associated with the ceremony.

Actually it was the coming of the white man that had created the peril by introducing venereal disease among tribes that had been free from it and knew nothing of its cause or danger. Its effects were only beginning to be noticed, for it was of recent origin and a government officer, with whom I discussed the matter, dated its introduction to a time when a certain ship, well known to us both, had lain for a week or more at anchor off Goaribari. As men and women in increasing numbers were brought to me for treatment when known methods were much less effective than now, I tried to make them understand the source of their suffering and in village after village warned the people of what was happening. My words carried no conviction, for the things I spoke against were bound up with the rites believed necessary for the preservation and strength of the tribe, rites which had been handed down from one generation to another. In the past they never suffered, so why should they suffer now? My task was made still more difficult by their firm belief that disease and death were brought about by malign spirits and that this new affliction was just another manifestation of their power. They would listen in silence but without conviction and to my surprise, the women whom I felt were outraged were the most hostile to any change.

I almost despaired of making any impression on them until one and another began to raise their voices in my support, not necessarily because they thought I was right, but because I was their friend and they felt I was trying to help them. Also among the younger folk there were those who were beginning to turn against some of the more disgusting practices.

All the same, most could see no connection between rites so long practised and regarded as absolutely necessary, and the disease now afflicting them, and would spend hours in discussing the question among themselves. Around the fires in the *dubu-daimo* the debate would go on far into the night. They could not understand why I should be so opposed to ways they had learnt from their fathers and it was suggested that if I knew more, my attitude might be different; but how could I know more without seeing the ceremony, and even if I were their friend, would it be right to break the taboo and let me into secrets long hidden from all strangers? The question led to much argument and the talk went to and fro while the grotesque *agibe* with its skulls looked down on the men. It was not an easy decision, but at last they agreed to ask me to come to the next *buguru* and learn something of its mysteries.

I was surprised and delighted, and at the appointed time ran down the river to Uboa, a big village not far from Goaribari. Preparations had been going forward for weeks with women working in the sago swamps, beating and washing out tons of sago, and others fishing or crab hunting or collecting yams, taro, sweet potatoes, and bananas from the gardens. Men and women were coming across the water from various villages and scores of canoes were lying off Uboa, each made fast to a paddle or long stake driven into the mud.

Most had heard that I was to be present and I was able to move freely among the people and learn from one and another what was happening or soon to take place. The *buguru* is mainly a marriage festival in which certain fertility rites take place and lasts for three or four days during which a number of different ceremonies are carried through in various parts of the village.

As we landed we could hear the beating of drums and sound of singing coming from the direction of the *ohio-daimo* and making our way towards it, saw a procession of dancing women. Their painted bodies were adorned with shell ornaments, necklaces, armshells and bright leaved twigs thrust in their belts and armlets, while their hair was decorated with red and cream hibiscus flowers. Some carried drums, others phallic emblems, and one of the latter, representing a man, kept making lewd passes at the girls among the onlookers. As they came dancing along, they would now and again break into a raucous chant which was possibly as lewd as their actions. Later they entered the *dubu-daimo* and processed up and down its length, singing and dancing to the rhythm of the drums. At one end of this building all the boys and young unmarried men were seated in a large group around one of their number, who was blackened from head to feet with powdered charcoal. He, as the groom, was soon to take part in the final ceremonies but had been undergoing a fast as yet unbroken. Two small boys, also with blackened bodies, sat with him and were known as *dubu-koiti* and occupied a place akin to groomsmen. The men and boys took little notice of the dancing women, in fact it looked as if they were deliberately ignoring them as the procession went up and down their home. This did not seem to disconcert the dancers who continued singing and later left with the drums beating steadily and processed all round the long house. I noticed three small boys, their faces hidden by masks, who seemed to be having a dance of their own and kept appearing at odd times and in different places, but was not able to discover what part they played in the festival, though, in some way, they seemed essential to it.

That night another ceremony was held in the *dubu-daimo* in which no unmarried folk were allowed to participate, and while it was in progress all the boys and girls were confined to their homes.

Within the great hall the men and women gathered together, and at times the dancing ceased and the place was plunged in darkness. Then from the far end of the building a man cried out, "I am Aibaro, and these are my wives." With them on either side of him he started to walk down the hall holding their hands until they were dragged from him by other men. Others followed, each announcing his name and bringing his womenfolk, until there had been a general interchange of wives. Then the fires were allowed to burn brightly for a time to give light for dance and song but during the night the whole ceremony was repeated several times with all present participating. At dawn the dancing stopped and the women streamed out from the great place and went to their clan houses or *moto* to rest, and for some hours the village was unnaturally quiet.

Later in the day crowds began to gather near the house, where the bride, like the bridegroom, was still fasting. The door of this was fast closed and there was mounting excitement as out from the crowd stepped two warriors, wearing pubic shells and head-dresses of cassowary feathers and nasal shells shining white against the brick red of their painted faces. They were carrying bows as if out for a fight, and taking their stand some distance from the house, they raised their bows and let fly their arrows at the closed doorway, shooting at it time and time again. These were representatives of the bridegroom's clan who had come to claim the bride, while the other side were simulating reluctance to let her go; and there was much shouting and a most realistic display of hostility, with one side wanting to take the girl and the other loud in protest. After a while things quietened and the opposition gave way. The shooting stopped and the shuttered entrance to the *moto* was opened up, and out from the house came a man bearing the girl straddled on his shoulders. After a few steps he stopped, so that the girl could slide on to the shoulders of a woman, who in the same way passed her to her husband, and he in turn to another woman and so on from wife to husband along a line that carried her right to the *dubu-daimo*, all taking care that the girl's feet never touched the ground.

Later, when at another village, I saw this part of the ceremony carried through by men only and noticed that a number seemed very anxious to share in the carrying of the girl, but in both cases I understood they were members of her clan, certain of whom, known as *mudu-abea*, were in some way related to either the bride or bridegroom. As far as I could sort it out, the relationship seemed to be that of uncle, and such men could claim access to the girl's person before the marriage was completed.

While she was being carried to the men's house, two small girls walked along on either side of her. They were called *noumu-koiti* and seemed to act as bridesmaids. I was told they were her sisters, though the words for brother and sister were very lightly used and often applied to quite distant relations, and these girls might have belonged to a different family but of the same clan.

Both accompanied the bride-to-be to the *dubu-daimo* and after entering it with the crowd, I found she had been seated upon an upturned wooden bowl, with two human skulls supporting her thighs while a *mudu-abea* stood on either side of her holding her hands. As she sat thus, various folk brought little offerings of food to break her fast and stuffed it into her mouth. She was doubtless hungry and at first ready to receive all that was brought to her, but there were limits, and when she could swallow no more she let the gifts fall from her mouth, and to my great astonishment, the two *mudu-abeamio* had to eat it up for her. It seemed a case of vicarious consumption, where they did their best to make up for her loss of appetite. The poor girl did not look very comfortable, for an upturned bowl and a couple of skulls could scarcely have proved a restful seat, but she had to remain there for yet another stage towards matrimony.

As a girl, her head was well covered with black curly hair and this had to be removed. One of the *mudu-abeamio* started on the task with a razor made from a piece of bamboo and it proved a lengthy and probably, for the girl, a painful process, though there was not even a grunt from the victim. The shaven head was a mark of her new estate and regarded somewhat as her white sister would regard a wedding ring, for all that much of her attractiveness had been shorn away. It took some time, but when at last the head was shaven clean, she was lifted from her uneasy seat and taken to the *moto* where the wives of her father lived.

Dancing was still going on and as the women processed up and down, the girl was allowed to go out and watch them, though her head and shoulders were shrouded by a tapa-cloth garment lest by any chance her prospective husband should catch a glimpse of her face.

Later she returned to the *moto* where various relatives set about preparing her and her maids for the final ceremonies with

an amazing display of barbaric art. The bride's face and body
were painted vivid red, with white and black markings. Long
strings of cowrie shells were hung about her neck and a crescent-
shaped piece of mother-of-pearl displayed like an outsized brooch
on her breast. To her ears were fastened ear-rings of white
circular shell, each about three inches in diameter, and through
a hole in the septum of her nose was thrust a magnificent nasal
shell about six inches long. The final touches were made by fixing twigs or small branches of bright leaved crotons and gay
hibiscus flowers into her arm and leg bands and belt, and by the
time the work was finished she presented a most striking picture
of wild splendour. The little maids were adorned as replicas of
their mistress, though with unshaven heads, so that it was possible for their hair to be gay with bright hibiscus flowers.

The sun had set by the time all was complete and as night
began to fall, she was led by two *mudu-abea* through an admiring
crowd back to the men's house where she was to be kept for the
night, her *mudu-abeamio* remaining with her all the time. The
dubu-daimo filled up when darkness fell and all through the
night those within were singing strange, wild chants while the
girl became the property of various men to whom tribal custom
gave the right of access to her person. At the same time there
was uninhibited promiscuity among the men and women filling
the place, mingled with a most disgusting rite, carried through
with definite ceremonial form as an integral part of tribal life
and considered essential to its continuance. These were the ways
of their fathers and if not followed, their very existence might
be endangered, and with such beliefs it was hard to convince
them that those ways were bringing them death instead of life.

Early next morning the horror of the night gave place to a
most imposing spectacle. A small platform called a *tetepe* had
been built on two long poles so that it could be carried on men's
shoulders. It was gaily decorated with flowers and croton leaves,
and a skull was hung from each corner. A number of warriors in
full war paint took up their stations around it as crowds of men
and women came pouring out from the great house and boys and
girls rushed from the various *moto* and *ohio-daimo* to join them.
Then a great shout went up as the bride came in sight, heavy
eyed after that night of bestial orgies, but presenting a wonderful picture in her barbaric trappings. She stepped on to the *tetepe*

with her two maids on either side of her, and as the rising sun lit up their painted bodies and shell ornaments and shone upon the warriors gathered round, I caught my breath at the wild beauty of it all. Then the air resounded with still louder shouts as painted fighting men lifted the *tetepe,* while the people formed a great procession, some going ahead and others following and all singing and dancing as the bride was carried through the village. As they passed, I noticed a number of sticks of sago and some arrows had been laid at the feet of the girls who, raised above all, stood on the *tetepe* beside the bride, now being carried to the *moto* of her husband's clan. It was a most colourful and exciting spectacle with all the people joining together in song and dance as they brought the bride to her new home. When at length they reached the house, the *tetepe* was lowered to allow the bride and her two *noumu-koiti* to step on to the entrance platform, and as they did so, a woman known as *mudu-mamu* lay down in front of them, whereupon the bride and her maids sat on her back. Then from all parts of the village mothers came hurrying, bringing their babies, and seating them first on the knees of the bride and then on those of the two small girls, but I could not discover whether this was to bring good luck to the babies or to ensure that the new wife would have a large family, and it is quite possible that the women themselves were not sure about this, for I have often found them unaware of the meaning of their customs, and when questioned, they could only say it was the way of their ancestors.

Though the *buguru* had reached what appeared to me to be the climax, the bridegroom seemed to have taken no part in it and after watching the women and babies I made my way to the *ohio-daimo.* There I found the bridegroom, still smothered in powdered charcoal which had been rubbed into his well oiled body. He was surrounded by boys and young unmarried men, with certain old men in charge to see that all was done correctly. They were singing one of the wildest chants I ever heard and their voices rose in a kind of frenzy so that the very air seemed charged with menace and devilry. Then as the chant increased in volume, the sound of shouting in the distance blended with the chanting and, hurrying to the entrance, I saw practically the whole village population advancing, and dancing wildly as they came. Out from the crowd came armed men who clambered to the entrance platform, and passing me, strode through the men and boys seated around the groom, seized him and started to lead him from the house. Immediately a boy jumped up and caught hold of the groom's hand, and then another and another, each catching the hand of the one before him, until the groom was at the head of a long line of boys, holding each other's hands and accompanying him to the *dubu-daimo*.

Here in the men's house the groom was prepared for the final ceremony. The signs of fasting were washed away and his various *mudu abeamio* set to work to make a warrior of him. His hair was shaven well back from the forehead and his face and body painted brick red and picked out with markings in white, black and yellow. A long nasal shell was thrust through the septum of his nose and a fine cassowary feather head-dress adorned his head. Gauntlets of plaited cane, decorated with cowrie shells and white feathers, were fastened to his arms and legs, and a bark belt fitted around his body with a white, triangular, pubic shell hanging from it. It was a long time before the old men were satisfied with their handiwork, but when at last they stood back for a final look, all felt their endeavours had not been in vain, for the lad was transformed, looked every inch a man, and a fighting man at that. As he stood thus with his *mudu-abeamio* beside him, various individuals brought small miniature brooms, known as *siuari*, wrapped in tapa cloth, and after receiving these, he broke his fast and waited with the men until late in the afternoon when the whole village came alive again for the final ceremony.

The men of the *dubu-daimo* had been preparing for this and had arrayed themselves in all the glory of their fighting attire. Fully equipped as for war they took their bows and arrows in their hands and, surrounding the young man, led him forth into the open, where an excited crowd awaited them. There towards evening another great procession formed, with all the men fully armed and magnificent in their savage trappings. Surrounded by a shouting crowd of women, boys and girls, they marched towards the house, where the bride and her maids awaited them seated in state upon the entrance platform. I watched the procession advance until the armed party halted right in front of the girl whose face was quite expressionless and without the least sign of welcome or happiness as she looked on the young warrior who was henceforth to be her lord and master.

He stood silently before her for a moment, then taking the little bundle of *siwari* that had been given him in the *dubu-daimo*, he slipped them on to the point of his bow and presented them to her. She took them off and in their place slipped on a similar bundle, and as he righted his bow he caught them in his hand. Neither of them said a word or even smiled, and straightway he turned his back on her and marched off with his comrades back to the men's house. Though both bride and groom were silent the crowd broke into low cheers as he turned away and these I took for their congratulations for now the *buguru* was almost at an end and the two were man and wife.

For these two, as for all their people, this was the beginning of a strange life of promiscuity and that night the custom of the tribe compelled him to take his wife and offer her to the men of his *dubu-daimo*, each making a gift of an armshell or necklace or some tobacco in return for her favours. Then on the following morning the two set out in their canoe to visit other villages where the same procedure was followed, and when at last they finally returned to their home, the girl would proudly display all she had won for herself and her man by her prostitution.

This was the *buguru* and I had at last seen what for so long had been hidden from the eyes of strangers, and later as I sat in the *dubu-daimo* the men gathered round and asked what I thought about it and what I felt they should do. I know how much it meant to them and how it was linked with age-long customs deemed essential for the preservation of tribal life, and I understood something of the significance of even the most bestial of their rites, but I also knew that since the introduction of venereal disease the practices associated with the *buguru* were bound to destroy them.

Even then outside influences were at work which were bringing utter corruption to what had once been an honoured tribal custom. As inter-tribal war ended and contacts with the outside world increased, the Kerawo tribe became notorious for the shameless traffic of its women, until we would sometimes come across companies of men and women travelling far beyond their ancestral lands and visiting what had formerly been unknown peoples, solely in order to trade the women for tobacco and other articles of barter. I knew what was happening but I did not want them to lose the colour and gaiety the festival brought to their lives, and felt that there was much that could be retained. The gathering together of the people, the celebration of the marriage, the feasting and dancing had much good in them and I urged them to retain the wonderful pageantry of the bridal procession, but reiterated my warnings concerning their sexual practices and it was here they found it hard to follow me, and I doubted if my words would carry much conviction.

I also wondered what would happen if they believed what I was saying, and if there would be a cleansing of the festival or its total abandonment; for when the government put a stop to headhunting, they wiped out a lot more than they ever intended and made a big contribution towards the breaking up of tribal life. Headhunting was associated with other rites and beliefs that made for the stability of the tribe and they could not separate one from the other, and all were lost. Later we learnt that this was what happened in Uboa in respect to the *buguru*. They abandoned everything connected with it; but when Christian marriage took its place we did all we could to introduce as much colour and gaiety into the ceremony as possible, and blend it with feast, song and dance. The old rites can never survive the impact of our Western civilization, but we can give to a people whose old ways are doomed something that will help them to a new and richer way, for through the ages Christianity has shown amongst most diverse peoples that it can do this.

21

WE BUILD A BOAT

SINCE reaching Papua, I had travelled far into unknown territory and now was asked to make another journey from west to east. For some years the site of our Institution for the training of Papuan teachers and pastors had been under criticism, and my colleague, H. P. Schlencker, known as Seneka, who had taken charge of the Orokolo district, was appointed, together with myself and R. L. Turner, the Principal, to explore the coast, with a view to finding a more suitable place with a good water supply and anchorage.

With the whole coast from Daru to Samarai to choose from, we did not anticipate much difficulty in finding what was wanted but we travelled for hundreds of miles in various craft, stopping at every likely spot along the coast, and found to our disappointment and surprise that a place that would meet all requirements was going to be much harder to find than any of us had anticipated. I had great hopes of getting what we wanted at Vilirupu, having anchored off there once or twice, but on careful investigation we discovered that though the approaches were all that could be desired, there seemed no place suitable for the Institution. My colleagues shared my concern, for we wanted the new site to be as central as possible and were getting further and further east; and it was not until we reached Isuleilei that our search was rewarded. We were returning from another fruitless journey when I was attracted by the look of a place where the land rose sharply from the shore. I suggested we climb up and have a look round. At once we realized that here was the kind of site we had been looking for since leaving Orokolo, and the more we explored it the more sure we were that no other so closely met the conditions that had been laid down for us.

Others wished, as we had, that it was more central, but all felt none other offered so much, and today there stands on that site a fine block of buildings known far and wide as Lawes College. The only place I know that is its equal is the site at

Veiru, and had its possibilities been better known, it might have been selected, but at that time the delta was regarded as a place to be avoided and Veiru was never considered. Our choice was often criticized by younger colleagues mainly on account of its being so far east, but in recent years when a serious attempt was made to fine something more central, a younger generation ended where we ended, and Lawes College remains at Fife Bay.

Back at Aird Hill work was extending rapidly and people from villages wo had never seen were asking us to visit them. Un fortunately the *Purari* needed constant attention and on one occasion sprang so bad a leak that we were in considerable danger of sinking. We put her on the slip and patched her up, but by then she was needed for the Urika district, so I decided to build a small launch in which to get around until able to secure a larger boat.

I had absolutely no knowledge of boat-building but after read-ing various books on the subject, decided to start on a V-bot-tomed launch some twenty feet long. It was a fascinating task, presenting many unfamiliar problems and numerous difficulties, but we marked out our frames full size and then fashioned them in timber, and little by little the boat took shape. Building the hull was one thing and installing the engine quite another, for the boat-builder had then to become an engineer and the instal-lation called for most careful calculations before the engine could be bedded down and the shaft lined up correctly. Fortunately there were various books to refer to and I gradually collected an extensive library in connection with the Technical School which I was later able to pass on to my successor. Each time I found myself up against some difficulty I would spend the night reading about it and the next day working out what I had learnt.

There were constant interruptions for boat-building was a spare-time job in spite of my having no spare time. I would be away for weeks among the villages, or spending hours on trans-lation and language study, or working among those making baskets and cane furniture, or at the hospital or school. In between, we worked on the boat and eventually all was ready for launching.

As far as I could see all was in order, but as I had never before built a boat or even seen one being built, the dominant question was whether our craft would sink or float. All our people were

down by the slipway to see the launching. We christened her
Neuri, and into the water she went with cheers from the crowd.
She was actually floating, but anticipating the worst, I clambered
on board, looking anxiously for gushing water, and to my infinite
relief and surprise found my boat absolutely watertight. In my
ignorance of boatbuilding I had been several times more careful
over joints and seams than any practical builder, and a white
visitor once remarked that I was doing cabinet work, not boat-
building, which is probably one reason why she lasted so long
and proved herself a first rate craft in nasty seas.

The name she bore was the native name for Aird Hill by which
my elder daughter had also been known among the Papuans; and
this added to our disappointment that Mamu was not present at
the launching, but away in Sydney. Four months later news came
of the birth of my second son, David, though it was another six
months before I saw him.

Meanwhile, the technical school had developed to such an
extent than the government gave us a grant which enabled us to
install a lathe, drilling machine and new bench, together with an
engine to drive it all. They were also interested in the cane work
and offered to meet the cost of a Chinese instructor if we could
secure one. It would have meant much to have a skilled man in
charge, but though we sought the help of influential friends in
China, they were unable to find a suitable man ready to come,
and the whole scheme fell through. It was one of our great dis-
appointments for such a man could have done great things for
the cane industry in Papua.

So many opportunities were missed through lack of staff, for
there was always more to be done than we could accomplish. We
had the only boat-slip west of Port Moresby and some boat or
other was on it most of the time. When engines broke down, our
workshop alone had the machinery and tools necessary to undertake repairs, and a labour recruiter said he preferred to get his
work done at the mission rather than in Port Moresby, as he
knew it would be done properly. Seeing I was a rank amateur
and my 'boys' one remove from cannibalism, we felt flattered,
but I grudged the time we had to give to work like this. Strange
to say, some of the Goaribari 'boys' handled machinery much
better than many who had had far longer acquaintance with
white men, and among these was Auwau, who quickly mastered

the big semi-diesel engine we had on *Tamate I*. Later he was put in charge of the four cylinder engine on the *Neuri* and while I was on furlough had to take her to Urika and back, a journey of about two hundred miles.

On the return trip the engine stopped and there was no one to help him locate the trouble. He decided, after much investigation, that the magneto was at fault and, quite undaunted, removed it, and after taking it to pieces, located the cause, fitted it back on the engine, timed the ignition and started up and finished the journey without any further incident. I am pretty sure that not one white man in a thousand, faced by this trouble, would have got away with it as did this son of a cannibal, though Auwau did not seem to think he had done anything remarkable. When asked how he had managed to put the magneto together again after taking it adrift, he replied most casually, "I looked," and he evidently looked to such effect that without books or advice, he got everything back in its place with no odd pieces left over.

We had had to treble the size of our workshops and at the same time were facing the need of enlarging our hospital accommodation. I accordingly drew up plans for a building with two small wards and a dispensary together with verandahs to serve as an out-patients department. The needed equipment was secured for us by a young school teacher in England. By organizing garden parties and sales-of-work, Kathleen Saw raised sufficient funds to ship out to us an operating table, six beds and other fittings and medical supplies, a remarkable achievement for which we were most grateful.

The building was completed about the same time as the *Neuri* and with the translation of Mark's Gospel ready for the press, I left Aird Hill for my second long furlough after twenty years of service.

We travelled to the coast in the *Neuri* and were delighted with the way she behaved, though we realized we still needed a boat on which we could live for weeks at a time if we were to get around our widespread district.

I had had a nasty bout of sickness and had suffered much from boils and was glad to be going south, though the steamer on which I travelled was rather ancient and not too comfortable. Moreover we ran into very rough water, striking the tail-end of a cyclone and later finding ourselves in the vicinity of another.

For me that journey is always associated with my first experience of radio. The younger generation who have grown up with wireless and television cannot conceive what it meant to us who had lived in a world without either. I had read of the new discovery with a sense of amazement that men could thus talk to each other. It sounded like a fairy story and it was exciting to find that the old steamer had been equipped to receive and transmit radio messages by morse code and still more to learn that the operator had a set able to receive Australian stations. It was very primitive by present day standards and earphones were necessary to pick up the broadcasts which could only be heard when we were near the coast but the officer promised to call me as soon as that happened and I waited impatiently for the call. The ship was pitching and rolling, and those of us who were not sick had wedged ourselves into odd corners of the tiny saloon to keep from being thrown about, when Sparks looked in and beckoned me. I followed him out into the night and clambered up to his office on the boat deck where he clapped the earphones on my head. Outside, the storm was raging, but through the wild winds there came the sound of music and nothing I had ever heard filled me with such wonder; wonder, such as the present generation will never know. A miracle was happening in the stormy darkness far from land, and since that night radio has been to me a kind of parable. As I think of the world filled with music and song, all unconscious of it until men switch on and listen in, there comes the thought of a world full of the wonder of the Eternal, who waits to break in upon us; but it is only those who stop and listen who can hear. That to me is a clue to the mystery of prayer, which can be as wonderful a discovery as was the experience of radio on that wild but unforgettable night.

Soon I was back in Sydney where I was introduced to my son David, and not long after we were on the S.S. *Maloja, en route* for England.

It was good to be home, in a world where for a time the noise of war was hushed, and during the next twelve months I was speaking and lecturing all over the country. My furlough enabled me to see the translation of Mark's Gospel printed and provided an opportunity to press upon our Directors the need of a boat to replace the *Tamate*. I suggested this could be built at Aird Hill and plans I recommended were accepted, and necessary material, including the engine, fitting and hardware, purchased.

A brother of mine suggested the possibility of lighting the station with electricity generated by a water turbine, and the more I thought of it the more attractive it appeared. The scheme as he described it sounded so simple that I began to make enquiries, fearing the cost would be beyond my slender resources, and was cheered by the way friends came to help. For a surprisingly low figure I secured a secondhand turbine and quantity of six-inch pipe, while a friend in the electrical business presented me with a generator, and with this generous assistance we went right ahead, and before my furlough ended everything was in order for shipping on a cargo vessel.

My visit to England was anything but a holiday, but it had been a very rewarding experience and friendships made then have enriched my life ever since. We left with grateful memories and once again were on our way to Australia but this time we had young children to care for and educate.

My children were too young to be put into boarding schools and my wife and I could see no way out but to face separation once again. Fortunately houses were cheaper and easier to come by in those days and with the assistance of the bank we were able to secure a cottage in Northbridge, a suburb of Sydney. The family were glad to have a home of their own and having seen them settled in, I prepared to join the *John Williams*.

It was not easy to set off alone, leaving wife and little ones behind, and it seemed as if even the elements were opposed to it. We preferred to say good-bye in the home rather than before an interested crowd, and a very tearful group saw me away from our new house, for we felt it would be a long, long time before we were together again. A crowd of friends had come to see us off and in between greetings and good-byes, I got my gear securely stowed, for a heavy gale was blowing and I knew we were in for a tossing. Prepared for the worst, we watched our friends leaving and then learnt that, owing to the storm, the sailing had been postponed until next day. I accordingly went back to the family who felt their sorrow had been rather premature, and when I set out the next morning, the parting was less tragic. This time there was no crowd at the wharf, but after a long wait we heard that the weather was still too bad and we would not be leaving until the day following. My second return created considerable mirth and when I again said good-bye, I was farewelled with smiles instead of tears.

It was still blowing hard and the wharf looked very empty but the *John Williams* was definitely leaving and we thought we were well away, until we swung into Watson's Bay and heard the anchor fall. The gale still raged and the port authorities were against our tiny ship facing it. It was Saturday. The prospect of a week-end with the family looked inviting, so I suggested to our captain that as a mission should not sail on Sunday, I had a feeling that he and the other officers would appreciate another Sunday at home, and as there seemed no strong opposition and before there was a chance of any arising, I slipped over the side into a small boat and made for the shore and eventually reached home again. Though welcomed gladly, my third homecoming was regarded as a glorious joke, but we had a very happy week-end and my fourth departure was far from tearful. Saying fond farewells was in danger of becoming a habit.

This time I did not return, not for three years, and when I saw the children again it was as if I were meeting a different family.

22

LIGHT IN DARK PLACES

BACK in Papua owing to the death of my old friend Baxter Riley I had to take charge of the work throughout the Western District in addition to that in the delta. This Western District was the largest in the country and extended from the Bamu River to the borders of Dutch New Guinea which at one point touched the western bank of the Fly. Northward the district reached far inland to what is now the Mandated Territory of New Guinea.

White men from the time of D'Albertis had travelled up the Fly, but given little information of the people, save that they were very hostile. I was therefore surprised when some men who had been looking for gold, called at my place and asked if I knew anything of a Christian mission in those parts. They told me that when about 500 miles up the Fly River, they sighted a village that looked very different from any other they had come across. They approached it cautiously and ready for a fight, but to their surprise received a friendly welcome and one who was evidently an educated native proudly showed them his church and school. They were ignorant of his language so could not discover where he had come from, while I had never even suspected the existence of a Christian mission in that area and found no one in Daru or Port Moresby who knew anything about it. I accordingly wrote to London, and as they also knew nothing, they approached authorities in Holland, who in turn made enquiries in what was then the Dutch East Indies. About twelve months later we secured the information and learned that a branch of the Church in Indonesia had formed its own missionary society and sent some of its members across to Dutch New Guinea. These had pushed their way on from the coast until 500 miles up the Fly River they established themselves among tribes that had been great fighters, a testimony to the vitality of the Christian Church in Indonesia and of its missionary outreach.

Another quite different story had also made us realize the

presence of the Dutch on the upper reaches of the river. Some men had come down the Fly, and on to Daru, claiming sanctuary, and the authorities learned they had escaped from a Dutch prison or concentration camp. We knew nothing of its position, but these were Indonesian nationals interned in this place in the wilds of New Guinea on account of their political activities, and I felt it an outrage when our government returned the escapees to the Dutch authorities.

Earlier, when visiting some western villages, I had another experience which emphasized the nearness of the Dutch territory. Across the border was a wild headhunting tribe known as the Tugeri who gave both governments a lot of trouble, and whose reputation was such that all the adjacent peoples went in fear of them. As we travelled, we were met by a group of men fully armed and very excited, who declared that the Tugeri were again on the war-path and not far off, for they had just come across one of their canoes. No one knew where the enemy was, but all were expecting to be attacked, and I was interested to see a house built at the top of a tall tree, and on its roof men with bows and arrows watching for the Tugeri warriors. As a matter of fact, no attack eventuated but I was glad to have seen the tree house, for until then I had thought such houses were only found among the hill tribes behind Port Moresby.

Although the country north and west was largely unexplored, the tribes around Daru were among the most sophisticated in Papua and had probably been in contact with white men longer than any others in the country. Contacts with Australia through the Torres Strait had existed long before Captain Cook sailed through these waters. The villages around Daru and in the Fly estuary were so constantly in touch with white traders, pearlers and government officials that simple English was understood and spoken by the majority of the men and many of the women, and the vices of the white men had been absorbed more readily than their virtues.

This was the district I had to take charge of, in addition to looking after the work in the delta. Fortunately, Riley had been given a stout little ketch called the *Ada*—for without her the task would have been impossible, as it involved journeys through what were often heavy seas, across the mouth of the Fly and along the coast where many shoals and sand banks made navigation dangerous. The little *Neuri* was quite unsuited to such conditions, but as a Papuan crew was in charge of the *Ada*, my work was considerably lightened. It needed to be, for I was trying to tackle a job that would have kept four or five men fully employed if it had been done as it should have been. I knew that, but set out to do the best I could.

The first task was to visit the villages, to help and advise the native teachers in charge of schools and churches, and generally grapple with the most urgent problems. It involved weeks of travel in all weathers under very rough conditions and when at last this exacting work was completed I returned on the *Ada* to Aird Hill and sent her back to Daru.

Back at Aird Hill I was almost overwhelmed by what confronted me. The school required daily attention, for the number of children was steadily growing and at times there were more patients in the hospital than I could deal with. The workshop needed my personal oversight, for in addition to those making the chairs, lounges, etc., we had to arrange gangs of cane cutters to collect the raw material. Always there was the urge to press on with translation work, for I wanted to give the people more of the written word in their language and it troubled me that the days were so crowded that I was never able to do as much in this direction as I felt I should. Here was more than enough to fill a crowded life but two other tasks confronted me. The hydroelectric plant and its turbine, piping and generator were on their way, and most of the material for the building of a motor cruiser had been ordered. I was facing work for which I had had no training and in the carrying out of which, no experience.

The building of a concrete dam and the erection of the hydroelectric plant proved a much bigger task than I had anticipated. It had seemed so simple and straightforward when my brother was enthusing about it, but only as I got down to the actual work did I realize what I had let myself in for. The picture he had drawn of the whole station lit by electric light at practically no expense was so entrancing that I had thought little of the difficulties and now found myself with a lot of unfamiliar equipment which I had somehow to transfer into a generating station. The look an engineer friend gave me in Sydney when I told him of the scheme expressed much more than his words, for when I confessed that my knowledge of hydraulics and electricity was practically nil, I sensed more than pity and incredulity, and had he said all he was thinking, I knew it would have been uncomplimentary. He was amazed, but whether at my audacity or ignorance, it was hard to say. I must confess to some very sleepless nights and harassed days, but having started, there was no turning back. I studied books on hydraulics and electrical equipment by night, and worked with the books beside me by day, thus learning more and more as we went along.

The first thing was to get a site with the necessary water supply, and we explored the sources of a small stream among the hills, and then decided on the best place for the concrete dam we had to build. It was not ideal, but the best we could find, and gave us a drop of seventy feet to where we hoped to erect the power house. The survey completed, we started on the dam with no equipment other than picks and shovels and a crowd of willing Papuans, who had no idea of what we were trying to do. We had no concrete mixer, so the concrete had to be mixed by hand, with sand and stones for the aggregate, collected by canoes, and carried up to the site in boxes. Having built a large mixing platform and got the foundations well in hand, I left Williamu to look after one company while I took another down to the site chosen for the power house. This we cleared and levelled and then set to work on the foundations and concrete floor and the tunnel beneath to carry away the water from the turbine. Holding-down bolts for the plant had to be embedded in the concrete floor, and this necessitated making templates to very exact measurements as once in the concrete, there was no shifting the bolts. Then came the difficult job of getting the heavy machinery to the site. We had no tractor or special gear. Everything had to be manhandled through the roughest of country, then lifted into position, lined up, and bolted securely down so that there would be no vibration. As I look back, I often wonder how we managed to complete this most exacting task and marvel at the strength and persistence of the Papuan helpers who carried it through to a successful conclusion. They worked with wonderful cheerfulness, and the power house was erected around the plant, and the dam at last completed. While work on the latter was still going forward, we started to get the pipeline in position. I had had to order more pipe from Australia owing to the lie of the land, and my friend the engineer, who had looked at me with such pity, managed to secure a quantity of used lengths of eight-inch pipe which saved us a lot of money but added to our problems, as we had somehow to connect it with the rest which was of six-inch bore. While trying to work this out in my mind, we cleared a run from dam to turbine through more rough country and lined up the pipes and started to fit them together, at the same time anchoring them securely. We started with eight-inch pipe and the work was fairly straightforward, for the lengths were flanged and only needed bolting together with suitable packing. The six-inch pipe was quite different, and connected by fitting the end of one length into the wider end of the other. I had had no experience with this kind of joint, but as a boy, had watched men in London connecting the water mains by caulking the joints and running molten lead between faucet and spigot, as I believe the different ends of the pipe are called. My boyhood memories were all I had to help me and I could find no information on how to join the eight-inch to the six-inch securely enough to withstand the heavy water pressure. My friend had sensed this difficulty and sent a flange to match those on the eight-inch pipe. Our problem was to fit this on to the smaller pipe. As we had only a small hand forge it proved very difficult, but after much time and labour, using the hand forge to its fullest capacity, we eventually succeeded, and the joints proved so satisfactory that we never had a leak or any other kind of trouble from it.

In this way, drawing on memories of what I had seen, and experimenting until we found ways of overcoming difficulties, the pipeline was completed and joined to the outlet from the dam and the inlet to the turbine. Then came the easier work of fitting the switchboard, running the cable from the power house to the station and wiring the church, mission, teachers' and Papuan houses, until at last all was complete. It had been a tremendous task for Papuans and amateurs to carry through and we felt we must have an official opening, so approached the Resident Magistrate and asked him to perform it. He was only too ready to oblige and decided to make it an impressive occasion. We also decided to do all in our power to see that no breakdown would mar the day, and to make sure of things, arranged a trial run. I had no idea how the turbine would behave when the valves were opened and after my experience with my

engineer friend and the many warnings from others who heard
what we were attempting, we were quite prepared for short
circuits and fires and even sudden death if that should result.
Pulling myself together as I stood in the power house I shouted
to those up the hill by the sluice-gate to let the water in. I heard
the torrent coming down the pipeline and rushing into the
turbine, and as it began to turn, I watched the indicator as the
voltage climbed, and then in fear and trembling switched on the
power, wondering if the whole thing would blow up or the
mission house become a blazing warning to all tempted to try a
similar venture. To my amazement nothing went amiss, there
was no explosion, no dreadful shocks, no fires, not even a short
circuit. The turbine was running beautifully and the generator
was soundless, and all on the station cheered at the sudden blaze
of light that filled the church and mission house and their own
homes.

With a load of uncertainty lifted from our hearts we now prepared for the great day and decided to combine it with an official
opening of the little hospital which was now in full use. A letter
from the District Magistrate gave us a clue to the importance he
attached to the occasion. He informed us that he would not only
be representing the Governor of the Territory but the King himself and would be bringing a company of armed constabulary
to act as a Guard of Honour. The whole of the white population
of the district, nine all told when I was included, together with
crowds of Papuans from the villages, rolled up for the great day,
and the Papuans viewed the native constabulary with mixed
feelings as they landed from the government launch and marched
up to the hospital fully armed and looking very smart in their
uniforms of navy blue edged with scarlet. The Resident Magistrate, also looking very smart in white uniform and topee, but
somewhat unsteady on his feet, lined his men up outside the
hospital and retired to my house after giving careful instructions
that as soon as he reappeared they were to come smartly to the
salute while the rest of us played God Save the King. Out of sight
he continued to fortify himself for the occasion with supplies he
had brought with him and when at last he made an appearance
it was evident that he was finding it somewhat difficult to
approach in as kingly a fashion as the occasion demanded. Somewhat unsteadily, he reached the saluting base where the con-

stabulary presented arms. The magistrate stood as stiffly as possible, and the rest of us in different keys did the best we could
with the National Anthem, the villagers joining in with their
own version. The result was indescribable. We were a long way
from England, but I believe the King died soon after. The hospital, then in full use, was declared open, and two hefty constables supported their commander and representative of His
Majesty, on his way down the hill, past the dam to the power
house seventy feet below. He found the going hard, but once
there, pulled himself together, threw in the main switch, and
with a mighty voice, declared, "In the name of God, and the
King, I declare this power station open." And open it was, and
everyone rushed to see the lights shining brightly, cheering
madly at the sight, while I heaved a sigh of relief as we hauled
the King's representative up the hill again and back to the house,
and found we had got through the occasion with nothing to mar
the day and quite a lot to chuckle over.

Looking back, I cannot help wondering how a crowd of
Papuans, one remove from cannibalism, led by an amateur who
knew little of electricity or hydraulics, managed to complete
such a task in such a short time, and were it not for the confirmation of my diaries, I would be doubting the record. In seven
months, we had built a concrete dam, lined up and secured a
pipeline about 200 feet long, built the power house, erected
turbine generator and switchboard, run the main cables up a
very steep hill to the station and wired all the houses. All this
was in addition to the normal work of the mission, for day by
day, we were teaching in the school and attending the sick, while
at times, I had to leave everything and get away among the villages. Daru was also on my hands and the accounts for both
districts had to be kept and supplies distributed among pastor
teachers in the different villages.

The arrival of the first book printed in the Kerawo language
had created tremendous interest and given new impetus to our
school work, for now young folk saw what learning to read
really meant, while some of the more advanced wanted to go on
and qualify to be teachers themselves; so while pushing ahead
with the hydraulic scheme, we had to build quarters for three
more married couples. We also needed more timber, and our
circular saw was not powerful enough to break down the logs,

so I had to teach the lads to use pit saws which meant time given to marking out the logs and sharpening the big saws. More orders for cane furniture were coming in than we could fill, and for most of the time the workshop and boat-slip were occupied by engines and boats under repair, with the 'boys' always looking to me for help and guidance. Fortunately I was blessed with a good constitution, but at times the going was very hard.

23

TAMATE II

WHILE working on the hydro-electric scheme, we had been interrupted by the arrival of the engine and much of the material for *Tamate II*. The thirty six horse-power engine was not so heavy as the turbine but heavy enough to set me wondering how we would get it from the wharf to our workshops which were situated on high ground quite a distance from the river. The Papuans, however, had no qualms. They fastened long poles to the casing, and gathering round like a swarm of ants, lifted it bodily without any help or suggestions from me and delivered it safely to its destination.

I had informed our Directors that as I had so much on hand, we would need a qualified boat builder to take over the construction of the new craft, but it was with the greatest difficulty that we secured such a man. When he came, he brought a young brother with him who was far from skilled. They arrived about a month after the completion of the lighting installation and by that time we had the frames of the hull completed and the keel on the blocks. I had hoped to be relieved of all responsibility, but the young men never really settled down, and at the end of three months left us. Most of the planking of the hull had been completed, but it was an unfinished shell and we amateurs had the task of turning this into a fully equipped motor launch.

I had introduced various changes in the design to meet the tropical conditions and terrific rains of the wet season, but the job requiring most care was the installation of the big engine, where any mistake in alignment would mean constant trouble and damaging vibration. My long experience with sailing boats and launches served us in good stead and one by one our difficulties were overcome and she was completed down to the last detail in less than ten months from the laying down of the keel. Then came the launching, when the magistrate's wife christened our ship with coconut milk and named her *Tamate II*. What I had longed for had come into being. I had at my command a craft that would enable me to keep in constant touch with the villages and from then on, much of my time was spent in going from place to place among the people.

Shortly before the launching, I asked my lads what they thought should be her first trip and Williamu suggested Dopima. I was glad, for I could think of nothing more appropriate than our ship *Tamate* commencing her travels by going with the message of God's love to the place where old *Tamate* had been slain. So it was that having got fuel, water and stores on board, we set off for the coast. It was fine to feel the boat had come alive and to listen to the rhythm of the engine and watch the way we were slipping down the river. We felt proud of her but our greatest joy lay in the thought that she was opening a way to all those scattered villages. It was a sheer delight to be travelling in a vessel on which we could depend and one specially designed for the conditions we had to face. Soon the broad estuary lay before us and in the distance the island of Goaribari where, skirting the mangrove-lined shores, we came to Dopima and dropped anchor. Canoes came speeding out to greet us and there was real warmth in the welcome the people gave. They had watched the building of the cruiser and one of their 'boys' had helped in it; she was their boat in a way no other had been and they were rejoicing to see her afloat with her white hull shining in the sunlight. It was towards evening when we went ashore and in the great house we gathered to talk of the little ship and of the message she had brought. We spoke of the old days and of the old missionary, and a stillness that could be felt came over the crowd as we spoke of his death; but it was good to point to the little craft on the river and tell of the church at home that paid back by giving more. There was much to say and I left my 'boys' still talking when at last I returned to the *Tamate*.

The sun had not yet risen as in the cool stillness of the morning I sat in the deck cabin thinking of all our coming might mean to the people. Across the water lay the place of tragic memories, almost hidden by the smoke from many fires, as women astir prepared the morning meal of sago, crab and fish. Slowly the smoke cleared and the village materialized through the blue. It looked much as it did when Tamate saw it from the deck of the *Niue,* but the swift flowing waters are eating out the soft banks and today sweep over the place where those early adventurers landed and laid down their lives. The old landmarks are disappearing and not least those by which the people once did guide their lives. The fighting days have gone, but life is not safer, because there is no fear that the stillness of an early dawn might be shattered by fiercer cries of savages bent on slaughter. There are other enemies threatening the existence of the people, new vices, or old vices rendered still more vicious, and as I looked across the water, I knew my work had only just begun. There was still adventure in it all, not the adventure of meeting a canoe full of armed and painted savages, but the adventure of trying out the Gospel and proving it to be in very truth a Gospel for the world.

We travelled far, visiting villages I had longed to know better. I took Makoni with others we were training and these shared in helping the people to understand why we had come. The 'boys' would take their sleeping mats into the great *daimo* of the village off which we anchored for the night, and for hours on end would be talking to the people. It was not preaching as we understand it, but it got further than preaching, for it was a meeting of man with man where questions were asked and answered and where the villages saw the new way of which my lads were speaking exemplified in their lives. They were different and the people saw and knew they were different and in my lads the Word had become flesh, something to be seen and not just talked about and I became more and more aware of the fact that my ways counted far more than my words. They watched and discussed us and got their ideas of what our faith meant from the way we lived, and saw God through what we were. It is so easy to work and talk, but as Paul said to the Corinthian Church "I may speak with the tongues of men and of angels, but if I have no love, I count for nothing." Too often we give people a poor idea of what God is, because of what we are, and these Papuans taught me much about myself that I needed to learn.

We went through the villages around Goaribari and the Omati River and on to Apewa where we saw the *dubu-daimo* crowded for a great occasion. No one will ever see the like again. What unforgettable nights they were when the drums began to beat and the women gay with specially made grass skirts and armshells and rows of white shell necklaces joined the menfolk and danced to sunrise. Yet as I got known, they would for a time sit around in the lights of the fires and join us in evening prayers. At first they thought it a strange custom, a white man's fashion, then they came to realize there was something that belonged to them in it all and sensed the presence of a Spirit who was near, to them as to the white man. This thought became so real that in village after village evening prayers were held, for though they were very ignorant, they had come to know that the Great Spirit addressed as *Imo Abea* or Our Father did not go when we went, but was never far from any one of them.

With a reliable craft at our disposal on which we could live for weeks at a time, we were able to go much further afield. Apart from the Poromi people around Aird Hill, our closest contacts had been with the Kerawo tribes with occasional visits to those of Urama. North of the latter were the Gope and Era River people of whom little was known. We therefore set off to learn more about them. We travelled along waterways well known to us until Williamu pointed to a narrow channel we had often passed, which, he said, led to the Gope villages. It was so narrow that we stationed two lads for'ard to hack away the overhanging fronds of nipa palm that almost closed the way. We broke through into a broad stream and up river saw big villages on either side with the roofs of the sacred houses towering above all the rest. As soon as we anchored, men came off and we found they were closely related to the Urama tribes and also acquainted with the Kerawo tongue, so that we could make ourselves understood. Everywhere we received a friendly welcome, for there were few villages that had not heard of Buta owing to the way news spreads among these people.

I was particularly interested in the *mene* or sacred houses which served a similar purpose to that of the *dubu-daimo* but were more like the *ravi* of the Purari Delta. Some were beautifully built, and that at one of the Kipi villages was particularly fine. Under the pointed roof that overhung the entrance platform hung the image of Iriwaki, constructed more carefully than many I had seen in Urama. The *awai*, with their skulls, totem shields and emblems were on either side, and within, when my eyes grew accustomed to the gloom, the house had a strange beauty all of its own. I stood looking down a vista of arches made of the giant fronds of the sago palm. To right and left were the totem shields, carved and painted in red, white and black, with other *awai* at different intervals. The end of the building was

hidden in shadows but I seemed to be standing in the cathedral of
a stone age race and looked around in wonder, touched by the
wild beauty of the place. Then accompanied by one of the men,
who seemed to hold a position of importance, I walked on slowly.
Boys were fascinated with us by my ability to speak a language
they understood and the men were delighted by my admiration
of their great building. But as we neared the gloomy end, the
boys forsook me and the men held back and I found myself going
on alone with no one but my guide. Soon I faced a wall of
plaited leaves, and parting these, saw nothing but a little empty
room. I had expected to see an image like the grotesque ones in
the *ravi* of the Purari tribes, but here there seemed nothing. Yet
the whole house was wrapped in silence as I stood there. "There
is nothing here," I said and my guide, speaking softly as if in
awe, uttered the sacred name Kaiia Imune and my heart was
touched with wonder. Here was no image, nothing we could see,
nothing but an unseen presence that made the place such that
only the one appointed could approach it. I too felt the presence
and entering the little room while a great silence filled the *mene*,
I prayed aloud in the language they could understand, and I
prayed to my God and their God though they did not know it,
and to my Father and their Father whose ways they had yet to
learn. Then I returned back through the building and out into the
sunlight where the men and boys crowded round and the women
stood below listening to our talk. After what had happened
within, we felt very near to each other and it was easy to talk to
them of the Unseen Spirit and of what we had learnt of Him
through Christ.

From the platform one could see other villages and after returning to the *Tamate* for a meal, I got into a canoe and made my
way to one where some old men met me and led me towards the
mene. There on the great entrance platform I saw one of the
finest group of stone age men I have ever met. In front of the
fringed curtain of sago fronds that hid the interior from the gaze
of women, were three chiefs, oldish men and splendid in their
savage trappings. The one on the right wearing his white shell
ornaments and feather head-dress, had his face marked out in
red and black, the patterns being most carefully drawn. The
central figure was every inch a warrior adorned in wild splendour
but without paint, so that one was able to admire his fine, in-

telligent looking face. The third was quite other, a wild looking
fellow who, in addition to all his other trappings, had his face
painted yellow and black. They sat there together, three of the
most striking-looking men I had seen in Papua and above the
head of the centre figure was posed the image of Iriwaki, with the
arrow of his drawn bow pointing at me where I stood. I've always
regretted not having my camera with me and have regretted still
more that it was before colour photography was known, for this
belonged to days that have gone for ever and no one will ever see
the like again: the great house with its strangely decorated skulls;
the soft fringed curtain with the awful image of Iriwaki on
guard above it and those three amazing men adorned with such
trappings as would, by contrast, make an old time Red Indian
look civilized. In another *mene* close by, we met three more
striking figures. I was told they were *nuda-abea*. These seemed to
have undergone some initiation ceremony, during which, I was
told, they had been stripped absolutely naked with even their
arm bands cut away, and not allowed to bathe. Then just before
we saw them, their bodies had been washed clean and oiled, and
men had gathered round them and painted their faces and
decked them in their regalia, and the effect was truly amazing.

Within the great hall near the entrance, a small one-roomed
house had been erected, and beside it sat a young male initiate
who I suspect was being prepared for marriage, as further back
was a young girl sitting beside another small humpy with her
father and *mudu-abea* on either side of her. I found it impossible
to get at the inner meaning of all that was going forward, but
that it had a religious background was evident from the name
given to the girl, *Kaia Imunu Behe* or Daughter of the Spirit of
the Sky. Here she was seated near the home of that Spirit which
was so sacred that only he who held high place among his fellows
dared approach it. Such scenes gave me a great opportunity, as I
tried to understand and appreciate their ways and outlook. I
would sit with them questioning about, and treating with
reverence the things they believed, and they in turn would question me. Their ceremonies were part of their religion and that
religion, like our own, was bound up with the search for the
meaning that lies behind the mystery of life and death, and as
we talked, I would try to lead them through what they believed
of Iriwaki and the Kaia Imunu and what we had come to believe

of God. I would stress that though we had different names for the Great Spirit, He was always the same Being, the Source of all life of whom we had learned much through Jesus Christ. There is no doubt in my mind that they find in the Christian faith the crown of all their religious strivings. Christianity rightly presented becomes truly indigenous, provides a spiritual foundation for the new life we must build as the old life crumbles under the impact of our Western civilization.

Back on the *Tamate* after long hours ashore, I sat watching the canoes passing me, laden with food from the gardens, or with groups of women returning with their nets and traps. Some of the canoes were beautifully made. One passed with fine relief carvings from end to end, and another was painted with a series of half circles in white and black the effect being most pleasing.

Among these people the making of canoes was a much more serious business than among the Kerawo tribes and the women were not allowed to see the work in progress. Going through the village, I came across the shipyard with a high fence round it to prevent the women seeing what was going on. To secure further privacy there was within the yard a further enclosure, and entering this I found no less than sixteen big canoes in process of construction. Iriwaki has something to do with the work though it was not clear to me just what part he played, but I noticed the same customs as I had found further west. A slither of wood from each canoe was fashioned into a figure something like a man and usually carefully carved and painted, for this was the Spirit of the Canoe. Some of these images finally rest among the totem shields beneath the *awai* with its rows of decorated skulls, and I got the idea that the canoes to which they belonged had been broken up, but the Spirit still remained. Near them I have also seen another figure that represented the spirit of the crocodile. My attention was drawn to this while wondering at the great size of a crocodile they had killed with their broad bladed arrows. They showed me how it was done, and then pointed to the roof of the *mene;* "There is its spirit," they said, and there it was, a rudely carved figure of a crocodile, but transfixed with a number of arrows.

A man who saw I was interested took me to see the canoe he was completing. The relief work on either side was splendidly carved, but the part of which he was most proud was the carving under the bows which is never seen save when the canoe is hauled out of the water and turned over to dry. It was there that he had put his finest work. To see it I had to kneel down on the chips from the carving and put my head almost on the ground as I looked up, but I thought more of that bit of work than of all the rest, and so did he. He told me as we talked together that it was the way of his fathers, and I felt it was a good way too, and let him know it.

Their long bamboo tobacco pipes provided further examples of their artistry and skill and while among them, I purchased a number of beautifully carved specimens. I wondered later if that was a kind and considerate action for these were among their treasures, and they only let me have them because they were hungry for tobacco and needed fish lines and hooks. Yet as I think of all that has happened since, I am not sorry. All these articles would have been destroyed long ago and so much of beauty lost for ever. Today, the Anthropological Museum of Sydney University has them in its care with much else that speaks of a life that has gone, and the unborn generations will some day come to wonder at them and maybe among them will be young men from Papua who, seeing them, will know that their fathers in their own way were great men. These treasures and reminders of the past are not lost as otherwise they would have been.

For weeks we travelled on and when amongst the Urama people we would often have to leave the *Tamate* and take to canoes to reach places hidden up streams so narrow that no vessel could traverse them. It was not long before our new ship had the first of many similar experiences in these uncharted waters. Speeding along what looked like a fine river, our engine suddenly began to slow down as it felt the drag of shallow water, and before we could take action, we were hard and fast on a bank. The tide was falling rapidly and there was no hope of getting free until it rose. We were anxious to see how our boat would settle when the waters left her, and delighted to find the hull well shaped for an experience we knew would be oft repeated. She settled down without heeling over, at an uncomfortable angle, and while I read, the crew went fishing until the tide came in and we were afloat and on our way once more.

24

A NEW HOME

AFTER two years of incessant work, during which I had been responsible for the conduct of two large districts, my colleagues agreed to my taking a short furlough and I reached Northbridge to be welcomed by three children who had grown up so quickly that I hardly recognized the youngest, only a toddler when I left. It was good to be with my wife and family once more, but the short time in Sydney was not a holiday. Two big construction jobs at Aird Hill lay behind us but a third awaited my return, and while south, I was preparing for it. Our old home of rough hewn timber with a thatched roof had stood for twenty years but was riddled with white ants to such a degree that in places one could push a finger through the paint and find the wood all eaten away. I had drawn up plans for a two storey building and while in Sydney discussed them with a builder who dealt in big contracts. He became very interested and set out to help me. His firm had been remodelling some city buildings and his yards were full of material taken from them, and at his suggestion, I spent days in that yard getting very grubby, but accumulating a wonderful supply of windows, doors and other items which I packed for shipment. I longed for the help of my Papuans for I had to do most of the work unaided, but it was worth it for it saved the L.M.S. hundreds of pounds. Not only did my friend let me have the material for a very low figure, but he also secured timber, cement, reinforcing rod, and roofing iron at prices only obtained by large contractors. Our steamer *John Williams IV* was loading cargo for the Papuan mission and we were able to ship everything freight free. This, combined with the generous help of my friend, resulted in the mission house costing far less than any other in the country.

When planning the house, I had seriously considered the advisability of building at Veiru, and in the light of all that happened since I left the country, the L.M.S. would have been saved some serious mistakes and heavy financial loss had I done so. At that time, however, it was difficult to decide the most strategic site for the mission. Geographically, Aird Hill is right at the centre of the delta and affords much closer contact with the Poromi, Gope and Urama peoples. Moreover, on Aird Hill we had the best equipped technical school in the mission, with a boat-slip that would take any of our boats together with boat-building and repair sheds fully equipped with all necessary tools and appliances. The station was lit by a hydro-electric plant costing nothing for fuel. There were homes for a dozen married couples in training for work among their people, a residence for my Samoan assistant and a fully equipped little hospital. A shift to Veiru would have involved the dismantling of eveything and a completely new start and at that juncture I felt I could not face so great a task.

Before we started building, Mamu, who had placed Hilary and Ralph in boarding schools, returned with David. Over five years had passed since she had left Aird Hill, and a great welcome was given to her and our little lad who was soon on the happiest of terms with his brown and black companions, the smaller youngsters regarding him as their leader and consequently getting into quite a lot of mischief. We were interested to note the quick way in which he picked up the language, for what we had slowly and labouriously mastered came to him as easily as speech comes to children when they learn to talk.

As soon as possible after their arrival we put in the foundations for a new mission house. Having seen the previous one destroyed by white ants, I decided on a lower storey of reinforced concrete and our experience with the dam and power house served us in good stead. As usual, the work was additional to the other activities in technical and day school and villages, translation and preparation of more reading matter, care of the church and attendance on the sick.

It was strenuous work but at last the lower walls and floor were complete and we set about erecting the upper storey. Here I think we beat all records so far as Papua was concerned. Heavy rains were threatening and we were anxious to get the work and workers under cover. While one gang under Williamu finished off the concrete work and erected the necessary scaffolding, Makoni and I, with other helpers, cut to size and shape all the timber required for the frame and roof of the upper storey and completed the fixing of joists and laying of the floor. Then one

Monday morning the whole staff set to with a will and by Friday night had completed the erection of the framework of a building fifty feet long by thirty feet wide and roofed the whole with corrugated iron roofing. They were five of the most strenuous days I have experienced, but from then on we could work steadily, unhindered by the frequent storms, and when completed, we had what many considered the finest house in the country. I think it was the first home in Papua to have modern sanitation connected with a septic tank and we had added a laundry just beyond the kitchen on the ground floor and a fully equipped bathroom for the bedroom above, while all the rooms were lit by electric light. Yet thanks to my Sydney friend and the use of so much secondhand material, it was easily the cheapest house in the country and apart from labour, had cost just under £300, which, as I write, sounds incredible when a house in Sydney, a quarter of the size, will cost ten times as much.

Soon after we had moved into our new house, we learnt that a young man had been appointed to take charge of the Daru District, and in 1930 I had the privilege of introducing the Rev. D. E. Ure to the people he had come to serve. He was not greatly impressed when introduced to the first of his parishioners. They had come from villages on the western side of the Fly River, a motley looking crowd arrayed in an amazing collection of old garments, many of which had done good service before being passed on to the present owners, and their general appearance was most depressing. When I remarked that Ure or Misi, as they called him, had not come to boss, but was a brother, they insisted that I was under a wrong impression and what they needed was a boss and not a brother, and knowing a bit about them I thought they might be right.

Mamu and David were with us and thoroughly enjoyed the journeyings, in spite of having to rough it very considerably, for the *Ada* had but one very inadequate cabin, while cooking arrangements were altogether primitive. They never forgot the visit to Parama, and I still have my wife's account of it in which she says it was a thrilling and rather eerie experience. "You sleep and eat on the deck and wash your face in an enamel bowl on the hatch with the native crew as interested spectators, while going to bed at night is beautifully simple. You spread a mat and a blanket or two and lie down, but sleep comes slowly, for the boards get harder the longer you lie on them.

"We set off in high spirits heading for the Tora pass, the narrow channel between Parama Island and the mainland and a very useful short cut to the Fly River. Near the Daru end is a village with a native teacher and his wife living there. They were expecting us and came out in a big sailing canoe. It was a beautiful sight as she skimmed over the water, sail up, flags flying and tassels on the rigging dancing in the wind. I was thrilled that we were to go ashore in her and so was our small boy, and sitting down on the deck, we watched them hoist sail. It was a lovely part of the journey, gliding so smoothly over the water that we almost seemed to have wings, and too soon we reached the shore where crowds of villagers awaited us. We stayed until well into the afternoon and then were off in the canoe for another delightful sail back to the *Ada* which was quickly under way, and eventually dropped anchor off Parama at a point where there was a path leading through the bush to the village. Mosquito nets, blankets, towels and a suitcase were sent ashore and we followed in the dinghy. Small David cheerfully proceeded to make certain of a wetting by trailing his hands through the water, while we sat tight and wondered when we would be wetter, for there was a nasty sea and the dinghy was overloaded. We kept a special eye on the food box hoping to keep the bread dry, though not feeling optimistic. Near the shore, half a dozen dusky men waded out to tell us the path through the bush was under water, and as it was now dark, it would be wiser to go round the island in a canoe they had brought. Not knowing the canoe, we cheerfully agreed. When it came alongside we saw it was a dug-out with two outriggers and a platform of widely separated strips of bamboo. We squatted on them with our precious food box and started off, after being assured that we had only to go round the next point. Later, we discovered that there were six points, but were mercifully unconscious of the fact when we started. Waves were tossing us around and our canoe men informed us that it was a little bit bad, which we felt was an understatement. I was glad I had put on my raincoat and wrapped David into a canvas coat I had made for him, but waves didn't stop for raincoats, and as we did not dare to stand up, we sat fast while the seas splashed through the bamboos and we were soon wet to the skin, all save

David whose canvas coat plus the shelter of his father's back, kept him fairly dry. Then it started to rain, so that both ends got wetter and our crew, finding we were in shallow water, jumped overboard, as they felt it was easier and quicker to push than paddle, and running and splashing beside us, helped us along. The waves were still shooting up between the bamboos and there was still another point to get round, always just one more, and we were feeling very sceptical as to the proximity of the village until our men startled us with long, shrill whistles and we saw a number of lights and men came crowding round, and before I could say or do anything, David was snatched away into the the darkness. Then the three of us were carried by strong arms through the water to the sand, though we might just as well have walked, for we were already soaked to the skin. I stood with the water dripping from me and asked for my small son and was informed that he was already at the house, so we set out in the darkness, stumbling over piles of seaweed and wondering what would happen next. The house was of native material and we reached it some time before our baggage, which was being carried overland, so were unable to get into dry clothes, but as we were needing a meal, I helped to get things going though we found it hard to decide whether to sit or stand as we ate, as in our soaking clothes both positions were equally uncomfortable. I found standing a little less miserable but we were all glad when we could strip and roll ourselves into blankets. We were so exhausted that we soon dropped off to sleep and when we woke the sun was shining and the night before seemed only a bad dream."

After such journeying through the widespread Fly River district, with rough seas, heavy rains and vast stretches of mud, it was good to be back at Aird Hill again. We were no longer as isolated as in the early days. Here white folk were coming into the country and labour recruiters were taking from the delta the most virile portion of the population. Papua was being brought into the main stream of the world's life and the results were not always good. We who lived among the people, spoke their language, working with them and sharing their joys and sorrows, were often troubled by the evil effects of these contacts.

25

THE *TAMATE* GOES PLACES

THE forces that were to destroy so much of the age-long tribal life were at that time only beginning to be felt and it was still easy to get beyond their reach and find oneself in primitive Papua. The country around us was largely unexplored, for the maze of waterways extended over thousands of square miles.

Sometimes our boat would thread its way through narrow but deep channels with nipa palm on either side, sometimes along fine streams which grew more beautiful the further we travelled from the coast where the forest land is entirely different from that near the sea.

The tribes differed considerably in their buildings and customs but could understand me for they were speaking different dialects of one of the most widespread languages in the whole of Papua, reaching from west of the Fly River to the Purari where the language but not its structure changes. As we reached a village canoes would surround us with many sufferers from yaws or tropical ulcers and we would line them up and give them intramuscular injections that brought about wonders of healing.

At night most of my lads would sleep ashore, for they were not just my crew but young men I was training, with the hope that they would one day settle in these villages as teachers. At Aird Hill they were learners but in the villages they were encouraged to pass on what they had learnt and would often be up at all hours talking and answering questions. Next day the strident roar of my klaxon horn which could be heard for miles would awaken them and I would go ashore, attending to sick folk, listening to various happenings and before setting off to another village, gathering all who would for a talk and simple act of worship. We got very near to the people on these journeys, and always tried to relate what we talked about with what they had learnt from their fathers, for God has never left the wildest savage without some knowledge of Himself and even through their strange, dark ceremonies, has prepared their hearts for the light that lighteth every man.

My elder children were at boarding school in Sydney, but about this time, I arranged for them to come and spend their Christmas holidays with us and it was an unforgettable experience especially when travelling from place to place on the *Tamate*. They were almost overwhelmed by the warmth of welcome they received from the villagers and through this I learnt of the highest honour the Kerawo tribes could show to anyone and which very few received. It was almost akin to spreading the red carpet, though the carpet in this case consisted of naked bodies. We had entered a big village and my children were gingerly making their way to the *dubu-daimo* along the crazy causeway built above the mud past the different homes. From these came women, who reaching the causeway, prostrated themselves before my youngsters, who stopped in amazement, wondering what to do, for their road was blocked by a line of almost naked women lying prone before them. Then one of my lads explained that they were being very specially honoured and were expected to show their appreciation by walking over each woman in turn. This shook them for it was a long causeway and there were many women, but when they learnt that the people would be very hurt if their welcome was not received correctly, they moved on looking very embarrassed and followed each other in a kind of slow hurdle race as they stepped across one woman after another until the *dubu-daimo* was reached. From there, a tall warrior emerged and prostrated himself in like manner, for he also had to be negotiated before they could enter. In all my wanderings I have never been honoured thus nor have I known it happen to any others of our race, for none of us, not even the Governor, seemed worthy of this, the highest honour they could pay. I have been met by bows and arrows and been surrounded by wildly shouting crowds, but have never received such a welcome as that accorded to my young family.

Those weeks were a wonderful experience and the presence of the children did much good, for the Papuans sensed that with all our differences of race and colour we were a family people like themselves, sharing together so much that belongs to family life. Christmas was a joyful occasion with the new house decorated with flowers and palms and the children awakened by young Papuans singing Christmas carols. After that came the sharing out of gifts, and everyone on the station, both young and old, received a Christmas present. Soon from villages all around, canoes were arriving laden with happy families, and while all were busy preparing the Christmas feast, there was a shout of "Sail O!" and round the point came the government launch with five white people who had been invited to join the festivities. One of them was known as a very hard case, but I was told that as they started on their journey back to Kikori, he informed the others that he never expected to have such an adjectival good time on a still more adjectival mission station, as he had had that day. He thoroughly enjoyed himself playing with the children and sharing in the feasting and fun, and when they left, the hundreds of Papuans who had come together were in the midst of a glorious dance that went on through the night. They danced tirelessly and with great vigour but usually with serious faces as if it was important business, though when I joined in, the whole company dissolved in laughter, since I was evidently not up to professional standards. Meanwhile the white contingent were on their way home. While with us they had nothing but tea and soft drinks and even the hard case seemed well content, but on leaving, they went up river to the home of a rubber planter and there made a night of it. So much so, that as morning broke, the magistrate had to be supported by two of his armed constabulary to keep him from falling into the river from the government launch. On arrival at the station they carried him to his house and put him carefully to bed. His night out had done him no good and he scared his associates by bringing up some blood while vomiting. I never discovered just what had happened but there was an urgent call for help and before I could do anything about it the launch arrived and I saw the sufferer carried ashore on a stretcher by four stalwart police who brought him to our house. We hurriedly prepared a bed and I took charge, and he slowly recovered. Some days later, when well enough to sit on the verandah, we were talking together, and I was very glad to hear him say, "You know, Mr Butcher, this will be a lesson to me." It almost seemed as if a brand had been plucked from the burning or a prodigal son had come home and I was wondering how I might improve the occasion and encourage him to persist in the ways of temperance, when he went on, still very gravely, "Yes, Mr. Butcher, it will be a lesson to me, I shall have to keep off plum pudding after this." Seeing it was my wife's plum pudding, I felt rather outraged, and told him very plainly that my wife's cooking had nothing to do with the condition he was in when returned to me for repairs. As a matter of fact the planter had given me details of the quantity and variety of drinks he had consumed and when I enumerated them, he looked both grieved and shocked, but never blamed the pudding again.

A short time before the children returned to their schools, a young girl from the adjoining village was taken by a crocodile which had swept her into the water and carried her off. The place was in an uproar and the air filled with the wailing of mourners. Canoes, with a man holding a spear in the bows of each, were patrolling the river and as they went along, the crews were beating the sides with their paddles and I was told this often attracted the attention of the crocodile who would come to the surface and investigate. Ralph and David asked me to let them go to the wharf with Makoni to see what was going on. To their horror the crocodile rose to the surface quite close to where they stood, still carrying the body of the girl in its jaws, but swiftly submerged again at the sight of danger. They never saw it again though for a long time the men continued to patrol the river and the sound of the paddles beating against the sides of the canoes came to us hour after hour.

The place seemed very quiet when the children left, especially as Mamu went with them, and I was alone once more. Fortunately there was much to fill the days as I was pushing farther and farther afield. Westward up the Omati, I heard of a great cave, and as caves have always fascinated me, we dropped anchor near the spot, and our guide led us through the bush to the hills where we saw the entrance yawning wide and high before us. They called it Awai and it was of no mean size. Hoping to explore it, we soon found our way blocked by a sea of liquid guana. High above our heads thousands of flying foxes were hanging and as the light of my torch disturbed them, the place became filled with vast numbers flying around and streaming from the entrance. I waded on until the filthy liquid reached to the top of my gum-boots, and the armpits of my two lads, but we could not get through, nor could my torch light up the end. Possibly it lies miles away, for between here and Veiru on the Kikori River are a series of caves and along the track a great hole leading down to one of these which the Papuans regard with awe and which no man has yet explored.

The Turama lies beyond the Omati and is a nasty river about thirty miles wide at the mouth, but for the first sixty or seventy miles, very shallow in places. Running up the river, we had a peculiar experience with the bore. The mouth of the Turama, being very wide and narrowing rapidly, causes the incoming waters to gather themselves into a great wave that roars up the river overturning canoes unlucky enough to meet it and capable of overturning or swamping a launch. It can be heard long before it reaches you and travels steadily upstream against the current, sweeping all before it. We had waited downstream for it to pass so as to get the benefit of the incoming waters as we went up river, and to my surprise the speed of my craft plus the strength of the current was greater than the speed of the bore and we saw a mass of broken water ahead of us and then a foaming wave stretching from bank to bank and soon were actually travelling over it with the tumbling waters all about us. Fortunately the tides were beginning to take off and though we had a bit of a tossing, there was nothing to worry about. In fact it was an experience I would have been sorry to miss, for to ride on top of the bore was a pleasant contrast to the time when on the Aramia River I went under it and nearly lost my life.

We found the villages on the upper reaches more like those on the Fly with the people living in long, communal dwellings hundreds of feet in length. Within were rows of rooms on either side walled off from the central passage which formed their dance hall. The tiny entrances to these looked as if they had been made for dogs, for in no case were they more than two feet high and in some cases less, and to get into their homes, the inmates had to crawl on their hands and knees. At first only the men put in an appearance. The women, who had never seen a white man, had carefully hidden themselves, so I made it known that if the men would fetch them, I would give each a fish-hook, whereupon, there arose a great commotion with the men shouting to the hidden females and the women protesting their fear of the stranger. Eventually, they sent one of their number to investigate and as usual the oldest and least useful was pushed forward, for if any harm came to her, it would not matter much. Consequently, I was not surprised when an old lady came crawling out with a good coating of dirt to make up for lack of other garments. She was very scared and needed much encouragement but when she found that I seemed harmless she took her fish-hook and went off to spread the news, and soon the rest were emerging from their hide-outs and sprinting down the house determined not to miss a good thing. The tiny entrances afforded privacy and protection from intruders, though a determined enemy could always smoke them out, as these great houses were built of most inflammable materials. This was vividly brought home to us as we travelled.

One evening, some seventy miles from the mouth, we reached Bahi, a village crowded with people. The erection of a new communal dwelling had just been completed, and from the surrounding districts men and women with their families had come to feast and dance in celebration of the ending of so great a task. They had good reason for making this a festive occasion and they must have felt very proud of their work as they looked at the great building hundreds of feet in length built by their own hands. It had been a tremendous task, for they had only the most primitive tools and no hammer, saw or nails to lighten their labour. A year or more had passed since the work started and now the building stood complete, and this was a time of rejoicing as well as ceremonial dedication. The dancing and feasting had been going on for a day or more before we arrived. A large crowd welcomed us though many were still asleep recovering from their exertions of the previous nights. Some twenty or more needed intramuscular injections and it was slow work, as each individual had to have the skin of their rump cleaned and sterilized, but we got through at last, and before we finished they were preparing for the next dance. None of the patients was standing out, for it would take more than a tropical ulcer or intramuscular injection to stop them. Then the drums began to beat, first one or two trying them out, then others joining in until the air was vibrating with the throb of hundreds beating out the rhythm of the dance. The dancers in long procession came prancing down the great new house and out into the open and round the building and then within it once again, with all the participants joining in a wild chant that rose above the ceaseless rolling of the drums. Hour after hour the dance went on and I hesitated to break in upon it, yet when in the evening I went ashore again they needed no pressing, but ceased their drumming and seated themselves on fallen logs and on the grass and listened with seeming eagerness as I told them of the purpose of our coming, and shared with them our evening prayer. The scene was unforgettable: that great crowd arrayed in all the splendour of the dance, their faces lit up by the light of fires where even as I spoke, women were cooking the evening meal and men warming and tightening the snake skin parchment of their drums. Yet there was no sign of resentment at the interruption of their fun, rather a wonderful silence after the noise of the dancing, and they made us feel we were welcome and were not only friendly but eager to listen to all we could tell them. Then they turned from the first prayers many had ever heard to the dance they had always known. It was a glorious moonlight night as in and out of the house they danced, and I watched the scene from the launch anchored close to the bank. I knew they would not cease until the sun rose, so feeling very tired, I turned in about eleven and was quickly asleep in spite of all the noise ashore.

How long I slept I cannot say, but in my sleep I seemed to hear strange cries and then awoke to hear my 'boys' shouting from the bank. Dancing had stopped, the drums were silent, but there was a queer sing-song crying and a strange roar filling the air and as I opened my eyes, I saw the cabin brightly lit and thought I had overslept. Half awake, I stumbled from my bunk and looked across the river and saw the great new house in flames. The air was full of smoke and burning debris. The fire had begun near the centre of the building where a torch, held high to throw light upon the dancers, had set the thatch alight and the flames were swiftly spreading in both directions.

It was a grand though terrifying sight, yet with something wildly beautiful about it as the forest all around was lit up by the glare. From the crowd came a continuous wailing mingled at times with excited shouts as parts of the roof came crashing down, filling the sky with blazing embers that showered upon them all.

We felt so helpless as we watched the catastrophe reach its climax and the fine new village home whose completion they had been joyfully celebrating, sink into a blazing heap of ruin. We had got into mid-stream well away from the flaming debris and as the fire died down I looked at the clock and found it about two a.m. I also found we had lost our dinghy and a frayed rope attached to the stern bollards told us why. We had had to pull out in a hurry and when going astern the propeller had cut through the painter and set the dinghy free to drift up stream. I called to our 'boys' ashore and they came across, paddled by some of the visiting dancers to whom I offered a fish line each if they brought my dinghy back. They were off like a flash and two hours later returned with the wanderer, having found it well up the river and still travelling gaily on.

While they were away I snatched a bit of sleep and on their return went ashore with them, for it was now daylight and I could see numbers of the villagers moving around disconsolately and I wanted to comfort them. I took a good supply of fish lines, hooks and tobacco to show them we really cared, and found them very sad but appreciative of our concern for them. The pluck of the men amazed me, for though the ashes of their village were still smouldering, they were already discussing where the next would be built. I gathered them together, the visitors on one side and the Bahi people on the other, and as the headmen came forward, I handed them the gifts I had brought, telling them how much we felt for them and of how these presents were just a token of our sympathy.

Then Makoni spoke, eloquently picturing me as almost in tears while their village was burning, and after commending all to God, we started to leave. I have never known a Papuan crowd so grateful. Their response was remarkable and they almost hugged me, and as the anchor rose and we got under way they lined the bank and waved and cheered until we rounded a bend and they were lost to sight. Much was lost that night but much was gained and we knew we would always find friends to welcome us whenever we returned to Bahi.

26

A HAPPY TRIO

SINCE my wife had taken the children back to school, life for me had been strenuous but the home very lonesome and it was with much gladness that I heard she was on her way back with a friend whom we had helped to get to Australia after the first World War. The months that followed were some of the happiest I spent in the country. Our place was crowded with young people and the problem was how to keep the numbers within our capacity to care for them. Five more young married couples had joined us, eager to be trained for work among their people. I told them there was no pay but they would face school work and tasks about the station day after day, yet nothing deterred them, and they settled in happily with the rest. Others I had to turn away and I hated doing it, but we already had more folk than we could well accommodate. I was more than thankful that our workshops, boat sheds and slip were fully employed for we were thus able to train and support scores of young people whom we would otherwise have had to turn away. We were repairing engines and launches, building houses, completing the framework for a church in the Orokolo district, sawing timber and making cane furniture, and the young folk found real happiness in the new things they were learning to do. They supported themselves by the work they did, but also shared in the life of the school and church and thus were under constant instruction. They might not learn much in school hours beyond reading, writing and numeration, but this alone meant a tremendous advance and opened a way for the Gospel to become a living force in their life.

Mamu and Eveline were good company for one another and the latter took an increasing interest in all that was going forward and seemed to enjoy sharing in the life of the people. They delighted in processional dances and Eveline would be in the procession with a fine, strapping and gaily decorated Papuan beating his drum in front of her, and a grass-skirted girl heavily

hung with shell necklaces following, while Eveline, with earnest
face, sought to imitate the movements of the rest.

Both accompanied me on my journeys, for the *Tamate* was
well equipped, and as I pushed even further afield, they became
the first white women to be seen in many of the villages. Our
company was a mixed one speaking four different languages or
dialects but working happily together. With Auwau as assistant
engineer and Makoni at the wheel we went down the broad
stretch of water north of Urama where at times I have seen tens
of thousands of great jelly fish (Medusa) covering the surface.
The water was a blaze of dazzling light as the sun rose ahead of
us, but in about an hour we swung north, entering a channel so
narrow that we had to cut our way through the overhanging
fronds of nipa palm that closed above our craft. Then quite
suddenly we debouched into the Era River at a point where it
was about half a mile wide and in the blue distance could see the
mountain ranges of the interior from which a cool breeze met us
and made travelling delightful. Everything was fresh and wonderful to the women and as we rounded a bend, we saw the first of
the villages we had come to visit.

Like most of those on the lower reaches, Wouwobo was built
above the swamp and a very shaky, rather rotten, wooden
causeway raised above the mud led from the river through the
village to the big *mene*. As I was the heaviest I went first,
gingerly followed by Mamu and Eveline with the 'boys' trailing
behind, and though there were times when we doubted if we could
make it, we eventually reached the *mene* but not before a kindly
old fellow wearing little save a smile, came to my wife's assistance
and in most gallant manner led her along the swaying causeway.

There, as everywhere, the two women were received with
tremendous excitement since they were the first white women
ever to be seen. The villagers gathered round us in the evening
hour and listened almost greedily to the story of the Good Spirit
who was not far away from any one of us, one old chap in full
war paint nodding his head from time to time in approbation,
while a big crowd of small girls were so interested that they remained quite unmoved by the antics of a small pig which my folk
on the contrary found highly amusing. Pigs are much prized and a
mother will show equal concern for her pig and her baby by suck-
ling either, and we got used to having both in our congregation.

From place to place we travelled up the Era, visiting villages where the crazy causeways were a constant menace and the rain and mud made for much discomfort.

The men, who usually ignored their own women, were always ready to help mine, and I'm pretty sure that in spite of all I might say to the contrary, they reckoned I was a well married man with two wives. They were also greatly intrigued by the singing of my company, who entertained them with some of the hymns I had written which sounded so different from their own wild chants. I was hoping, when later I translated a number of the psalms, that we could wed them to their own strange music, but in this I never had much success, though I hoped my successor would do better for there is something in their singing we should try to retain.

Leaving one of their villages one evening, as we set off for the *Tamate,* everyone seemed to be accompanying us and I felt doubtful about the stability of the causeway which was creaking ominously. Two men supported my wife by holding her more firmly than she found enjoyable. They meant well and she accepted their help with due expressions of appreciation and then caught a glimpse of Eveline that filled her with delight. She was coming along arm in arm with a fine young man dressed in shells and feathers and little else and looking as if he never wanted to let her go, while Eveline accepted his protection as happily and unconcernedly as she would have accepted that of one of her fastidiously dressed male friends in the City of London.

The further we got from the coast, the more primitive we found the people, and their costumes, or the lack of them, created considerable amusement. One wore a kind of peaked hat of tapa cloth and another appeared wearing a red cap that made him look something like a pirate, but the most admired wore a beautiful head-dress of cassowary feathers and plumes of the bird of paradise which were greatly envied by both ladies. The women were largely unadorned, and their clothing reduced to the absolute minimum, but the raffia baskets they made were beautifully woven, and seeing my wife admiring one, the owner presented it to her. Mamu, as a token of appreciation, gave the woman a fish-hook and the resulting rush shook her and Eveline considerably, for from all quarters women came hurrying with baskets large and small, good and bad, all eager for hooks which were evidently of great value in their eyes. We had the greatest difficulty in stopping the rush and left the place with more baskets than we knew what to do with.

We were among people I had never visited and when we heard of a tribe of inlanders who were settling on one of the higher reaches I decided to make contact with them. On and up the river we travelled with splendid high ground on either bank until ahead of us we saw a number of people clearing some ground for a village. As soon as we appeared, the women ran into the bush but the men held their ground, and thanks to our guide we were soon on friendly terms. I was glad Mamu and Eveline were there, for it made contact easier as their presence gave confidence to these very timid folk. Mamu wanted to see their women and asked why they had run away. "I am a woman," she said, "and have two boys and a girl and I want to see your wives and children and be friends with them." Upon this, there arose much shouting on the part of the men while expostulations from the women could be heard, though none appeared. Then Mamu went after them, calling to them not to be afraid, and after a lot of persuasion a few came near to her, tremendously interested in this woman who in dress and in colour of her skin and eyes and the texture of her hair was so unlike themselves. One thing created considerable comment among my 'boys'. We were familiar with the almost universal custom of piercing the septum of the nose so that a nasal shell could be thrust through it, but this tribe had gone one better and the men and some of the women had each bored a hole in the tip of the nose into which a curled feather or a long piece of stiff grass had been stuck. The operation must have been both lengthy and painful and these Sesa people are the only ones I have ever known to practise it. Meanwhile, the women were approaching my wife almost as if she were a lioness about to spring, but the tobacco she held out to them had a magnetic effect and they were soon around her with their fears forgotten. Not so the children, for when they saw Mamu at close quarters they shrieked in terror and their mothers had hard work to pacify them. I had always thought my wife a very attractive woman and she knew she was not lacking in good looks, but remarked that it made you wonder what was wrong when people screamed at the sight of you. One woman was leading a little girl by the hand Mamu declared her to be the most beautiful Papuan child she had ever seen, but it was sad to see so pretty a face contorted by fear. The group sat huddled together with the head man in front of them to keep guard and as I tried to tell them the reason for our coming, one started to talk about us, whereupon he gave her a fearful nudge in the ribs with his elbow and silenced her effectively.

They were different from any tribe we had met before with customs so unlike those of the Kerawo tribes that we wished it had been possible to stay longer and learn more of them. We were told that when a daughter married, her mother must never look on her son-in-law, and as soon as a child is born she has to leave the village and make her home in the bush away from all her relatives, living a lonely life until she dies and is then buried just where she lay. Gotadou drew my wife after her to see one such in the bush. She was sitting under a tree with her back towards us and her head shrouded by a hood of tapa cloth lest she should look upon our guide who was her son-in-law. Mamu went up to her and gave her a friendly greeting and handed her some tobacco and she smiled and seemed greatly pleased, but never looked round towards her people and my wife's heart was heavy as she left her; it seemed so unutterably sad. For such, there was no home, no fellowship, no comfort, but a life of wandering in the bush until she died.

Another custom which we were assured was absolutely true, though it sounded incredible, was that when married, the woman lives on the ground beneath the house while the man lives above and there is a hole cut in the floor through which the woman passes the food to her lord and master. She serves him and works in the garden and goes fishing with the other women, but like them, when once married, she must not look upon her husband's face. Mamu was very keen to learn more about this and urged our lads to find out all they could, for it seemed to her that that kind of husband was not much good to any woman and that kind of marriage more like keeping a strange animal in a cage. I am quite sure that there was more to it than we were able to discover, and it is possible that this strange way of living was really part of the marriage ceremony and though they may have had to live thus for months, there came a time when the marriage was consummated and they lived together normally.

We were all sorry when we had to say good-bye to these most

interesting people and they seemed reluctant to let us go and lined the banks and flapped their hands as if imitating the flight of birds as we went away.

Later, we ran down to Urika and on to Orokolo to see the erection of a church, the framework of which we had been preparing in our workshops and had sent ahead of us in big canoes. My lads, now used to such work, set to with a will, and in six days we had the roof on and the greater part of the church completed and within another week we were on our way back home. Soon after, we were among the Gope people again and found them preparing for a great festival at which twenty couples were to be married, and the amount of food that had been collected amazed us all. Great bundles of sago, ten feet or so in height, stood at the entrance of the *mene*, forty of them in all, as the relatives had to provide one of these bundles of sago, and a pig for each man and woman to be married. The *mene*, whose painted overhanging roof was some forty or fifty feet in height, was splendidly finished and it was awesome to look down the length of it where on either side the carved and painted totem shields were standing, and decorated masks hung from the roof.

The memory of those days is touched with sadness now, for never again shall we share the change and beauty of the endless waterways or wonder at the loveliness of the fire-flies holding high court, transforming the banks into a fairyland where the trees were lit up with myriads of pulsating lights. Never again shall we walk together those crazy wooden causeways past the palm thatched homes to the amazing sacred houses with their wild beauty, and never again shall we share the discomforts of seemingly endless rain and mud which made a return to the *Tamate* so full of rest and cleansing.

Those months, crowded with experiences grave and gay, came to an end as Eveline left us for Australia and England, and Mamu went with her as far as Sydney to spend Christmas with our children.

27

BACK TO A SILENT HOME

AIRD Hill seemed very desolate and I was glad there was so much to fill the days and so little time for self pity. The work was expanding rapidly and we were in contact with some eighty widely scattered villages and reaching out to new tribes on the Turama, Paibuna and Era Rivers. More and more of my time was spent in itineration but when back at Neuri, I gave all the time I could to translation. Everything was going well and we were expecting Mamu to return within another month, when a cable from overseas upset all our plans. The Directors wanted me to address a great meeting in the Royal Albert Hall, London, and I had to leave at once to reach England in time. For many reasons I was sorry to go, for the work was full of promise and it was with a rather troubled heart that I set off in the *Tamate* to join the ship that was to take me to Port Moresby and the south bound steamer. The young folk and the people from the villages gathered for a great farewell and crowded on to the little wharf carrying bunches of flowers, tossing them ahead of us as we moved off, until the river was bright with many coloured blossoms. Shortly after, the good-bye to my large family in Papua was followed by a glad reunion with my small one in Sydney where we joined the S.S. *Barrabool* and reached England ten days before the meeting at which I was to speak. During the voyage I was lecturing and taking services, but for the children, the journey was a lovely holiday which they hoped to continue when they reached the old country. But I immediately set about getting them into schools which had been founded for the sons and daughters of missionaries, at Eltham and Sevenoaks, and five days after our arrival, my youngsters found themselves settled in as boarders. All their dreams of an English holiday were at an end.

The Albert Hall meeting was a wonderful occasion and I found the audience of ten thousand a great inspiration, and from then on was launched upon a strenuous programme that took me all over the British Isles. The crowded months slipped by and soon I was facing the prospect of another long separation from wife and children, as the doctor had advised against Mamu's return to Papua. I decided to return via Canada and visit some of our churches there, as well as my youngest sister Amy whom I had not seen for many years. It was a decision I never had cause to regret, for it opened up a new world and gave me an opportunity to meet our people on that side and speak in some of their churches. The merger of the Presbyterians, Methodists and Congregationalists into the United Church of Canada had brought a new freedom and spirit of adventure to the people. No longer was their witness stultified and their resources wasted in keeping three separate organizations going, with never enough to carry forward the expansion a rapidly growing country called for. Now as one Church, they planned together and shared the joy of adventure in new areas. I have always been troubled over the hesitation of our leaders elsewhere who, faced with similar problems, cannot bring themselves to follow the Canadian lead. Our divisions are not only a scandal, but sheer folly. Our leaders complain of the shortage of resources but fail to use aright the resources they possess. Every denomination longs for a united church, but each wants it on its own terms, seeking unity in doctrines where it will never be found, for doctrines and creeds divide, while only love and trust can unite.

Back in Sydney, I found myself the target of reporters, for Papua had at last become a place of increasing interest to Australians and many were eager to learn all they could about it. This led to my receiving a request to address the Millions Club, and right up to the time I left for Papua, I was addressing one meeting after another in various parts of Sydney. I was anxious to get back to my people, and left by the first available steamer, but owing to various delays did not reach Aird Hill until a few days before Christmas. It was the dullest I have ever known, with not even time to organize festivities for our young people, but on Boxing Day I opened up my baggage and was able to give a Christmas present to every one of them and arrange for a good feast and dance. They danced until Gotadou brought my morning tea, and then the crowd, having first thanked God for a lovely time, went cheerfully to bed. It did my heart good, for I felt that prayer was for them as natural as speech and God as near as I was and religion bound up with all their work and play.

I was in closer touch with world affairs than I had ever been, for on leaving England a friend had presented me with a short wave receiving set built for the tropics and an expert on radio reckoned it was the finest he had known. With it, I could travel round the world and London often came through loud enough to hear right through the house. I was no longer cut off from the world's news, but it was news that filled us with deep concern, for day by day we sensed the building up of those evil things that eventually came to a climax in the second World War, and were dismayed at the inability of our leaders to cope with the forces threatening the peace and happiness of all. We seemed to be listening to time-serving politicians and short-sighted states-men who, with no clear-cut policy, were leading the people to disaster, and day by day as the news came to us, the dark, angry clouds of war began to darken all the ways of men.

It was 1935. I knew I had but a few more years of service in Papua. Others would take up the work where I laid it down, so I spent more time preparing reading matter and building up a vocabulary and grammar for the use of those who followed me, though it was only with the utmost difficulty that I could get the time I needed. The technical school had become widely known and orders for cane furniture came in far more quickly than we could deal with them. We needed more timber and always I had to supervise the marking of logs and sharpening of the saws.

The boat-slip was constantly in use. We laid it down for the slipping of the *Tamate,* but on my return built a longer and heavier carriage to take bigger craft such as the *Ada* which came over from Daru for extensive alterations and repairs including the fitting of a new false keel. Before I left for England I had sold the *Neuri* to a small company trying to use nipa palm for in-dustrial purposes. Like so many other ventures it ultimately failed, but meanwhile the *Neuri* had been in constant service and suffered a lot through misuse and after the decease of the company, I bought her back, and after repairing her, got her into service again. She proved invaluable as the work in the villages extended and the Samoans took a greater share in it. We needed all the help we could give, for the industrial work alone provided a full time job for any man and in addition to the cane, wood-working and engineering workshops, there was the general upkeep of the station and only those who have lived in the tropics know what that involves. The excessive rain, the burning heat and the silent ravages of white ants are constantly attacking work that in other climates would stand for years with small attention.

We were erecting a terrace of houses for eighteen married couples who were in training. Originally we had not planned for so many and the first two houses were some eight feet in front of the rest. We wanted them in line and grudged pulling them down, so with the aid of skids and jacks shifted them bodily and congratulated ourselves on successfully accomplishing a difficult task.

The turbine driving our generator needed attention and on dismantling it we found the blades had been damaged by a faulty deflector, and Auwau and I had the tedious job of fitting new tips to them all and then reassembling the heavy casings. It was a worthwhile job, for after it the plant ran better than it had ever done before. We nearly suffered disaster soon after when a storm bringing fourteen and a half inches of rain in a day, tore a tree from the hills above the dam and sent it over the spillway and down the seventy foot drop to the power house, which it nearly wrecked. Such setbacks, however, were in the day's work and the lads at once started clearing up the mess and in a very short time all was shipshape again.

Fortunately I had two splendid Samoan helpers. The wife was an outstanding woman, once a head girl at the Papauta High School and a credit to the Institution from which she came. These two gave themselves to the school work with enthusiasm which was fortunate, as educational work of other kinds demanded attention and medical work was steadily increasing. I was surprised to see how frightened Papuans were of my scalpel, seeing how abominably they would cut themselves about with an unclean knife or a bit of broken glass or shell when making tribal marks upon their bodies or trying to cure a headache by bloodletting. A lad came along suffering from a bad inguinal abscess and there was consternation when I opened it and stuffed the cavity with antiseptic gauze. The next morning when dressing it, Makoni came to lend a hand. Hearing a nasty thud, I found my assistant had fainted at the sight, and was glad to think these people's skulls were thicker than mine, for he hit the concrete floor with a horrible bang.

With my wife away, housekeeping devolved on me, and I frequently forgot about meals until it was time to have them, but as time went on, Gotadou and a couple of small boys became more efficient cooks and I was usually able to rely on them to see I did not starve. I say usually, for the Papuan is unpredictable and often oblivious to the passage of time, though Gotadou, in spite of occasional lapses, was one of the most reliable Papuans I ever came across. If she happened to be away or when I was travelling with the 'boys', I had to keep a much stricter eye on the food, for to eat with unwashed hands was the done thing among our people. Kiso, one of my cook boys, was making an orange salad for my evening meal and I was amazed to see the change that had come over his hands by the time he had finished! I realized that orange juice must be a wonderful cleanser, but it spoilt my appetite and I told him not to worry about salads in the future. Even when Gotadou prepared it I would sometimes find the oranges flavoured with onion or kerosene and was very glad when Rarotonga showed them how to prepare fruit without handling it. Such experiences made me very insistent on the use of soap and water and they marvelled at my being so particular.

On the whole we did quite well for food. After a day's fishing I would often find myself with more fish than I could eat and most weeks there would be a pigeon or a fowl to roast, while as a rule we had plenty of eggs, as my fowls had multiplied since I first introduced them and seemed quite at home in our tropical climate.

Unfortunately snakes were very numerous and a constant menace. Some were big fellows and others deadly. I once saw a rooster peck at a very small one. The reptile turned and bit it on the comb and the fowl died as if it had been shot and I could hardly believe my eyes as it fell. Once when roaming the hills Dauwa shot the largest snake ever seen at Aird Hill. They laid the body on the ground and put marks at its head and tail and according to these, it was twenty feet in length and twelve inches in girth. In little more than a week I myself shot as many as five snakes ranging in length from nine to eleven feet.

Flying ants and sand flies were pests of quite another kind. The ants came out in swarms, especially when soft rain was falling, and when they did, the only thing was to go to bed, for if you were using a lamp they swarmed round it and down the chimney and put it out, or if you were using electric light, they swarmed round you and put you out. Sand flies also came in swarms and when they did, the wise sought refuge under nets of cheese cloth, for though smaller than a flea, they have a bit like a tiger.

Snakes and sand flies, however, were but incidents in the daily life at Aird Hill where a very happy crowd from many villages were being brought together into a Christian fellowship we hoped would be a growing influence throughout the district.

28

LEARNING NEW WAYS

THE translation of St. Mark's Gospel was now in the hands of the people who were awaking to the wonder of the written word. Somehow, the book seemed to make things that I had talked about come alive. Even the possession of the book without the ability to read it gave some of them a sense of belonging to a new way of life. At one of the most distant villages I was surprised to see an old man with a look of delight on his face as he walked towards me holding aloft a copy of the Gospel. He could not read a word but to him it was a treasure of great worth and in some dim way he seemed to feel it made him one of us. I urged him to come and let us teach him how to read it, or send some of his young folk that we could teach them and so make the book come alive, for that was my practice wherever I went. If we could get one or two from each village to come and learn to read, they could take the word to their own people and the book would teach them, and through it and their simple prayers they would come to sense the nearness and wonder of God. That was my aim, but it required steady teaching at the station and constant itineration. They were the first generation of Christians, largely illiterate but passing on to others what they had learnt and the change in their way of life spoke more eloquently than their words.

In the old pagan world, as in Papua, the difference made by acceptance of the Christian faith was much more marked than it is among people whose outlook has for centuries been leavened by Christian standards, and those who gathered round us were marked men and women, so different that people took notice of them. The problem that always confronted me and which I felt had never been solved by the mission, was how to bind these believers into a fellowship that would be both self-propagating and self-supporting and at the same time essentially Papuan. I never solved my problem, but I caught glimpses of what it might have been had it had time to develop and what the witness of untutored men could mean.

Masi of Uboa was a case in point. He had worked with Dimi, a young Papuan, who, with his wife, had come from Hula to help us, and from Dimi, Masi had learnt something that sent him to his own folk with a desire to help them. I did not know this until I heard he was gathering the people of his village for morning and evening prayers. They would meet in the *dubu-daimo* where the *buguru* was celebrated or where in the *hawa-gama* they had danced with the skulls of their victims, and there Masi would talk to them of what he had learnt and lead them in simple prayer. I took the first opportunity of running down to see him, and recently I came across my wife's description of the visit. "They had," she said, "been dancing through the night, but at midnight Masi ceased beating his drums and stepped out from the procession of dancing men and women. 'It is Sunday now,' he said, 'time for quiet, for it is God's day,' and with that he left, and others, moved by his example, did the same and only those of us who know the delight the folk find in their dances can appreciate what that meant to them. Early Sunday morning we arrived and Masi met us as we left the *Tamate* and led us along the shaky causeway, over the swamps to the *daimo*. The long building was very quiet. There was an eerie silence broken only by the breathing of sleeping men worn out by long hours of dancing, and by the soft steps of those who came to join our group. We seated ourselves beside a clay hearth in front of the *agibe* with its cluster of skulls, and looked down the gloomy *daimo*, its shadows broken here and there by doorways framing dazzling pictures of sunlit palms and trees with a background of blue sky." In this unlikely spot all joined in worship, and the setting and service were quite other than anything we civilized folk are accustomed to, and for my wife, a moving experience that warmed her heart as she sensed the changing spirit of these people who talked and prayed with us. As we closed, there was a whisper from one of the crowd, "Buta, tell us more," and questions followed one another as we talked together and they gathered some new thing to pass on to their friends. Masi was very ignorant, but when we shared that morning with him, we learnt that for three or four years he had, in his simple way, been passing on the thought of God that had come to mean so much to him and leading his people from the fears and hates of primitive life towards a faith in a Father Spirit who cared for them.

Some time after, he came to see me. He was not only sick in body, but sick at heart with a rankling sense of injustice. He had been in the Kikori prison for a month, for being involved in a village brawl. Actually, he was not one of the culprits. He had rushed into the fray to help his friend who was being set upon, but he was not engaged in the fight. It was his loyalty to his friend that had got him into trouble but the fact that he was not one of the brawlers counted for nothing; he was in the middle of them and with the rough justice that sometimes resulted from the magistrate's reliance on interpreters, he was gaoled with the rest. He knew he was innocent and had suffered wrongfully, but it did not shake his simple faith and he surprised me by saying that he felt it did not matter what the government did to him, for the government had killed Jesus on the cross and so he was quite ready to go to gaol. This, from a man whose fathers had lived in days when headhunting and cannibalism were accepted as normal, revealed how far he had travelled. He also told me that since the Uboa people had invited me to see their *buguru* ceremony, they never held another. It had been cast aside, and again, only those who knew how central it was in their tribal life, could realize what a transformation had taken place in his village. Masi could neither read nor write, the little knowledge of the Christian way of life had been gathered mainly from another Papuan, but he had learnt enough to make him an influence for good among the people of his village and that meant much, for too often a prophet is without honour among his own people.

A similar case was that of Ema, a lad from the tribes east of Aird Hill. He also, quite on his own and without my knowledge, started to gather the Kumukumu people together and lead them in prayer and worship. His method, if such stark simplicity and lack of organization could be described as method, was much the same as that of Masi, and I often deplored the fact of his illiteracy; but he was passing on to others all he had learnt, and had gone farther than Masi for he not only brought various men and women to us for further instruction, but fired his people with the ambition to build their own place of worship, the first

church building ever erected in the delta by the people themselves. We were invited to the opening ceremony and the
Resident Magistrate also received an invitation and made a
special trip with his wife to be present. The *Tamate* arrived
about the same time as the government launch, and we found the
road to the village decorated with arches and all the villagers
lined up to receive us. With my party were Fau and Rarotonga
who had done much to encourage Ema and to teach the boys
and girls who had come from his village, and the work begun by
Ema owed much to their interest and support.

We walked to the church and as the magistrate arrived, all
sang the National Anthem, and thanks to the teaching of Rarotonga, did it really well. Then Mrs. Chance, the magistrate's wife,
cut a string of flowers that hung across the entrance and after
Fau had offered a dedicatory prayer, we processed into the
church. It was a well built place and a credit to the builders and
Mr. Chance spoke briefly, but right to the point, on "A good
church, a good village, and a good people", while I translated.
Everything went well and the Kumukumu villagers were most
elated. We returned to the *Tamate* for lunch where my Papuan
helpers had excelled themselves. We were in what a few years
before had been a very wild part of Papua, but we sat in our
little deck cabin, waited on by the children of those who had
known the old life, who served us with prawns garnished with
lettuce, followed by cold fowl and asparagus tips and topped off
with fruit salad, all of which goes to prove that in Old Papua
life was not always full of hardship.

That day seemed to promise the fulfilment of a dream I had
always cherished: a dream of a Papuan church so simply
organized as to be an integral part of the life of the people and
needing no outside financial help to keep it going, yet a church
that possessed within itself all that was needful to help them to
go on learning the will of God. I could not see why men of
proved Christian character, with a gift for leadership, should not
celebrate the sacraments, why they should not be recognized as
true ministers, and why the church, under their leadership, should
not be encouraged to work out forms of worship and ways of
supporting their minister along lines suited to their conditions.
But they needed more than Masi possessed. Men like these two
exercised a remarkable influence in their villages by the life they

lived, but their work was seriously limited by reason of their illiteracy. Yet such a mastery was essential in the new world the people were discovering and we had recognized that from the first. We were reducing the language to writing at the same time as we were clearing the forest and building our houses. Now, with much of the pioneer work behind us, we were able to give more time to the preparation of reading matter for the increasing number able to use it.

I was constantly putting Bible stories into their language and translating or composing hymns. Many of our English hymns need re-writing anyway, but I would use the old tunes and theme, and adapt them to Papuan conditions or thought forms. I often wished I had some musical talent, for I longed to adapt their native chanting to the psalms I was translating but I never made much of a success of such endeavour. Left to themselves, however, they will so modify the tunes we teach them that they become essentially their own. Thus transformed, they become part of their life and are often charged with strange beauty and excitement and are a sheer delight to hear. The hymns I was writing were not just words set to tunes but vehicles carrying a message, and were in themselves ways of teaching by song. That, of course, is one of the most ancient methods and has been followed by all races down the centuries. The Old Testament stories were probably handed down in this way long before they became embodied in the written word. Thus I was following a very old tradition as I taught them to sing what I had written and though unable to adapt Papuan tunes, I found I could make use of their sense of rhythm. I had often noticed the way they cared for their drums, and one day as a crowd gathered round us on the great platform of a *mene*, I saw some drums hanging by the doorway, and as I started to teach the songs I had written, I took one and beat out the time, much to the delight of the assembly. Then I gave one to Natai and he joined in and made a huge success of it, for he was a better drummer. It improved the singing considerably for though my helpers knew the tune, the villagers seemed quite indifferent to it. Each went his own sweet way in a different key, until the air seemed full of discord. The drums, however, brought them more in line, and improved matters considerably and I felt we had hit on something worth developing.

When we returned to Neuri, we got six of our lads to bring their drums and practise beating out the rhythm of the tunes. Toloa, who with his wife had recently come from Samoa, undertook to train them and it did not take long for them to accompany our singing as effectively as they did their own chants. On Sundays, the drummers, wearing special *ramies* or loincloths, would file into the church at Aird Hill ahead of Toloa and myself and take their appointed places, and when the people sang, the drums helped the rhythm and made the hour of worship more akin to their own ceremonies.

In their old life, there were no Sundays. They had never kept a day of rest, in fact, they had no such thing as a week in their calculations. All days were the same to them and their year was marked by the changing of the seasons and the month by the moon. Possessing no calendar, they had difficulty in planning ahead but fixed the date of dance or festival by some form of tally such as a bundle of sticks or a serrated palm leaf or notches cut into a piece of the midrib of a sago palm. I used their system to help them to remember Sunday, not because I am a strict Sabbatarian, but because it would bring some order or system into the planning of their lives and still more because I believed that if one day of the week was kept differently from the rest, it would help them to give expression to their faith by dropping business and coming together for the worship of God.

The tally was as like their own as possible but consisted of seven notches in a length of midrib, the first being larger than the rest and each having a hole beside it into which could be thrust a pointed stick. The duty of the time-keeper of the village was to shift the stick into a new hole each day and each time it reached the first or largest notch, they would know it was Sunday. The idea soon caught on and I was interested when I next went through the village to find the tally carefully hung beside old Iriwaki and the people enjoying a new way of living with a break from normal routine every seventh day. I was pretty sure that a day would occasionally get missed through the time-keeper forgetting to move the peg or moving it too far, but that would not trouble them, and after all, it was not the day, but what it stood for that really mattered.

Strangely enough, it was our introduction of the idea of Sunday that gave the Seventh Day Adventists their chance of coming in and telling the poor people they had been wrongly instructed and that Saturday was the right day on which to worship; as if the Lord of the Universe would be concerned with such trivialities!

Makoni thought their keeping of Sunday on Saturday rather a joke, while none could understand why they should forbid their followers to eat pig or smoke tobacco. A taboo on these would in the eyes of the Papuan rob him of two of the best things in life. The matters they put such stress on seemed to me largely irrelevant in the delta, where I was trying to teach the people that Christianity was a way of life, and not a set of rules and prohibitions. I introduced the idea of keeping Sunday and the practice of talking to God as simple beginnings from which they could go on to make greater discoveries. Unfortunately, the Adventists, like the Mormons and others, are so sure we are on the wrong track that they spent large sums and much effort trying to disrupt our work. Like the rest of the multitudinous sects, they claim Biblical authority for their tenets and without such books as Daniel and Revelation and a belief that the whole Bible is the Word of God, they would be unable to sustain their strange and often misleading doctrines. Yet among them are men and women whose lives are full of love for others and some day we shall find that we who now are so divided are in the same family and the children of the one God and Father.

29

OUR YOUNG FOLK

THROUGHOUT Papua, a generation with a new outlook was slowly displacing one that still cherished nostalgic memories of old days. The young folk around us were learning much that made life happier and more carefree and wanted others to know it too. Those who could read would set off in their canoes and spend a week or so travelling from village to village and no evangelists fulfilled more literally the injunction Jesus gave to those he sent among the villages of Palestine. They had "neither gold nor silver; and into whatsoever villages they entered they abode till they went thence and received the food the people offered". With even less than the men of old, our young men would set out with the Gospel in their hands to tell their people what it meant to them.

In the great gloomy *dubu-daimo* where, among the shadows, the skulls hung before the *agibe*, these lads, whose knowledge and equipment were of the slightest, would gather the people for a friendly talk and end the day singing their evening hymn and commending themselves and those who gathered round, to the God and Father of us all. They were not great preachers; they just talked about the ways of God and His love for men and women and tried to help others to find what they had found.

Old Dauwa, of Dopima, one evening ushered into my study eight men and five women with whom he had been talking. They had been in the habit of coming to his house where they would sit and smoke and talk far into the night; now he brought them to me, for they had come to want what he had found and wanted their names added to those seeking more instruction. Auwau came along with his wife, both wanting to join the church, and I have seldom seen a Papuan woman look happier than she did that night. Auwau was anxious to get along to his village to help them build a *tana moto* or sacred house, their name for a place of worship, but I suggested that other things were necessary before he could do that, and he saw the point, so went off and found his friend Irumi and brought him along to have his name added to the growing number seeking instruction in the Christian way of life. Then Gotadou got busy and found her brother Dimi and his wife Naari together with another young woman, and in this way numbers of people were being influenced by their own folk and I heard of villages where, without any outside leadership, many were gathering daily for simple worship.

Such happenings occurring spontaneously in various places set us the problem of how best to give fuller instruction to these people. They belonged to widely scattered villages and it was impossible for me to stay in these long enough to give the instruction they required, so I tried to get them to spend a week with us once a quarter, when with the aid of a simple catechism we could teach them more fully what it meant to be a Christian. The scheme did not work very well as it proved very difficult to get the villagers together at the same time and we knew much more was needed. The instruction had to be given in their villages, and in response to the need, some of our lads were now ready to go back and stay as teachers. These young men with their wives were not highly educated but they had learnt to read and write and had travelled and shared with me the work among the people. They had the Gospel in their own tongue and with the ability to read it could go on from there. We called them *hiwaa-oubi*, the nearest word we could find for servants or ministers, and I had hopes of seeing such men at work in many places living with the people, sharing their daily life, supporting themselves as did the rest, by fishing, hunting and gardening; but in addition, gathering the people for worship, reading the Gospel to them and teaching their children to read and write. They were not trained pastors but very simple Christians, who like ourselves, often failed, but who were also very like the majority of first century Christians from whose witness grew the church we know today.

While teaching them at Aird Hill I began to train them in the practice of silent prayer, that they with us might come to a deeper realization of the nearness of God, and at most services the opportunity would be given when we had a time of silence before joining in the Lord's prayer.

The Unseen Presence was sensed by them more readily than by many white folk, for their fathers had always been conscious of unseen and inescapable spirits round about them, though until we came, this spirit world was touched with fear and a belief in malign powers that brought sickness, disaster and death. That is why the Christian faith brought a sense of release as they learnt that the unseen world in which their fathers believed was friendly after all and full of the presence of One who cared for them. He became to them *Urio Abea,* the Spirit Father or Father Spirit, and they talked to Him as children to their parents. I shall never forget the carefree, happy look on Gotadou's face one morning when she arrived rather late and explained matters by saying, without the least trace of embarrassment, "I've been talking to God". Just that, as if it were the most natural thing in the world and I could see the truth of what she said, written where all might read.

Natai, who eventually took over the work commenced by Ema, became one of the *hiwaa-oubi.* Like Ema he belonged to the Kumukumu tribe and I well remember the day he came to me. There had been a great dance at Kumukumu the night before and Natai had evidently been having a grand time, he was in full regalia and splendidly adorned and I was struck by his alertness and the happiness lighting up his dark face. His appearance was so unusual that I wondered what had happened to him. He did not keep me waiting, for he was eager to tell me of an experience that had transformed his outlook. Amid the drumming and dancing, God, he said, had spoken to him and he had come straight from the dance to my study to tell me he wanted to follow the way of Jesus. Mamu, who at that time was at Aird Hill, had from the verandah seen him coming up the hill and been impressed by his appearance, and when I told her what had happened, was not at all surprised, for she had felt as she watched his coming, that only such a purpose could possibly explain the look on his face. Natai was the son of a high chief and from that day he never looked back. He quickly learnt to read and write and with his wife became members of the band I was training for service in the villages. They shared in work on the station and Natai often came with us as we travelled through the district. Later he took over from Ema and through the years has served so faithfully that since I left the country the Papuan mission has honoured him for his long service by ordaining him as a fully accredited pastor.

Two others who had come to me as lads and had been trained

in the same simple way were also ordained on that occasion. One was the son of the first man in the delta to become a Christian. Dauwa, his father, as mentioned earlier, was at Dopima when James Chalmers was killed, and had probably shared in the cannibal feast that followed the massacre. He came to us later and tried to learn to read and it was touching to see him sitting with the small children in the school, but somehow these older folk found the mysteries of reading and writing too hard to master. But though he could not read, Dauwa had listened to the Gospel stories so intently that he knew them well, and could often repeat them word for word, and was never tired of telling others what he knew. He was a quiet, faithful gentleman in the best sense of the word and won the respect of white and brown alike and it was not surprising to find his son Wanua following in his steps.

Wanua was not brilliant but he began the work among his own people at Goari and one notable result was the first break from the *buguru* ceremony by a couple who wanted to be married. Only those who knew the awe and mystery surrounding this ceremony at which marriages were made binding can appreciate the significance of this. It was the most complete break with ancient tradition that had ever been made and the decision to make it was the decision of the villagers themselves. There were, of course, those who still wanted the *buguru* and made their voices clearly heard, but after much discussion the councillors said, "No". They had an *hiwaa-mere* with them now and this wedding would have to be a Christian wedding, and preparations began forthwith. It was to be a native wedding, i.e. one arranged and carried through by themselves, but would be very different in character, and many wondered what would happen.

The *dubu-daimo* was filled with an excited and deeply interested crowd to whom this was an unheard of venture. Makoni and Wanua conducted a simple service, after which they had a splendid feast and the next day and night a great dance, and according to all accounts, they greatly appreciated the change. Makoni, who led the service, was with Natai and Wanua, the third to be ordained. He was as dear to me as a son and regarded me as a father, though he did not love his own father any the less for that.

He had good reason for holding him in respect, for Makoni's father was one of the finest village men I ever met. Living the life of his people, he seemed to have an awareness that there was something better, and encouraged his son to stay with us and learn all he could. He would visit him on occasion and I was impressed by the quiet dignity of the man, one of nature's gentlemen, who never begged and never cringed, and met me as an equal.

Makoni was worthy of him and fulfilled what I believe his father hoped for him. He was one of the finest lads I ever had and one of the truest. He became a capable carpenter and later was coxswain of the *Tamate* and as we went from village to village he took an increasing share in the evangelistic work. With other members of the crew he would spend long hours talking with the villagers and they would be at it long after I had gone to sleep. Like his father he had a quiet assurance and natural dignity and I was often gladdened by the interest shown by his audience when he got up to speak.

We had many good times together. I watched him one day as he stood at the wheel conning our little craft down the river. A smile was lighting up his face and his lips were moving, and I asked him what was making him so glad. I had been writing some new hymns and one to the tune of the Old Hundredth had captured his imagination, and there he was silently repeating it to himself. But I saw him standing thus again and he was anything but happy. We had been speaking of the time when I would have to leave and the tears were rolling down his cheeks for we two had shared much together and both of us dreaded the day when we would have to say good-bye.

Makoni married a remarkable little woman. She had been brought to us as a small frightened child after the death of both her parents, and was a wild, untamed creature. As she grew up she was quick to learn and clever with her fingers, full of fun and affection, yet very jealous with a temper that seemed impossible to control. Gotadou was one of the most mixed characters I have ever come across. She could be more stubborn than a mule and as helpful as a ministering angel; she could pray like a saint and at times act as if possessed by seven devils. I have seen her raging and shouting aloud in anger, but I have sometimes heard a soft voice in the hospital and there was Gotadou praying by the bedside of a patient. In spite of all her contradictions her faith was a living thing and though she would exasperate and drive us almost to despair, she could be most lovable and full of surprises. She often took a service in the church and I wondered what she would make of it when I heard her speaking about Peter and his denial of the Lord. Gotadou was talking of the way we all fall short and fail like Peter and remembering her own sulks and public displays of temper, looked across her audience and remarked, "You all know my ways," but not being meek enough to wear the white sheet in solitude, added very meaningfully, "and I know yours." I chuckled to myself, but everyone else was listening seriously and there was no doubt about the way she got her points home. I often wished others were as effective in their addresses and as much to the point in their prayers.

With all her tumbles and many failings she had a clear idea of what was fitting and after a bad time with her temper would acknowledge her wrong by coming to church and sitting with the unbaptized women from the villages while members of the church were sharing in the Communion.

Mamu had trained her until she was a good cook and better in the house than many a white maid, though bitterly jealous of anyone who came to help in work she reckoned was her job. Even when Mamu was away she kept the home neat and clean and followed most faithfully the routine my wife had taught her. This was the more amazing to those acquainted with the lack of home life, order and cleanliness in the villages.

Reading over a letter to my wife, I came across an account of what Gotadou had been up to during the day. "She has been through all the bedrooms, cleaned the bathroom and gone through my study, getting rid of any amount of dirt the hornets had brought in. She prepared me a fine dinner and now is wiping the bathroom floor and fixing my room for the night and through it all has been as cheerful as can be with never a hint of feeling tired. She is a testimony of your training. Just now she is very delighted for she has found on top of the bookshelves a book without a cover. It is a child's life of Jesus with many illustrations of the Bible stories she knows so well, far better in fact than the average white child, for she has helped me to translate them into the language of her people. For her this discovery has been a great ending to a day's work she seems to have thoroughly enjoyed and she has just gone off to her little home with her find which I let her keep."

Her home was vastly different from the village *moto* in which she had been born. Makoni had made a couple of cane tables and some chairs and they had a well kept little cottage which at night look most attractive when the lights were on for all these homes received current from our plant.

One sensed in Gotadou the latent possibilities that are in these delta women who at first sight seemed so degraded, but who often proved to be so much like their white sisters.

As I have said, her stubborn temper, an inheritance from her wild ancestry, was a trial to her as well as to us and once almost ended in disaster, though the adventure it led to had a wonderful effect upon her and her people. There was some excuse for her outburst that day. She had been ill spoken of and her character impugned and she came to me in blazing anger, and with flashing eyes said she had done with us all and was going back to her village. No one could turn her from her purpose, and gathering her small possessions together, she set off with her adopted child.

Paddling down the river and through streams where the trees met overhead, there was a sudden rending crash as a great bough fell upon the canoe, just missing Gotadou and the child, but tearing the paddle from her hand, splitting the hinder part of her frail craft and tossing them both into the water. They righted the canoe and swam around, collecting all they could of her possessions, and then climbed back and sat breathless and frightened. Then as she began to realize how near to death she had been, she whispered to herself, "That was God. I tried to run away from Him and He has found me out." Though her experience made her feel she could never escape from God, she did not seem to have had any thought of returning to us, but having pulled herself together, continued on her journey; but when at length she reached her village she was a very different girl from the one who had left us, and her wild heart was strangely subdued.

She stayed in the home of her father-in-law and could not have stayed with anyone better than the quiet, understanding father of Makoni to whom she recounted the story of her flight. I do not know what passed between them but later when evening came, she went with him to the *dubu-daimo* and as the people gathered together, she told them what had happened, and how she had found she could never run away from God. For days on end she stayed with her people and every evening read to them from the

Gospel, answering their questions as best she could and offering an evening prayer before she left for her mother-in-law's *moto* where she slept with the women.

Later came the day when she felt she must return to us. I took her apart and spoke to her of the shame her wild conduct had brought to us all and suggested that when we met for morning prayers she should confess her wrong before them. It was a very difficult thing to ask so proud a spirit but after a while she agreed to do it and I shall never forget that morning. She stood before her people with whom she had grown up and quietly told them of her going and of all that had befallen her. "I was bad," she said, "and angry, just like some of you. I was bad and angry, and I ran away, but I could not run away from God," and as she went on with her story the words of the 139th Psalm came to my mind: "Whither shall I go from Thy Spirit? or whither shall I flee from Thy presence? If I take the wings of the morning, and dwell in the uttermost parts of the sea; even there shall Thy hand lead me, and Thy right hand shall hold me. If I say, Surely the darkness shall cover me, even the night shall be light about me. Yea, the darkness hideth not from Thee, but the night shineth as the day." Gotadou had learnt what the Psalmist discovered over two thousand years before and the experience of men and women down the centuries had come to her wild heart and she was never the same again.

She still had her ups and downs, but became a leader, and once a week with other of our women would set out in canoes for the villages and gather the women and children for instruction and worship. Among people whose women were trained to minister to the lusts of men, with no rights to their own persons, Gotadou and those with her lived a new life and brought with them a new idea of marriage and home.

She often travelled with us when visiting the people and when I was working on translation was of greater assistance than any other Papuan, for no one was quicker to note a mistake in grammar or keener to get a sentence into the real language of her tribe, and it was through her that the words of Christ, translated into their tongue, took on a richer meaning, and her people heard Him speaking as one of themselves.

She was a born preacher and for dramatic power I have never heard any Papuan come near her. I remember her taking a service in our church when she told the story of the deaf and dumb man Jesus healed. I wondered what she was going to make of it but she soon warmed to her subject and spoke of the way we grow deaf to God because of the sin that closes the ear of the heart. She illustrated this from her own experience, telling again the story of what had happened to her when she ran away from us.

"You know," she said, "I ran away from here because I was bad. I could not hear God's word because I was bad and so I cleared out and left you all. But though I was bad God had not left me," and she told again the story of her travelling through the narrow stream and of how near she was to death. She was, she said, running away, but God knew all about it and now she knew that He was true. She went on with deep emotion speaking of the way God had dealt with her and of how when she reached her village she knew she had to witness for Him and told of how one of the leading men opposed her because she was only a woman. Knowing her, I knew no mere man could keep her silent, and she went on to tell how she had withstood him and told him that he talked like he did because his heart was so dark that he could not hear God's word. His bad ways had shut his ears as bad ways shut the ears of all of us, and we are deaf and dumb until Christ can heal us. I have seldom been so gripped by a Papuan's words as I was that day. It was a simple but most challenging utterance and I felt what a power she could be in the villages when the time came for her to work in them beside her husband.

She was one of the pioneers and I am not surprised at the way the Papuans of today are taking an ever greater share in the government of their country and in the conduct of its industries.

They have never lacked those who could lead. When travelling through the Gope villages a young man named Girou came and joined us. He was a natural orator but I did not discover it for some time. As was my custom with those I hoped would some day be *hiwaa-oubi*, I used to take him with me when visiting the villages of his tribe. He would listen to us as we talked to his people and one day when I asked him to emphasize something I had said, was amazed at the competent way he went about it. He proved to be a very fluent speaker and as time went on, literally bubbled over with what he had to say, and every visit increased his power. Apart from Cotadou I have never known a

Papuan more effective as a speaker. He made no attempt to preach a sermon, but spoke of what he had come to believe and said it with power. At his own village of Goiiravi it was most interesting to watch the crowd, and especially the women, and see the deep attention with which they listened. No one seemed to want to go away or even smoke, which was still more remarkable. Later, an old man got up, not to ask a question but to add a word of his own, and I was interested to hear him say that the women would find God before the men, for they believed, while the men loved their old, dark customs. I had always felt the women were more conservative, but one of the women, with any amount of character in her face, backed the old man up by saying it was the men who should listen to this talk. They were, she said, sitting away near the entrance because they loved their old ways and did not want to change. They were the ones who were spoiling their womenfolk, so did not want the word brought. Some of her audience found this hard to take, so started to leave, whereupon she had another shot at them much to the delight of Makoni and Girou.

While there, a little blind boy was sitting at my feet and it was touching to see the way he felt my clothes, shoes and hands as he tried to comprehend the appearance of this stranger he could never hope to see. My shoes puzzled him and when I took one off, the sock left him still bewildered until I took that off also and he felt my foot. Like a little dog, he smelt hands and feet and shoes and clothes with a questioning wonder on his face and my heart went out to the little lad as he sat there in his darkness.

Days and weeks spent like this served a double purpose, for they taught my 'boys' how to lead their people in simple worship and how to put into words the faith they sought to bring to others.

It was to give them further guidance that I was now spending all the time I could on the preparation of a Book of Worship. We decided to call it the *Tana-moto Buka* or Church Book and in addition to the hymns I was writing, it was to have a Psalm for every day of the month, a very simple creed or statement of the things we believed, linked with a Catechism which could form a basis for Christian instruction. In addition, there were to be orders of service, which would help the *hiwaa-oubi* in the conduct of daily worship, baptisms, marriages, funerals, etc., together with special readings for Christmas and Easter, and sundry prayers that I hoped would help the people towards a richer understanding of what prayer can be. Day after day we pushed ahead with this task, giving all the time we could to it, for the need grew greater as the numbers seeking instruction increased week by week.

When at last the whole had been completed in the Kerawo tongue, revision commenced and we went through it time and time again and still were not satisfied; nor do I think we can ever be completely satisfied with our work, for there is always much that we feel could or should have been put into richer or more appropriate language.

As page after page was gone over, I typed out copies and continued revising and retyping right up to the day I left for Sydney to see it through the press.

I had not expected to go south just then but wanted to get the book into the hands of the people as soon as possible, so made this journey in order to hurry on the work.

My brother-in-law, Dr. Arthur Davidson, with whom I stayed was one of the founders of the printing establishment controlled by the British Medical Association of N.S.W. He put me in touch with the manager who was greatly interested and glad to have the opportunity of producing a work in a Papuan tongue. His staff backed him up splendidly and kept me busy at proofreading and correcting with the result that the whole task was completed most expeditiously, for in about six weeks I was on my way back to the delta with the first batch of printed copies of the *Tana-moto Buka*. They were well bound in bright, attractive colours and became the prized possessions of our people.

30

A DYING CULTURE

Wɪᴛʜ our young people in the villages and the *Tana Buka* in their hands, I hoped to see a truly Papuan Church take shape, organized and supported by the people themselves along the lines with which they were familiar. I knew the old tribal life had to go, but I did not realize how quickly it would be destroyed, nor did I foresee the upheaval of the second World War. So many revolutionary changes had taken place, that those who followed me are grappling with conditions we scarcely dreamed of. The Papua I knew is fast disappearing and with it much that was wonderful and worth preserving.

Missionaries have often been criticized for interfering with the life of simple folk by people woefully ignorant of their work, but the critics seldom seem to realize how much greater interference comes from themselves and the Western world. I had been where white men had never been before and was not ignorant of the good in the life of the people among whom I worked, and the more I came to know of these so-called savages the more I came to like and respect them. They were men and women like ourselves, with their hopes and fears, their simple joys and wild excitements, and all the business of their tribe, who through the centuries had roamed the forest, hunted and planted, paddled down the glorious rivers, danced and fought, untroubled by rivalries of our restless Western world. But that world could not be kept from their country and through the years I watched the twentieth century breaking in upon them with shattering effects, and I think of a day that brought it home to us with dramatic force.

It was a glorious morning and in the warm sunshine a peaceful drowsiness slowed the tempo of life until a strange sound brought alertness to these stone age people and startled us upon the hill. It came across the trees of the delta forests, where in all the centuries no sound like it had ever come before. The still air seemed to be vibrating and old folk in the village stopped to listen. Wild men, carrying their long bows, waited, wondering. Women and children rushed from their homes or clambered from the creek with nets and fishtraps and we ran from our house and looked towards the horizon.

The queer noise had become a drone, rapidly growing louder and then in the far distance we saw a speck which shaped itself into an aeroplane that roared above and past us and so on out of sight. The old men hid in fear, the young warriors trembled, and women and children fled shrieking into the forest or ran to us, weeping aloud and seeking protection.

From many villages in the days that followed they came to us, with hearts full of fear, asking what this strange creature might be that tore through the air as no other bird had ever flown. Whence had it come? What did it mean—this apparition that had brought such consternation to them all? I told them something of man's conquest of the air, but I could not tell them all it meant and would mean to them and to their children in the days to come. It was the white world coming to the brown man's land. The white world with its hunger for things that only the brown man's land could give; the white world with its power, its greed, its ruthlessness. Already they were feeling something of its touch and the second World War was to bring still greater terror in its train; and looking at this world the Western races have done so much to shape, with its fears and hates and rivalries, I have sometimes wondered if it is much fairer than the world the Papuan knew before we came.

I remember being put to confusion when at the beginning of the first World War, a brown-skinned girl came along with an English illustrated paper and pointed laughingly at a picture and asked me what those funny looking people were. I looked and was dumb, for she was pointing at a crowd of men of my own race, hideous in the gas masks they were wearing, and how could I tell her of the horrors planned by the so called civilized, which made the worst in a savage life seem as nothing.

Had the Papuans known all that was to follow the coming of the aeroplane, they would have hated us. Yet the white man had to come, and if there is blame, we all share in it, for we all want so many things that only the brown man's land can give. Tea and coffee, soap and rubber, copper and oil, gold and diamonds are won for us by men of many lands and few stop to ask what it means to those who win the things we seek. In Africa and Papua, our demands have swept the young and virile from the villages into the mines and plantations. They are there in their thousands, living their lives under what are to them unnatural conditions, doing strange and unfamiliar tasks but working for us who seldom think of them. They are no longer members of the tribe, part of the village community, they are only hands or labour, labour that wins for us the things we want, and the old Papua with its colourful ceremonies and wonderful buildings is doomed.

I have often stood in their villages wondering at the size and beauty of their temple homes, but they are gone and their like will not be seen again, for the strength that built them is being spent in meeting our demands, and the young men will never rejoice as did their fathers in the great works of their own accomplishing. They made wonderful canoes fashioned from the trunks of mighty trees and spent long weeks beautifying them with carvings wrought with loving care; they wove patterns into their cane and raffia baskets, and decorated all their implements and articles of daily use; but the old arts and crafts are dying out and a tin bowl takes the places of one fashioned with skill and care from wood. They had colourful festivals, and for many a week the villages would be filled with happy workers who, in joyful anticipation, would be preparing for them; but now the youths who should be taking their place in the life of the tribe are away working for the white men, and the festivals grow duller and more sordid with the passing years.

I spent long years among the people of the delta country, and in the early days they seemed so gay and strong and confident and the villages were full of children, but towards the end of my time I came to one of these, one of the prettiest on the Paibuna River, gay with croton bushes and bright hibiscus blossom, with palm trees by the waterside. The men gathered round me in the *dubu-daimo*, and as we sat talking, the women drifted in. There was a dull listlessness about the place and I missed the shouting and laughter of children at play, and after we had talked a bit, asked them where the children had got to. There was silence and then one answered as if in shame, "There are no children, only this one," pointing to a solitary child beside its mother. I found it hard to believe, but they assured me it was the truth and that they could not understand it. I knew, for this was what I feared would happen as a result of their promiscuity. My warnings had been unheeded, for they were but following the custom of their tribe. They did not know that the venereal disease brought by the white man was making the custom of the tribe a deadly threat to their existence. No wonder the Kerawo tribe which, when I first made contact with the people, was at least ten thousand strong, now, according to the latest figures I can get, numbers only some two thousand.

In Port Moresby, not far from the large, white population that has come here since the war, another settlement that had come into existence some years before I left the country has grown enormously, and is a place of ill repute and a source of grave concern to all who have at heart the welfare of the people. Here are herded together men and women, boys and girls from many tribes. Here, too, are brothels, gambling dens and opportunities for drunkenness and ways of life unknown in old Papua. Here are those who, drawn from many villages and thrown into a strange environment, have lost all desire to return to the homes of their people and have become detribalized, learning new vices and contracting diseases never known before among their people. All this has come through their contacts with the Western world and as I learn these things I see the end of a life these people knew and loved. We have all helped to end it; we do not know what we are doing and few tell us of the cost of the things we get so easily; but as we hear of the great houses falling into ruin and of the broken tribal life and scattered people, we do well to remember that we all have a share in it.

Fortunately, just after I came from the Paibuna, Sir Hubert Murray arrived at Kikori and I put before him the facts I had observed. Later the Resident Magistrate told me the Governor had been very disturbed by what I had told him and it soon became evident that he was taking energetic action, when two medical officers arrived from Port Moresby with orders to do everything possible to clean things up.

What was needed, however, to make their campaign a success was a new outlook in the villages and I was tremendously encouraged when Kebaau, the great chief of the Kerawo people, came to talk things over. He was troubled by what was happening and by what I had told the villagers of the dread results of the disease that had spread among them. He had scouted my words when I first warned them, but now he listened seriously as once again I spoke of the steady destruction of his tribe which was being hastened by their promiscuity. "Yes," he said, "I know now that what you say is true. You are right. The old custom must go. Send us a teacher to stay with us and stop my people when they want to start these ways again, and help us to be good." It was an unexpected word from such a man who in addition to being a great chief had the reputation of also being a great sorcerer, and I longed for more men to send, and wished it did not take so long to teach them to read and write. I did not aim at much more than that, provided they would read with understanding. I felt if they could go to their villages with the written word in their hands and the love of God in their hearts they would still be better equipped than many of the early Christians who overcame the pagan world.

The early administrators never had a tithe of what they needed to carry on such work but they did all that was possible with the limited funds at their disposal and of them and those who now direct affairs it can be said that few governments have administered the affairs of a territory with more concern for the rights of the native inhabitants than has the government of Papua, but no government can save them from the impact of a world that becomes ever more closely knit together.

Sir Hubert Murray realized that, and once, when we were discussing the break-up of the old life, he turned and said, "That is where you come in. We of the government can protect these people and administer their land but only you can give them a new basis for their life. I am a Christian man," he went on, "but it is only an accident that a confessed Christian is at the head of this government, the next may make no such profession; but whether he is a Christian or not he will still have to support the work of missions, for only in what you have to bring can these people find a new foundation on which to build a new life to take the place of that now falling into ruin." What Sir Hubert said on that occasion he repeats in different words in his book *Papuan Story* where he writes: "Unless the missionary is there to help him, the native is left like a ship without a rudder and will run a great risk of being wrecked in the sea of alien civilization."

This was what I was feeling more keenly with the passing years and it brought an increasing realization of the greatness and urgency of the work to which I had been called.

31

THE DAILY ROUND

SOME of the lads we had been training were now ready to go to the villages as *hituaa-oubi* or teachers, and at the same time as I took Wanua and his wife Ihaha to Goari I installed Ubuauma and his wife at Uboa and Iadia and his wife Cuima at Dopima, one of our most difficult villages whose people we found very hard to reach. A number of our young men helped them in the building of their homes, but when we left them to carry on without our presence I knew they would need much encouragement and frequent visits to keep them up to the mark in places where men with much richer equipment would find the going hard. They needed further instruction and all the help and advice we could give them, and it was the lack of this after I left that led to much failure and loss of contact with many villages that at one time were eager to have teachers. Where one man is trying to do the work of two or three only the most rigid division of his time makes it possible to meet the demands of the widespread district. Always there is the pull of the school, workshops and hospital and a hundred jobs that tend to keep one on the station, but the need of the young teachers was so urgent that I felt we had to visit them at least once a quarter.

It was during one such journey that Ubuauma and his wife lost their daughter. I had set out to visit the villages around Goaribari and particularly the three where Wanua, Iadia and Ubuauma were working. I had been to the first two and was on my way to Uboa where Ubuauma was expecting us. Taking his small daughter with him, he went to the shore, and while looking across the estuary to see if the *Tamate* was appoaching, his little girl went to the water's edge and was snapped up by a crocodile. I arrived to find the parents overwhelmed with grief and brought them both back to Neuri to stay with their friends and recover from the shock, but they had not been on the station many days before we had more trouble, and Dauwa's sister suffered the same fate as Ubuauma's daughter. The women had gone fishing and had slept in a hut by the river and early in the morning Otoiia when preparing the morning meal had gone to get water. The others heard her screams, and running out, found she had disappeared and immediately guessed that a crocodile had carried her off. The guess was right and later they found the mangled body and brought it to the station for burial.

Two such deaths in so short a time brought sorrow to us all but Dauwa faced his loss in a way so different from most of the others. He came to see me after the tragedy, his face all lined with grief, but as we talked of our faith in a life beyond the gate of death, the lined old face changed and lit up with hope and I knew that through his sorrow and loss he had found something he could pass on to his fellows. For him death was no end but just a going on and though there was so much he did not know, he had no fears, for he was one with those who see life in the light of eternity.

He was so different from the rest who let the whole world know of the grief they felt by their loud wailing. Their sorrow was so vocal that you could hear it a mile off and I believe they rather enjoyed such occasions, as they could let themselves go without restraint. Gotadou was among them and though Otoiia was but a very distant relative one would have thought she was the chief mourner. She was a typical primitive in the expression of her emotions and would continue howling until her voice was gone and for days after would be scarcely able to speak.

More people than ever were coming to the hospital, and the ignorance of patients and their friends added to our difficulties. Dauwa's boy Dodo was very ill and running a high temperature, but when after lunch one day I went to the hospital to see how he was getting on I found him out of bed and on the verandah. Worse still he had had two cold baths that his mother had insisted on his taking and now under her direction was sitting with a strong south-east wind blowing on his wet body to cool the fever. I told the woman what I thought of her and hustled Dodo back as quickly as possible, and having got him safely tucked up in bed slipped down to the workshop to attend to matters there. Shortly after, his sister rushed down to tell me Dodo was very bad and would I come at once. Hurrying up the hill I found the hospital crowded with his relations who were already starting the death wail. His mother's folly had brought about a sudden relapse and the wailing was adding to the trouble by scaring the boy who felt his end was near. All wondered at the hardness of my heart and my indifference to their very vocal grief as I hustled them off the premises before getting to work on the boy. He had completely collapsed and it was with difficulty that we got him round, and after that we took care that his mother did not get another chance to try any other of her remedies. They had twice nearly killed the lad with their tricks and I was very mad.

Soon after that I was mad with a woman's husband for quite a different cause. Some people brought me word that the son of Aisoi, an old sorcerer, had attacked his wife and beaten her up so cruelly that she was nearly dead. Those involved had tried to keep the news from us and had carried the woman off and hidden her in a humpy down the river. I sent some of my men to find her and bring her in, and she was brought to the hospital in a shocking condition with her arm and leg both fractured and a mass of mud and blood from head to foot. We cleaned her up and I set the broken limbs, and while she was lying with her head bandaged and her arm and leg in splints I relieved my feelings by sending a letter to the magistrate at Kikori in which I expressed my opinion of Aisoi's son in no uncertain terms. It was a most brutal assault and I was not sorry when the culprit was arrested and received a stiff sentence which even the villagers felt he richly deserved. That meant something, since among them it was the done thing to give one's wife a thrashing now and then.

On the other hand Aisoi, the father, was most indignant and out to cause a lot of trouble, but when he threatened to use his sorcery on me I let the people know I had invited him to do his best or worst and had told him that nothing he could do could hurt me. Naturally everyone was keen to see the result and it was an object lesson to all when I continued in good health.

The next hospital case was very different. A man came asking if I could do anything for a friend of his whose hand had been bitten off by a pig. It sounded strange, for it would have to have been a very big pig with an outsize bite and when I asked when it happened I was amazed to find that no one seemed to know save that it was a long time ago. It was so long ago that I felt it could not be an urgent case so finished the work I was doing before I went to the hospital. The man was there and it was clear that he had lost his hand and I set to work to clean up the stump which was a bit of raw meat in a horrible condition. After we had fixed him up I got the story. It began about three months before. They had been hunting and had speared a pig, and this man, thinking it dead, went to take hold of it when it turned and bit him hard. The hand must have been badly mangled but instead of coming to me, he did nothing and his people did nothing. It started to mortify and still he did nothing. The fingers dropped off one by one and then the whole hand and not till then did he decide he had better come and see me. One is left amazed at such apathetic folly and endurance, for what he must have suffered passes comprehension and it is still more incomprehensible that he suffered thus for months without making the least move to come to us for the help he knew we would be ready to give. There is much about these people and their ways that we white folk can never understand.

Somewhere about the time the man lost his hand a boy was murdered on Goaribari Island and the murderer was captured and tried at Kikori. His very laboured explanation of the reason for his crime was that he had found the lad wandering about after having run away from his village. The boy, he said, was very hungry and he felt very sorry for him so he killed him.

It seemed a queer way of putting an end to the boy's hunger and the excuse was less understandable than that of another culprit, also a murderer. He was charged before the Governor with killing his own wife, and when asked why he had done so evil a thing gave as his explanation, "He talk, he talk, he talk, he talk too much, so I kill him?" "him" of course being the wife. It is whispered that the Governor, a man of deep understanding and incidentally twice married, let him off with a light sentence.

For some reason there were about this time several cases of people disappearing without a trace and after some men had come to us seeking news of two boys who had once stayed on the station I began to make enquiries and eventually got hold of a queer stoy. I was told that after they left us, they were met by a Kiribara man who took them to Irimuku, a village a few miles above the Kikori government station. One of them landed and was killed among the coconut trees and the other murdered in the canoe, the Kiribara man helping in the killing, while a woman from the boys' village saw the crime. It all happened the best part of a year before even a whisper of it reached us, and had it not been for the very belated enquiries about the two lads we would probably have heard nothing. I reported the matter to the government but they were never able to convict anyone, though the boys were never found, and the mystery of their disappearance never solved.

It was 1937 and I knew my time in Papua was coming to an end and I was most unhappy about the prospect. I had pledged myself to this service when a lad of twelve, and never felt there was any other for me, but letter after letter from home made it plain that they needed me very urgently. I knew I was nearing retiring age but nothing would have persuaded me to leave had my wife's health been better and the needs of the family less pressing. At the same time there was much to be done before I could get away, and most of all I wanted to complete the translation of the four Gospels and as much as possible of the New Testament.

The presence of our lads now teaching in the villages made this work assume ever greater importance and I handed over to my helpers all the tasks in school and workshop that I felt they could possibly undertake, while I gave myself more fully to it. Through the years I had had to spend so much time in exploration, building up the station and ministering to the sick that my study had seen far too little of me. Now I was trying to make amends and felt if I could stick closely at it for another twelve months or so I could not only give the people the Gospels and some of the Epistles in their language but also leave my successor a grammar and vocabulary that would enable him to go on from where I left off.

In the two thousand years of Christian history the Bible or part of it had been translated into little more than a thousand languages and it was a high privilege to be a member of that very small company who have given a people a written language and the Scriptures in their own tongue. Often I wished I were a more worthy member. I did my best but did not expect my successor would ever realize how great were the difficulties. He would find many mistakes and wonder why I was so ignorant. In the early years mistakes are inevitable, especially when first learning the language. It is always difficult, when questioning your helpers, to be sure the word you get is the one that expresses to the people the thought that is in your mind. Many words we use without thinking have no counterpart in their tongue and I discovered that the word we were using for prayer conveyed something quite different to the people. The mistake had been made when we were learning the language. Seeking a word for prayer, we had tried to show what we were after by talking with our eyes closed, and they had also watched us when we began the day's work with a short act of worship, and seen us praying with closed eyes, with the result that the word we got for "Let us pray" was "Shut your eyes". We changed that to *Iehovaido wade aromoi* or "Let us talk to God" and sometimes added *kirodumeaito,* "with eyes closed". I have been interested to find other translators who have made the same mistake and in some of the translations it has never been corrected, as the word soon received the new meaning in the minds of the people who become familiar with the way their white friends use it.

As we pushed on with the task, it took an ever greater share of my time, and when on the *Tamate* among the villages, we snatched every hour we could working on the manuscript.

By August 1937 we had translated all four of the Gospels but knew there would have to be revision after revision before they would be ready for the press.

At school and in our worship I would read from the manuscript, and the work came alive when we saw how the words gripped the hearers. As I read passages from John's Gospel it sounded to me as if it was the best bit of work we had done. We had found it fairly easy to translate, but when we turned to Paul's Epistles we were staggered at the difference. We found Paul terribly difficult to render into our people's tongue, which is not surprising, for quite a lot of his writing is hard to put into straightforward English let alone Kerawo. When one reads such a letter as that to the Ephesians, asking oneself what many of the sentences mean, one soon realizes how difficult it is to make his argument come alive in so limited a language as that of the Papuan. Ephesus and Dopima are as far apart in thought as they are in miles, save when Paul refers to women. It went against the grain to translate the words, "Wives submit yourselves to your husbands in all things" and "The husband is the head of the wife" for I disagree with Paul on this matter. He puts women where the men want them put, firmly kept in their place with a lord and master over them. The words of Christ are simple compared with those of Paul yet He dug more deeply into our humanity and knew us better, and the Papuan will understand Jesus but will find Paul far from clear at times.

32

CLOSING DAYS

ALTHOUGH giving first priority to translation, other calls upon my time seemed endless. The oil-search companies were asking for chairs, lounges and tables to be delivered in such quantities that we were hard put to it to fill the orders. It was, therefore, a great relief to be able to place Toloa in charge of much of the work of the technical school and to find him proving himself as a very capable superintendent, though I still had to be on the alert to see work was not scamped.

When I returned from Sydney with the *Tana Mota Buka* I had also brought back additional machinery, including a power grinder and guillotining machine for keeping the pit and circular saws in order. This was soon in great demand for they were also using pit saws on the government station and rubber plantation and their saws were sent to us to be reconditioned, though we ourselves were complete amateurs at the job.

I also added a small oil mill for treating the increasing quantities of palm nuts we were now getting from Veiru and soon we were using the oil thus extracted to make soap, and very good soap it proved to be. The Samoans had had some experience in this work though they use coconut and not palm oil. The soap-making process is the same with either though the palm oil is so thick that it looks like grease.

The oversight of Urika was again on my hands owing to the illness and later the death of Moir Smith, and I was not surprised to see Misifoa, Moir Smith's very capable Samoan assistant, arriving in the *Homu*, the launch that had replaced the *Purari*. I was also very troubled when I discovered the boat needed extensive repairs and would have to go on the slip. The stem was in a bad condition and had to be removed together with the interior supporting timber known as the apron. I sighed, for it was a job that could not be left to the 'boys' and would mean my spending a lot of time with them, which I could ill afford. It meant precious hours away from my translation but there was no way out so we got on with it at once.

The L.M.S. would have been involved in very heavy expenditure if a boat builder had been called in but the work was carried through far more expeditiously and with infinitely less cost on our slip, which highlights the disastrous errors that were made after I left, when the slip, winches and all other gear were removed before there was anything anywhere in the mission to take their place. With the Homu repairs out of the way I was soon among the villages again, taking my manuscript with me to work on while travelling or at anchor.

The need for closer contact with the people was increasing as oil-search boats and labour recruiters made their presence felt. Few of the white men had any sympathy with our work and some were openly hostile. In the eyes of the Papuans white men belong to a social order as closely knit as their own, where all are motivated by the same beliefs, and it must have been hard for them to realize how profoundly we white folk differ from one another. After years of contact with the mission it must have been a shock to find that we missionaries were a tiny minority and the things we tried to pass on to them were ignored and even scoffed at by so many of our race. There was evidence that those antagonistic influences were having an increasing effect and some of the Kerawo villagers were openly scoffing at our boys for believing in God. Knowing the tremendous grip of their old beliefs, it seemed incredible that this should happen, but they see and hear more of the white men who ignore God than they do of the missionary who honours Him. These white men can pay them and give them what they feel is wealth, and many are eager to get the things that money can buy, and are ready to let go the things of God if these seem to stand in their way. Here and there a few are added to the Church but progress becomes more akin to that in our own land where the seekers are few and the many indifferent, and the Kingdom of God seems slow to come. Yet a journey through the villages usually took me back to Neuri with renewed hope and a confidence that things were on the move.

We anchored at Kiwaumai and Maika, the wife of one of my old 'boys', came off to see me. She was a bright, happy looking woman and seemed delighted to have a word with me. She also seemed quite oblivious of the fact that she was naked save for a belt and a very tiny whisp of grass. I showed her Mamu's portrait and those of the children whom she remembered and she was most excited and eager to hear more about them. She chatted about them and the folk at Neuri as naturally as any friend of my own race might have done, for white and black have so much in common in spite of this one's amazing lack of clothes.

The great house in her village possessed the biggest totem image I ever saw in Papua. It was in the form of a snake and was about twenty feet long and fourteen inches in girth. The head with its wide open mouth and protruding tongue was beautifully carved and the carvings extended along the neck while the eyes made of bright scarlet seeds gleamed wickedly. The whole body was painted and decorated and I appreciate their pride in it for it was a splendid work of art.

After my experience in some of these villages of landing on my back in the mud with all the debris of a broken causeway falling on top of me, I was not surprised at what happened when men and boys of the village crowded on to their crazy jetty to watch us anchor. With scarcely any warning, there was a tremendous crash as the whole thing collapsed and flung them into the water. The noise was terrific and the sight of that mixed assembly struggling in the water or through the mud was unforgettable, but no one seemed hurt and soon all were laughing together or at each other until someone missed a tiny tot about four who had been with them and had disappeared. At once the laughter gave place to consternation for many feared he was drowned and started a search for his body. Papuan youngsters, however, are adept at looking after themselves and this one had got out of the water so quickly and streaked off to his mother so sharply that no one saw him go and it was only after the rest had been thoroughly scared that someone found him safe and sound at home.

Work in these villages was being made more effective now that Fau and Toloa were sharing in the itineration of the district; Fau among the Kerawo and Serebi and Tolea among the Urama and Gope tribes, and both were doing well and finding it gave new meaning to their work on the head station.

Toloa returned after a most successful trip far up the Era River where he found himself among people speaking the same language as the Kumukumu tribes around Aird Hill and what intrigued me was the fact that the Kumukumus seemed to know nothing of their existence. If I had had the time, I would have gone along to investigate, for it looks as if the Kumukumus originally came from up the Era River or that long ago some of the tribes had broken away and settled in the country where Toloa found them. That he did find them is a tribute to that real pioneer spirit that urged him on to reach new villages, and when he returned I was delighted to receive a written and most encouraging report of his journeyings and the number of people with whom he made contact.

I have always been critical of the policy of putting South Sea men as pastors of Papuan churches, feeling it led to the formation of a church built up on traditional methods unfavourable to the development of one truly Papuan. To my way of thinking the work of the Samoan should be that of an assistant missionary sharing in the head station activities and supervision of work in the district while training the Papuans to be the leaders of their own people. That was our policy at Aird Hill right up to the day I left and I consider any departure from it fatal to the growth of a truly Papuan directive which has to come into being if Christianity is to be indigenous. My Samoan colleagues co-operated with me in this, and though they introduced much that was new to the people, it all added to the enrichment of their life and not a little to their happiness.

Their presence and help enabled me to spend more time on the translation, but there were few days when we could give uninterrupted attention to it. Looking through my diaries, I note that about this time we were having an average of twenty or so men and women coming each day to the hospital for treatment, some of which were serious cases that demanded a lot of attention, and others not as bad as one feared they might be, for I find myself writing, "I had a nasty accident to deal with today. The 'boys' were skylarking and bumped one of the smaller lads off the verandah. He fell on a stone and made a terrible hole in his forehead. I don't think the bone is fractured but it looks pretty nasty. I fixed him up and made him lie down all morning but he wanted to go back to the boys' house at lunch so it was not as serious as I thought it might have been. He is a dear little chap and I get more and more fond of these folk. With all their savage ways they can still teach us a lot. When I see with what few possessions they are content I'm not surprised that they think we white folk are greedy and call us *hogoi oubi* or hungry men."

Describing another day, I wrote: "They gave me a lovely birthday. Rarotonga, Mutaago and Aiula were, in spite of the rain, standing at my front door with all the small boys and greeted me with Many Happy Returns of the Day and sang Home Sweet Home in English and then recited the twenty-third psalm.

"The women had made a cushion for my study chair, with a lovely blue 'B' decorated with yellow flowers, beautifully worked in the centre. The men gave me a walking stick so well made that I shall be proud to use it wherever I go.

"Later the Samoans invited me to afternoon tea and after that the children gave an entertainment with action and South Sea songs, games and dances. The Samoans are a delightful folk, friendly and gracious and most hospitable, and I shall be very sorry to leave them. I think they will also be sorry for I'm told that when I last left for England the whole station was full of wailing."

Rarotonga, the wife of Fau, was one of the finest helpers we ever had and her contribution towards the training of the young folk hard to overestimate. Under her leadership they seemed to develop all sorts of unsuspected talents that surprised their own people and often amazed our white visitors.

Sunday school as run by Rarotonga was very unconventional but a sheer delight to the children. One Sunday, for instance, I heard shouts of laughter coming from the building that served as church and school. It seemed to me they were having a very hilarious session and on enquiry found they were acting out the story of the man with the legion of devils. The shouts of delight were when the demoniac broke his chains and went dancing all over the place. Later, I saw all the smaller boys running from the church as fast as they could and asked if school was over. "Oh no," said Gotadou. "It's only the pigs; they are running away." I'm not sure about the reverence, but there was no doubt about the story getting home, and later I heard Makoni mentioning it in his prayer. Maybe he thought the devils sometimes got into his wife but I'm quite sure if my grand-daughters had any say in it they would be regular attendants at such a school as Rarotonga ran.

Papuans often surprised us with their dramatic talent and

among them one comes across delightful mimics and born actors. I have seen the Governor convulsed with laughter at an entertainment given in Port Moresby when some of our young men from Lawes College gave a burlesque of a District Magistrate presiding over a court case. Sir Hubert, who had a keen sense of humour, told me later that he knew quite well which magistrate they were mimicking. Rarotonga was quick to notice their talent and did her best to develop it.

We had a wonderful instance of this at Christmas when a Nativity play was produced under her direction. I knew great things were being planned, for she and Mutaaga, Toloa's wife, were constantly seeking coloured pictures of Eastern people, Roman dignitaries, soldiers, priests, etc. They were also drawing on me for all the brightly coloured cotton print and loincloth that I could spare from the mission store. There my assistance ended for I was not allowed to have anything more to do with what was going forward. Something out of the ordinary was under way for rehearsals seemed endless and I understood why, when I heard the lengthy parts they had memorized, and witnessed the action of the play.

Christmas at Neuri was always a great festival and the white folk from the government station and jubilee plantation and the trader on the river and any others who might chance to be in the neighbourhood, were always invited, and there were no refusals.

When the great day arrived the church was packed to overflowing with villagers from all around who had come to see their children in the play and share with us in the festivities. As the white visitors came in with me we saw scaffolding reaching from floor to roof, packed with black faced, white robed angels. These joined as one in reciting the Christmas story as I had translated it for the *Tana Buka*. It was a long story but repeated without faltering, and we were all amazed at the children's memories.

The Madonna, a shy but pretty Kerawo girl, was discovered sitting below the angels grouped above her, and as she sat with downcast eyes, the angel Gabriel cried from among the white robed figures, "Fear not, Mary, for thou hast found favour with God", and after her response, all sang together the angels' song.

As the scene changed, Mary had gone and in her place came the shepherds and their sheep. These were the young fry dressed in white with white ears fastened to their little black heads and each with a little white tail. They were evidently enjoying themselves as they crawled about on their hands and knees, while the angels' song went on as the singers descended from their high places and moved among the shepherds and the sheep and still singing returned to their stations above them. As the song died down, the shepherds tried to lead their flock away but the latter were having such a good time that the keepers found the task rather difficult, one of the lambs being especially active in acting the wandering sheep, and putting a strain on our gravity.

When the ground was clear a thatched hut and a manger were brought, and Mary, Joseph and the babe appeared, the little black baby sitting up in the manger, thoroughly interested in what was going on as the shepherds came back with their flock, and after gathering round the manger went on their way again.

The next scene showed us Herod with his soldiers and the Wise Men coming to ask him where Jesus was to be born. The page who was with Herod was immediately sent to fetch the Scribes and Pharisees who came in to tell the king how the prophets declared that the Christ would be born in Bethlehem.

The manger scene was then repeated, but this time with the Wise Men gathering round to pay their homage to the baby who was no longer in the manger but seated happily on his mother's lap, while the Wise Men most gorgeously arrayed presented their gifts to the child. Then, as they stood beside Mary and her babe, the angels began to descend, singing another song that I had written and it was taken up by the other actors who came trooping in singing, "Praise to Jesus, our Lord". They grouped themselves around the central figures, angels and shepherds, the wandering sheep, Herod and his court and the three Wise Men and last of all the Scribes and Pharisees, all joining together in singing the same glad song.

We thought it was the finale until another procession appeared. They were singing a hymn they had asked me to write that brought in by name the various nations of the world. It was so unexpected that even our white visitors seemed spell-bound and my heart was touched with deep emotion as into the building came representatives of the different nations paying their homage to the Babe born to be King. I was as unprepared as were all the rest, for I had had no word of this innovation. They came along, family by family, introduced by the different verses of the hymn, Indians and Chinese, Africans and Malagasy, the South Sea islanders and the wild Papuans and last of all the Europeans with old Dauwa as a white man wearing white ducks and a helmet, and his wife in a gay dress. Some may have smiled but I could do little but watch and wonder as they approached the Holy Family until all were gathered there around the Babe whose birthday we were celebrating, and there they joined together in a final hymn of praise.

I was spending my last Christmas with them and my mind went back to the first when I was surrounded by savage men and women, and not far from our home a canoe load of people had been set upon by a rival tribe and killed and their bodies carried off to a cannibal feast.

At that time there was little to suggest that I would live to see such a scene as this and as I looked upon the glad faces of those taking part and saw the happiness and pride of their relatives who were the descendants of those who had fought on that other Christmas Day, I thanked God that He had let me spend my life in their service for it had brought great reward.

Christmas over, we settled down once more to the steady routine, but for me it was interrupted by one of the worst attacks of malaria I had ever suffered. It put an end to my activities for some weeks, but fortunately for me the wife of my friend, Mr. Foldi, then assistant magistrate at Kikori, was a trained nurse and my 'boys' carried me on a stretcher down to the *Tamate* and across to Kikori, where she took charge and looked after me so well that I was soon on the mend though it was some time before I was able to put in a good day's work.

It irked me the more for I knew I would soon be leaving the people and the work that had claimed the best years of my life. I had pledged myself to it when a lad and I never felt there was any other life for me. I had come to love these Papuans and to feel I belonged to them, and they felt it too and we were all troubled.

The one cheering factor was the knowledge that a young man and his wife would be taking over before I left. This was not the usual practice, for owing to financial stringency no new appointment could, as a rule, be made until a missionary had retired and ceased to be a charge on the funds of the Society. This meant that a district was often left for a year or more with little supervision, and the work frequently suffered considerably. Knowing this, I had for some years been putting aside what money I could get together so that the stipend of my successor could be met and in view of this, a young man, E. R. Fenn, and his wife had been appointed and were to arrive some time before I left in order that I might help them find their footing. Early in April 1938 a canoe brought word that they had reached Kikori and I hurried over in the *Tamate* to pick them up and bring them to what was to be their home. I was glad to see them but my heart was heavy at the thought of leaving the people; it seemed as if I were coming to the end of everything, for the future was hidden and I could not know what God had in store for me, nor did I dream that when well over eighty I would still be doing a full day's work. The Samoans and our young people crowded down to the wharf to welcome the young couple who were tremendously impressed by the place and rather overwhelmed by the magnitude of the task that faced them.

Mrs. Fenn was a trained nurse and used to the Australian bush and immediately took full control of the hospital, and I knew I had no need to feel any concern about this side of the work. She gave herself to it with the utmost devotion and the people around Aird Hill, and especially the women, were cared for with trained skill such as I never possessed.

Fenn, who quickly received the name of Teri, was quite at home in the workshop and I knew he would see that the activities of the technical school were not neglected, but I was not so happy in the thought that the nurturing of the emerging Papuan Church had to be left in young, inexperienced hands, for I soon sensed that my way would not be his.

His wife told me that he realized the greatness of the work with its many-sided activities but though he had great responsibilities he was starting where I left off. What he would make of it none of us could tell. Like others new to the country he was very conscious of what seemed the gulf between his way of life and that of the Papuan. Maybe I also felt that way when I was young but during the years as I came to know the people better I learnt how much we had in common. They had their sense of need, of failure and of sin. They had their hopes and fears and knew what it meant to long for the better and follow the worse.

To me they were my brothers and sisters and sometimes my children, as they came with their troubles and fears or wept before me in their contrition. Only time would teach Teri these things, but at first he was more conscious of the difference and shocked by what he saw. Meanwhile I was doing all I could to help him to grapple with his task, at the same time preparing to leave him to it.

At the last conference I attended in Port Moresby, the white residents took leave of me at a big gathering attended by Sir Hubert Murray, the heads of government departments and members of the business community. I had seen the tiny township grow into a busy port and each time I went there, had welcomed one and another new to the country and it was good to feel they thought of me as an old friend and were sorry I was leaving.

Back at Aird Hill there was still much to do in finalizing on the station and at Urika, and in addition I had to introduce Teri and his wife to the village people and take them through our wide-spread district. We travelled far and as we went from place to place there was no such happiness as I had found on other visits, for I was saying good-bye to men and women, once hostile or suspicious but now my friends. These were the saddest journeys I had ever taken and as I returned from the different villages, my heart was heavy with the knowledge that never again would I be coming that way. Then I faced the greatest wrench of all as I said good-bye to our people at Neuri.

The Samoans gave me a great tea to which they invited all the *hiwaa-oubi* and their wives, and their speeches moved me very deeply. The day following, everyone on the station came together for a farewell feast on the lawn at the back of my house. They brought little parting presents and dear old Dauwa made a speech. He was no orator but a wonderful friend and a very simple Christian gentleman and we both found this parting hard to face. Then for the last time I went down the hill and boarded the *Tamate* and set off to join the little coastal steamer that would take me the first stage of the journey to Australia and England. My people and crowds from the villages were there to see me off and the ship was surrounded by canoes large and small, and there was so much wailing that I was glad when the anchor was weighed and we steamed slowly down the river passing canoes laden with men and women waving their last farewells.

Makoni and his wife Gotadou came with me to Port Moresby where I took leave of more friends in mission, government and commercial circles, but the friends I found the hardest to leave were those two Papuans who had worked and travelled with me through many years and to whom I owed far more than I could ever repay. They too were full of grief, and as they left me on the ship, I watched them walking down the jetty, with lingering steps and bowed heads, two lonely souls looking friendless and forlorn. I, too, felt lonely and bereft for I was leaving so much that had brought meaning, purpose and challenge to life and those two now lost in the shadows were my children, members of a great family gathered from many tribes, who had become very dear to me and thought of me as *Abea*, or Father.

There was still some further service I could render them, for I had with me the manuscript of the Gospels and Epistles and these I took to a London darkened by the shadow of war and soon to experience its horror. Work was held up owing partly to a heavy programme of meetings that took me all over Great Britain and also to the outbreak of the second World War. The British and Foreign Bible Society undertook the task of printing and publishing, and in spite of many difficulties pressed on with the work. Finally, after months of proofreading and re-reading, the books were ready for despatch to Papua, and it was a great day for the Kerawo folk when they at last arrived. As for myself it was soon clear that a new and rapidly enlarging sphere of service was opening up which finally took me back to Australia and eventually led me to the highest office the Congregational Union of N.S.W. could bestow on its sons.

Meanwhile my people in Papua had had to face the horror of war such as the land had never known before. The first great war had touched Papua but little, the second had a shattering effect upon it. I had lived with cannibals, my predecessor had been killed by them, but never had there been such indifference to life and human rights as the conduct of the war revealed to their children.

In my day government and mission were united in our efforts to lead divided tribes into friendship with one another and to bring an end to inter-tribal fighting. Now the white man was teaching their children how to use far deadlier weapons than they had ever known and to destroy and massacre wherever possible. All this by white men among whom the Christian way of life has been known for many centuries. No wonder Buddhists have small respect for Christendom. Often I wonder what would have happened if instead of formulating the unprovable creeds and doctrines about Jesus which have filled the Church with division, the priests and clergy had sought to know and practise the religion of Jesus which he summed up in one great sentence, "Thou shalt love". That is God's way but it is too simple and too hard for most of us, yet there is no other way of hope for humanity. Maybe my Papuan friends also find the simple way too hard at times, but they, with other Papuans, throughout the land, have never ceased to pray to the God and Father of us all, and that gives purpose and direction to their lives.

When war came, devastation spread among peaceful villages. Homes, schools, churches, all the outer symbols of their way of life, were destroyed and the people scattered, but this story is told of some of the survivors returning to their tribal lands. Strangely enough they returned with much money, a commodity almost unknown among them in my day, but won in work done for the armies of Australia and America. Around them was a desolation which they planned to transform and messages were sent to all the tribes to bring their gifts to a common fund. There were churches and schools to be built and books to be bought, but the size of the offering amazed them and a great meeting was held to decide how to use it. Three days were spent in long and earnest discussion and at the end they made their decision. "This is what we will do: half of the money must be spent on our villages, building the churches and schools and buying new books; but half we will send to Japan that they may learn to be a helping people and not a killing people. This is what God would have us do because we are His children."

They were remembering words that Christendom seemed to have forgotten or found too difficult—"I say unto you, Love your enemies, bless them that curse you, do good to them that hate you, and pray for them which despitefully use you and persecute you, that ye may be the children of your Father which is in Heaven."

"This is what God would have us do because we are His children." These were the children of those who, like the head-hunters of the delta country, marched out to their tribal wars, but like Makoni, Gotadou, and the many I had come to think of as my own folk, were travelling along new paths. As Western influences press upon them they are beset with a thousand new temptations but many are learning to distinguish between the evil and the good and are banded together into a growing Christian fellowship. A new government with a new outlook has taken the place of the military powers of the war years and millions are being spent on medical, educational and social benefits in place of the inadequate thousands the government of my day had at its disposal. It is a different land but in it is a Church, growing in power and finding its leadership among its own people, who, in spite of the wars that have disgraced Christendom and the increasing impact of a materialistic civilization, are learning what the white man also has to learn: that this is God's world and it will only work in God's way. No other way will ever work. Lord Bertrand Russell sensed that in his message to posterity: "Love is wise—hatred is foolish." He has yet to learn what the children of cannibals have learnt, that "God is Love".

And with that I close my story. I seem to be the last living link with the earliest pioneers; now I am an old man looking back, remembering the days that were. But I am an old man in a new world which with all its achievement faces the threat of annihilation; an old man wondering if it will learn in time what some Papuans have come to sense, what Jesus proclaimed two thousand years ago and the great philosophers of today know as truth: "Love is wise—hatred is foolish" for "God is Love".